WHAT IS GOD SAVING YOU FOR

MICHAEL KELLY CARROLL

What Is God Saving You For?

(One man's search for the truth.)

By Michael Kelly Carroll

with Charrie Foglio

Table of Contents

Preface

I know what you think when you see a book written by a former Navy SEAL. It has to be filled with action-packed stories of covert operations from around the world during the war on terrorism. Although some well-written books from SEAL warriors, fiction and nonfiction, exist…I loved the Jack Carr series; this isn't one of them.

It's true, though; I've spent 20 years serving our country as a Navy SEAL; the first round was 16 years, and the second, after the attacks on 9/11, was four. I learned a lot during that time, enough to write a book like the one mentioned above. But oddly enough, those experiences weren't the ones that people had asked me to recount most often; those stories were about the times when I nearly lost my life, how I survived, and how they changed me.

Perhaps you've had a brush with death. If so, you may already know how it feels. I've had five, which were outside of my military service during the war in Iraq. It may surprise you that these weren't haphazard accidents involving me being in the wrong place at the wrong time. I've undergone rigorous training in whatever I was doing at that moment, yet I still managed to breach the point of no return more times than I'd care to think about in one sitting.

And, no. In case you're wondering. I don't have a death wish. I love life, and I value life. I wouldn't want my children or grandchildren to remember me as an adrenaline junky who put himself in one dangerous situation after another just for the thrill of it because that's not the case, or at least I don't think it is. It's just who I am. My parents and siblings would tell you that I've been the same way since I was a kid.

1

Be that as it may, I hadn't seriously questioned my life's circumstances until this last rub in August of 2022. I crash-landed an airplane onto a city street during rush hour without hurting anyone other than myself. I'll admit that I didn't think I would walk away from this one.

Looking at the photographs, neither Robin nor I understood how I survived with only a gash on my forehead and seven breaks in my right leg when the force of the crash peeled away the plane's front end like the lid of a soup can.

When the paramedics pulled me from the scene, their expressions and those on the faces of the doctors and nurses in the ER at Scripps Memorial had me worried. What did I look like? Was it as bad as I felt? As bad as the airplane looked? How am I still here? What was God saving me for?

In between surgery and recovery at the hospital, I couldn't help but look back on my life and ponder that question. What was God saving me for? I felt as though I was already living a just life. I loved my wife; I loved my family. I loved God, I loved my church, and I loved my country. What was left? What was I missing?

I gave it a lot of thought and jotted down some notes. I recalled my earliest memories with my parents, brothers, and sisters and fixated on what it was at the beginning of my life that molded me into the person I became. The decision to join the military was easy and fit me like a glove. It pushed me to the best of my abilities and opened my eyes to the true meaning of patriotism and the role America's values played throughout the rest of the world. Meeting Robin, falling in love, and the challenges of turning me into us.

The turning point came in 1987 when I attended my first World Wide meeting in Las Vegas and gave my life to the Lord at a Sunday morning service. That was when my existence transformed from being one of pleasure to one of purpose. I had been a believer but was grateful that God gave me grace until I realized that the ultimate role of my life was to serve him.

You know, the bible does say that God gave us these incredible imaginations and the ability to dream in a way that would lead us and prepare us to serve his purpose. The more my life passes, the more I am assured that I was born for his glory. Perhaps God wanted me to share my experiences that testify as to how He guided me for His purpose. Even during the events when I thought my existence was coming to an end, I felt that God was there to save me because he wasn't done with me. What other reason could there be? After much contemplation, I think that God spared me to add to his kingdom. That is the explanation that suits me above all others. Mark Twain said it best, "The two most important days of our lives are the day we were born, and the day we figure out why!"

So I started floating the idea of writing these stories down to close friends I respected—those who would give me honest opinions on whether a book was a good idea. I wanted to save my time and, even more so, the time of others who would have to help me since this was the first time I'd ever written a book. Second grade, the most challenging two years of my life, would tell you I don't have the skillset.

I reached out to a very close friend, Charrie, the daughter of Joe Foglio, my mentor, and coach for over 30 years. I valued Charrie's input because, from my experience, she is knowledgeable and an accomplished writer. We were having a phone conversation about my idea, and immediately, she started an interview process to help me shake these stories loose. She was very encouraging and told me where to start, "Write for one hour every morning when you wake up. Let it free flow, and the words will come," she said.

So, through collaboration, Charrie would read what I wrote every morning and prompt me to dive deeper into my life's journey. As I wrote about my past, the black-and-white history started to turn to color. I could tell that God was at work guiding me as I was writing.

Sometimes, I would second-guess myself, thinking I'd gone too far in the weeds with my adventures. But anytime I doubted my writing, I thought that, at the very least, it would be an extraordinary memoir for my children and the generations to follow, and that was reason enough to continue. Then I started to worry that perhaps telling these tales would come off like a self-licking ice cream cone. What would be the point? I didn't want these stories to be so-what stories. Then God spoke to me and said your life isn't a so what story. It is my gift to you, and what you are doing with your life is your gift back to me.

I remember a discussion I was having with my mentor, Joe Foglio, about how much God sees into the future, and he said, "God knows all; he knows your life before you are born to the end." Inspired, I said, God sees the beginning and end of the parade. From then on, Joe would remind me whenever the subject came up about what God knows; he would say, "As you said, Mike, God sees the beginning and the end of the parade." I was always blessed when he would use my analogy.

You are about to read the story of my parade thus far. My deepest wish is that you find value in my story. It may inspire you to look at your life from a different perspective and remind you that your life matters.

Now, on with the parade.

4

Chapter One
May Day, May Day, May Day

1097D: Gillespie ground, this is 1097D.

Gillespie ground: Go ahead, 1097D.

1097D: I am at Safari Aviation with information Echo, taxi to 27, right.

Gillespie ground: 1097D taxi to 27 right, taxi way Alpha, taxi way Delta to 27 right.

1097D: ground 1097D taxi to 27 right, Alpha, Delta to 27 right.

As I pushed the throttle forward, there was a puff of white smoke as though the Jacobs was clearing its throat after sitting on the sidelines for so long. The radial engine started talking to me through the roar of the round engine that sang its song with the power of many classic airplanes dating back to pre-World War II. I felt like I was sitting in that part of that history when everything seemed to make sense. These 275 horses were powering this beautiful polished silver Cessna 195 highlighted in royal blue; I couldn't help but notice what a perfect day to test fly after being down for nine months.

Taxiing out to the runway, I relished the beautiful new interior. It had just had its last bolt put in the day before. Everything seemed so clear; the windshield and all the windows were also brand new, and the colors outside never looked so brilliant.

Even though this aircraft was built in 1951, it looked brand new inside and out. I felt like I was a steward of a piece of history.

Taking care of and maintaining such a thing of beauty, attempting to make it better than it was when I took possession, was a joy. It was my responsibility to preserve it for the next generation to enjoy.

After two years of owning the Cessna, Robin and I decided to sell it. I loved the airplane and the attention it received wherever I landed. It was named one of the nine most beautiful airplanes ever built, and there were not that many flying. Robin loved it, too, but it scared her. She couldn't see over the nose and was concerned that if she had to take the controls and land it for whatever reason, she wouldn't be able to. So that was the reason we were selling it. When the timing was right, we would get something she felt comfortable flying and landing.

I felt perfect about the plane's condition for the next owner, but I wanted to check everything before throwing a sign on the windshield. This flight would be a concise test to stretch its legs to ensure it performs as it should after the repair and upgrades. A take-off and an extended downwind, then a base turn to land, should tell me everything I need to know.

N1097D handled great taxiing to the runway. Pulling into the run-up area, just short of the runway, you do your final checks before taking off. The engine was nice and warm to conduct the magneto check. I ran the engine at a higher RPM and switched the mag to the left and right, ensuring they fired the spark plugs on all cylinders. After checking all the systems and ensuring everything is green, I am ready for take-off.

N1097D: Gillespie tower, this is 1097D ready on the right for take-off and downwind departure.

Gillespie tower: 1097D, you are cleared for take-off on 27 right; after take-off, make a right downwind departure.

N1097D: Gillespie tower 1097D rolling.

Releasing my brakes and pushing the throttle forward just enough to get the airplane moving, I taxi onto the runway and line up on a heading of 270 degrees, matching runway number 27. After increasing the throttle slowly, the aircraft accelerates, picking up speed as the power increases. I'm now at full throttle; the tail comes off the ground. Ahh, now I can see over that big radial engine. Being tall enough to see is much better than using my peripheral to keep the aircraft on the centerline of the runway. I can see why, at 5' 4", Robin was a bit apprehensive.

Airborne, I have a beautiful view of San Diego; it has never looked this good. Winds were calm, and there wasn't a cloud in the sky. Looking to the right at my freshly polished, shiny wing, I notice that gentle bouncing motion when the air flows over it, creating the lift it needs to keep me in the air. The plane is handling perfectly and in the right shape for a new owner to enjoy as much as I have.

I start my right crosswind turn, my head on a swivel, looking for traffic that might have wandered into my airspace. All clear, and now I am making my next right turn to start my downwind departure that will parallel the aircraft with the runway I just took off from. Looking down at the tower about 1500 feet below, I know that the man who just gave me clearance to take off was watching me do what he instructed. I continue to climb another 500 feet. Everything feels good; it's 10 am on a sunny August morning. The temperature is a mild 75 degrees; it's a great time to fly.

Everything was so beautiful that I didn't want it to end, so rather than staying in the pattern to land, I decided to take it out a couple more miles towards our home in Alpine. It had been nine months since I felt the incredible freedom of flight; maybe Robin would be out by the pool, and I could wave my wings to her. The mountains looked like I could reach out and touch them.

Ten minutes later, after getting my fill. I decided it was time to head towards the field. The tower had kept an eye on me, and as soon as I started my base to final, they reached out;

Gillespie tower: 1097D. Are you making your right base to land?

N1097D: Affirmative.

Gillespie tower: 1097D. Make straight in for 27 Right; you are cleared to land runway 27 right.

N1097D: 1097D is cleared to land 27 right.

Five miles from the runway, I started going through my landing checklist, "GUMP." G stands for gas; ensure the fuel tank selector reads both. Fuel selector switch on both; check. U is for undercarriage; if you have retractable gear, ensure the gear is down and locked with three green lights. Since my aircraft is fixed gear, I don't have to worry about that. M is fuel mixture; make sure your mixture control is fully rich unless you land at a high-altitude airfield, which I am not doing today. Mixture full rich, check. P is prop; make sure prop control is in to ensure it's in the position for a possible go-around. Prop, check. I will put my flaps down when my airspeed needle is in the white area of the gauge; this is the allowable speed to lower flaps without structural damage.

I am 4 miles out, dropping below the desired glide slope; I add a little power to get back on the desired glide path to the runway. I push the throttle forward; there is no change; what's going on? I don't hear the roar of the 275 horses. There is something wrong. I tried again, pumping the throttle, but there was no change. I then go to mixture control, ensuring it is operating; I pull out the toggle and push it back in, but still nothing. What else? Switch fuel tanks; I reach down on the left side bulkhead by my knee and turn the fuel selector to the left tank . . .nothing . . .right tank . . .nothing.

Exhausting the checklist, I look forward through the windshield towards the airport. I am still three and a half miles away from the runway. It's too far, I need more time. I already know that I can't make it. I'm familiar with this area; I need somewhere to go, but the streets are full of cars. Engine failure is a pilot's worst nightmare, especially with no place to land, not even a flat piece of ground.

N1097D: Gillespie tower, this is 1097D; I have lost all power and am going down!

Gillespie Tower: 1097D. Are you declaring an emergency?

N1097D: Yes, I am!

Immediately, I started thinking, what does declaring an emergency mean? Are they going to send somebody to save me? Is Superman on standby, flying in at the last second to lower me safely to the ground?

Gillespie Tower: 1097D. How many souls are on board?

N1097D: Just me!

At that Moment, I was thankful that Robin was not with me on this flight. Thank you, Lord, nobody is with me. Yes, I am the only soul on board.

I look down and forward, estimating how much time and distance I can cover. I am about 1500 feet above ground, so I have about 35 seconds before running out of airspace and ideas. I have over 3000 skydives under my belt, with over half performing in airshows with the Leap Frogs. I am accustomed to landing in very tight areas and have extensive experience estimating glide slopes into landing areas; that is how I know I have no options here. I have trained for this for forty years; even as a student, the instructor pulls out the mixture control without warning, the engine quits, and he says, "Your engine just quit; what are you going to do?" I go through all the steps while picking out a safe place to land, but there is no place to land safely this time. The only option is crashing into the very rough ground below me. Help me, God!

I see Interstate 8, which is approximately three miles from the runway. I could put my wheels on an asphalt patch on the freeway. I have just enough altitude to make a slow left turn; I am descending; this will be close. No good; there is too much traffic on both the eastbound and westbound lanes; I can't land there. But I see a gap between the freeways. This open space looks like a black hole, with no light getting to it; it's an overpass. I can't see what's down there, but no options are left.

To land an airplane, you must have a forward view to set up for the landing; the Cessna 195 needs about 1000 feet to land and roll out properly. The airplane has to be at the right altitude with the right speed, and then a controlled stall of the aircraft, with perfect timing to touch down and roll out, controlling the airplane until it stops. But that's not going to be possible.

I have enough time for a tiny correction, not for a landing but for a crash, and hopefully minimize casualties from hitting any cars. After the minor correction, I am about to disappear below the overpass. Flying lower, almost even with the bridge, I still couldn't see what I was flying into.

I am making a slow left turn and running out of airspace; the ground is coming up fast, and I am doing my best glide, 75 knots. I feel the wing hit the overpass…my eyes instinctively close to protect them from the debris. I am now in a hurricane of crunching metal and breaking glass; the sounds are deafening. I am waiting for it, death, that is. Will I feel anything, or will I just be gone? I am conscious and at peace; I will open my eyes in heaven any Moment. Within seconds, it is quiet; I hear nothing.

Chapter Two
My Parade Begins

I was born in Rockford, Illinois, on March 18, 1957. I shared my birthday with my twin sister, Kathy, as she was born seven minutes behind me; I blame her for our early arrival of nearly two months for pushing me out from behind. Weighing in at three pounds twelve ounces, I was a premie. In 1957, they didn't have the medical technology that they have today to keep premature babies alive. Despite all that, God had a plan for my life.

My parents were born in the pre-WWII era in America. My mother was a nurse by trade, and my Dad was an ironworker. My Dad served in the Navy on a supply ship in the South Pacific during the war. After the war, my parents married and started contributing to the baby boom. Doing their part, I was number five in our food chain of eight children.

My Mom and Dad had their hands full, and six children were born within five years. There were four of us in diapers before disposables were the norm. It seemed my Mom was always doing laundry. They raised us like most post-war parents, and our lifestyle was typical. My Dad had a new home built, which was comfortable for our family of eight. Although my Mom was a nurse, she knew, like most mothers back then, that her most important job was taking care of her children. I am very thankful that our mother could do that because of the economics during that generation.

It was a great time to grow up in America; my impression of life in the late 50s and early 60s as a young child was that everybody seemed very happy. A decade removed from WWII, America was very unified. We won the war, and our future was bright and hopeful. Having parents who grew up during the Depression made them very frugal with their money. My Dad would always say that our mother was so cheap that she would jump over the gate to save its hinges.

Life was simple and uncomplicated. The focus was God, country, and family in that order. We lived in a neighborhood with no fences that separated the half-acre parcels of land, which gave us baby boomer kids plenty of room to play. Whenever we wanted to play a team sport, all we had to do was start, and kids would come running. Whether it was baseball, football, kicking the can, or capturing the flag, we played outside until supper. Then, after supper, we would be outside until dark. Our parents had peace, raising their children during that time; we could be out after dark without worrying about being kidnapped. Before driving age, we would hitchhike to town eleven miles away without a care; life was good!

I do remember the night that complacency and innocence started to crumble. My sister Maureen's best friend Susan Brady came missing. That night, we got a knock on our door; one of her older brothers was looking for Susan. He and the rest of her family were canvasing the neighborhood to find her. After several months, they caught the guy who had taken her while she was walking home from school. The police had found her remains in an incinerator at the perpetrator's home. Our quiet, innocent community was never the same. Nothing like that happened again while we grew up there, but the death of Susan took our innocence from us. As a child growing up without the internet, you didn't know evil existed unless it came knocking on your door. In today's world, children learn about evil at a very early age.

Post WWII, parents were not always the most affectionate, and ultimately, with eight children, there wasn't much one-on-one time to build those special bonds with Mom and Dad. Like most siblings, we fought and competed for their approval and affection.

Despite the weaknesses I had created about myself, I don't remember being unhappy. Children don't know what they don't know; we weren't aware if we lacked anything. I didn't realize I was skinny, especially in the leg area, until the other kids called me chicken legs. I hated to wear long pants in the summertime, but my Mom always tried to get me to wear them because of my skinny legs. These are the indicators that start to make you feel inferior. What does a kid do to fix the problem? In the skinny leg department, you try to fill them in by eating; obviously, this is a no-win solution.

Looking back, I see that my parents made some mistakes but did their best with what they knew. One of the greatest attributes of my Dad was that he decided to quit drinking when he had children. I had heard many stories about my Dad drinking from our grandparents and even the tales our Dad would share about his drinking and fighting while in the Navy. My Dad had enough sense that he didn't want that kind of exposure to his kids. I will always have a grateful place in my heart for the decisions he made to be the best Dad he could be.

Life seemed somewhat normal until I hit second grade; being with my twin sister during kindergarten and first grade was nice. Attending a catholic school could be tough on a kid during that time. The nuns had full permission to discipline how they saw fit; rulers across the knuckles or a simple slap in the face was not uncommon, at least not for me.

One strong memory that sticks with me is when I was clowning around like most days. Sister Alyssa had just about enough when she called my name, "Michael Kelly Carroll, bring your desk up here." When I got to the front of the class, I thought she wanted me next to her desk to keep a better eye on me. But she was standing in the doorway. "Keep coming," she said sternly, motioning me across the hallway toward the janitor's closet. There was no way my desk would fit in there. Well, sure enough, it slid right in. I thought she must have done a trial run with some other kid. She told me I would spend the rest of the day in the closet and proceeded to shut the door; thank God she left the light on.

If not for the fun I had after school, I would have never been able to endure my school years. The winters were terrific growing up: ice skating at the local park, building snow forts, and having snowball fights. The Carroll kids were pretty mischievous; we would hide between the houses, wait for cars to drive by, and then pummel them with snowballs. Most would stop very quickly from the shock of the thud. Stopping a vehicle with a snowball was fun—the power we had! Things would get exciting when they would stop and try to chase us. Our hearts were pumping like crazy from running and trying to get away. It was hard for the chasers to catch us because we knew the neighborhood backyards and all the hiding places.

Once in a while, the younger, slower kids would get caught, and the chaser would scold them, but other than that, it was pretty harmless fun. Another favorite winter pastime occurred after a fresh snow. We would stand by a stop sign, and when a car would stop, we would grab hold of the rear bumper and go for a ride unbeknownst to the driver. We would take the ride as long as we could hold on; we called it skitching. Depending on where you grew up, you had your name for it. All the same fun, though.

One year, this winter storm started with heavy rain, then the temperature dropped below freezing. All the streets and sidewalks transformed into one huge ice skating rink. Our entire neighborhood was out that evening, ice skating from house to house. It was so much fun and beautiful; the rain froze on the branches of the trees, which turned it into a winter wonderland. It was one of those magical memories that I will never forget.

The transition from winter to spring was my least favorite time of year. The snow would melt, and everything would turn to slush—no snow to play in, but still cold. Being wet and muddy limits our options for outdoor fun. That is why summer has always been my favorite season of the year. I knew summer was getting close when the temperatures warmed, and the teachers opened the classroom windows. You could hear the janitor mowing the grass, and the smell of fresh-cut grass in the spring would fill the entire classroom with excitement; it was a telltale sign that freedom was near!

The last day of school before we were out for summer couldn't have come soon enough. Sister Alyssa was at her wit's end, trying to keep me focused; all I could do was stare out the window, daydreaming of what I would do during summer vacation.

Freedom, in itself, was the best part of summer. Just getting up in the morning and not having to be under control all day long was heaven. Being cooped up was difficult for me, being the high-energy kid that I was. I longed for new adventures and learning new things.

One of the best achievements in every kid's life was learning to ride a bicycle. All the older kids that had bikes were at another level of freedom. They could go places that the younger kids couldn't follow. I learned quickly by observing and watching the techniques of the older kids. Mounting and starting to pedal my bike was beginning to click. So one morning, when my older siblings and their friends were riding their bikes, out of the blue, one of them asked if I wanted to learn to ride; maybe it was for entertainment value to watch me crash and burn. Whatever the reason, it didn't matter; with great enthusiasm, I said, boy, would I.

Like magic, a bike was next to me, and I received instructions. "Whatever you do, just keep pedaling." Sherman Avenue ran perpendicular to Johnston, where we lived. Sherman had a slight decline to it, and if not careful, a bicycle could get going pretty fast.

They lined me up, pointed me down the hill, and gave me a running push as they yelled, "Mike, keep pedaling!" I did. The speed was increasing, but I kept pedaling. The bike started to veer out of control towards this house, but I didn't know how to correct it, and the inevitable happened: I hit the house broadside, going 20 mph. The agony of defeat replaced the thrill of victory. As I limped towards our house, I heard some kids laughing. My big brother Tom was the first to reach out to me to ask if I was okay. My memories of my older brother Tom were that of the encourager. He was always watching out for me. He was four years older, which seemed like a lifetime when you're young.

When we returned home for lunch, the six of us piled into our designated seats at the table. Mom, being a nurse, noticed I wasn't my agile, graceful self. She said, "What happened to you?" Before the words came out of my mouth, my brothers and sisters said I ran into a house with a bicycle. After a quick examination, Mom said, "You stay off those bicycles." To this day, I wonder why she said that. That is part of success; you fail, you try again. She probably meant to say, stay off the bicycle today because you're hurt. Either way, I didn't listen.

After lunch, we all went back out to play; within a couple of minutes, all the older kids left a friend and me alone. He already knew how to ride; having a taste of success and believing I could, we decided to ride down to our church/school parking lot. I picked up the bike that I crashed on and started riding like there was nothing to it. We went down to the playground, where I rode around like the wind in this ample open space. It was one of the greatest feelings of speed and freedom I had ever felt. Looking back on it, this was probably the beginning of my need for speed.

Five or ten minutes had passed, and I noticed this car parked in the middle of the parking lot and learned that your head and body follow whatever your eyes look at. This car was like a magnet; after every turn I made, it seemed I got closer and closer, and then bam, I hit the car!

The first point of contact was my eye hitting the end of the handlebar where your hands go, which would have been fine, except there were no rubber handlebar grips. There I lie again; I should have listened to my Mom. Within seconds, two nuns sitting outside their convent on this beautiful summer day, sipping lemonade and watching these two young boys enjoying their freedom, came running over to me to see if I was okay. They walked me to their convent and offered some lemonade. I had a cut over my eye that needed some doctor's attention, so they called my mother, and in a few minutes, my Mom showed up in a taxi since our family only had one car. She graciously thanked the sisters, loaded me in the cab, and swept me off to the doctor, where I got my first stitch.

I don't remember my Mom scolding me that day for my disobedience; I'm sure she realized then that there was no stopping a child from learning to ride a bicycle and falling. Getting back up was part of the process. From that day forward, I acted like one of the big kids. I rode where they rode. There were exceptions, though; sometimes, they didn't want to hang out with the younger kids. They were probably doing things they shouldn't be doing, and they didn't want us little tattle tales opening our big mouths.

Like most large baby boom families, there were a lot of hand-me-downs, clothing, ice skates, and bicycles. I remember my Dad came home one summer evening, pulling into our driveway with our station wagon. With this excited look, he jumped out, opened the tailgate, and there were two brand new Schwinn 10-speed bikes. It wasn't anybody's birthday, and not even close to Christmas. All six of us gathered around my Dad and Mom, trying to figure out who these beautiful bikes were for.

The suspense didn't last long; my Dad said, "Tom, Colleen, these are for you." I don't know how my other brothers and sisters felt, but I was excited for them. They were the oldest, and all the old bikes would move down the food chain. I am trying to remember the bike I was riding or my brother's, who was eleven months older. But wherever it came from, my bike was good enough; it got me around.

As my Dad presented the new Schwinn to my oldest brother, Tom turned to Pat and said, "Here you go." I knew the sibling order of things had to be followed, but it didn't stop me from being envious of Pat, who was given the bike I always wanted: a royal blue Schwinn Sting Ray. I wanted it badly. Patience was something I didn't have, like most children my age. I would have to bide my time; one day, the Sting Ray would be mine.

One of the most memorable summer highlights was our vacation to Turtle Lake in southern Wisconsin. We would stay at our grandparent's cottage. It was a two-story, wood-stained structure that stood proudly on a hill overlooking the lake. I don't know how my grandparents put up with another eight people in their lake home, six being wild, little, energetic curtain climbers. The two younger siblings came seven and eight years later, so other than waking up in the middle of the night for feeding or a diaper change, they were problem-free. Swimming and boat rides on our grandparent's pontoon boat were some of our favorite things. I don't remember doing much more than that because we were all so young.

At that age, you are along for the ride; we did whatever the grandparents wanted. We were in their world, and that was limited. I loved the smells of the spring-fed lake and the activity and energy from the people who came from all over to spend some of their summer vacation, fishing, water skiing, and swimming. We didn't experience nightlife other than playing dominos with Grandpa or card games our grandparents would teach us to play. I will remember and appreciate that our parents and grandparents didn't get a babysitter and run to the resort bar, leaving their eight responsibilities alone. The time at the cottage was all about us and building those quality memories, and we built quite a few.

Writing this chapter helps me reflect on my life and how I was blessed to grow up during one of the most significant times in America with parents who had their priorities and values correctly in place. I admit that I was judgmental of my Dad and Mom, and I focused on some of the mistakes they made raising their children. But revisiting those times has made me realize how grateful I am that I had parents willing to take on the responsibility of raising and caring for such a large family and protecting our innocence as long as they could.

Mike's far left with brothers and sisters

If you are reading this and feeling that you weren't as blessed as the Carroll kids, I can say that God created you for a specific time and place for His purpose.

I just watched the movie about Bart Millard, lead singer for Mercy Me and composer of the song; I Can Only Imagine. He had a horrible upbringing, and through the grace of God, he became a victor and not a victim. Take this time to make one of the most critical decisions in your life, to live your life as a victor!

Chapter Three
Adversity Makes You Stronger

I could always tell that summer was ending when our Mom would take us shopping for school clothes; it was just about that time when my Dad and Mom called me into the kitchen, where most of the severe talks would take place. The three of us sat at the kitchen table big enough for ten.

Growing up, I was on the receiving end of plenty of serious talks, but something was different this time. You could tell my Mom and Dad were a little nervous about what they would say to me. My Dad spoke, "Michael, we have something important to tell you. "Your principal, Sister Owen, has recommended that you repeat second grade, and I and your mother agree."

I couldn't believe what I was hearing. Those words were like daggers penetrating my heart. All I could think about was spending one more year with sister Alissa. It couldn't be true; how would I survive? I was so embarrassed; my twin sister Kathy would go on to third grade while I stayed back in second; what would our classmates think? What would my brothers and sisters think?

Second grade was a very uncertain time for me. I was seven or eight years old, trying to figure out life and feeling like a failure. I was a sensitive child, especially during that time. One night at the dinner table, my siblings were picking on me about something; maybe I had knocked over my glass of milk. My older brother Tom said, "Leave him alone." Everybody got quiet because they knew they were wrong. I felt so moved by my brother standing up for me that I became emotional. Rather than embarrass myself even more, I acted like I dropped my fork and ducked under the table so nobody would see me cry. My brother was like my guardian angel. Throughout the years, he would always be there for me; when someone bigger hurt me, he would step in like a sheepdog and kick their butt!

Thinking back, I realize this was one of the most pivotal stages of my life. Years later, my Mom and Dad always told me that holding me back was a big mistake in their parenting decisions. I would always encourage them when I explained that it was the very thing that helped me be the man that I am today. You see, I made a choice; I could roll over and be a victim or use this setback to show the world that I wasn't some stupid failure. I developed an "I'll show you" attitude.

I want to say that I applied that attitude in academics but did not; I became rebellious toward the whole school system. I did just enough to get to the next grade. I maintained that same attitude through the end of my junior year until my career counselor sat me down and told me that if I didn't buckle down in my senior year, I would not graduate. That was all it took; I rose to the occasion and, for the first time, realized that I wasn't stupid when I applied myself. After years of poor grades, Cs, Ds, and Fs, my senior year was As, Bs, and Cs.

In fourth grade, I had a very positive experience that gave me a glimmer of hope that I wasn't stupid. I had a knack for spelling. Every Friday afternoon, our class would have a spelling bee. Even without studying, I would end up in 2nd or 3rd place. I couldn't wait to share my talent with my Mom. After all of the hard times that I put my Mom and Dad through, worrying that they had a kid who wasn't cutting it in school, it was encouraging to her that I excelled at something.

Since I was doing so well, I started to study. My Mom gave me this book with almost every word listed from A to Z. I would study every night. Even though I would work hard to win, I always came in second place. There was this one kid who always beat me; his name was Tim Denari. I would go home and tell my Mom that Tim beat me again. My Mom looked me in the eyes and said, "If you beat Tim Denari, I will give you five dollars."

I went to work, studied harder, and was ready the following Friday. That day, I was victorious. I ran into the house yelling. Mom, I won! I came in first in the spelling bee today. My Mom said, "Michael, I am so proud of you; here you go, here are your five dollars." I didn't have the heart to tell her that Tim Denari was home sick with the flu.

That was also about the age when my friends and I were always looking for different things to do. We lived near some fields that had these hollow reeds growing. We got some matches and would pull a reed out, light it up, and smoke it like a cigarette. You know where this is going; yes, reeds are the gateway to cigarettes, and by the time I was ten years old, I was hooked. One summer day, we had just finished lunch, and my friend and I were getting ready to jump on our bikes and ride to the local park when my Mom caught us. "Michael, what do you have in your pocket?" Trying to ride off before she could stop me, she grabbed on the back of my bicycle and stopped me cold in my tracks." What is this?" It was a pack of cigarettes.

"Let's show your father what you have." In the house we went, my Dad was still sitting at the kitchen table. "Ronnie, look what Michael has!" My Dad said, "So you smoke, Mike? Let's see, light one up." I thought for a minute; this is cool; I am smoking in the house in front of my Dad and Mom. I could not imagine what this exercise was all about. After I finished smoking the cigarette, I put it out in the ashtray that my Mom had put in front of me. As I wondered what was next, "Light up another one," my Dad said. So I pulled another out of the pack and lit it up.

About halfway through the second, I started to understand; I didn't feel so good; "Keep going, Mike." My Dad started to see his plan working; I'm sure I began to change colors. I was starting to lose it, trying to control it, but it wasn't working; pressure started to build, and suddenly, I was projectile vomiting my lunch all over the kitchen table. I looked up at my Dad, who grinned from ear to ear. I want to tell you that my smoking habit was broken that day, but it wasn't.

By completing my 8th-grade year of schooling, I would have nine years in the Catholic school system. The summer before 8th grade, my mother met this woman who had her son attending a Catholic seminary high school for young boys who felt they had the calling to be priests. I believed my Mom wanted one of her sons to be a priest. It seemed to me that in my Mom's heart, I was the best hope for her dream to come true. My Mom came to me and asked if I would be interested in attending a couple-day open house for the seminary school. My Mom was so happy when I told her yes; I thought it would be fun.

Maybe this was my calling, and I am being guided here. The boy who would be my sponsor was in his second year and excited to share his thoughts about his calling. It was a couple-hour drive, and on the way, he answered most of my questions, primarily those about recreational things to do; again, I was still all about having fun and probably didn't hear a word that he thought was important.

When we arrived, I was shown some essential facilities where I would sleep and eat. I immediately believed this would be fun and different, but it was not my calling.

After getting home, my Mom asked me how it went. I told her it was okay; she didn't press, and I really didn't have much more to add. I think she was a little disappointed.

As I got older, especially in my teen years, my heart grew farther away from God; I hadn't learned or desired how to build that relationship with him. I was probably taught that in my years of Catholic school, but I probably wasn't listening.

After buying the Turtle Lake resort, my Mom and Dad were separated from their duties to take their children to church. One had to tend to the resort, meaning they had to church at different times. My mother would take my younger siblings with her; my brother Pat and twin sister Kathy would always want to go with my Dad; the reason was, on the way to church, my Dad would tell us that we couldn't tell our mother about us going to breakfast instead of the church service. Please forgive me, Dad!

As we got older and could drive ourselves to church, we had a lot of breakfast stops, if you know what I mean. Our mother reminded us of our responsibility to God, which was attending church, and confessing. Our mother wore out many pairs of knee pads, praying for her children.

She always reminded us about services to attend besides Sunday service. Ash Wednesday was a big one; our Mom wanted to see the ash cross as proof that we attended. We would always find a distraction from fulfilling our responsibility. After about the time Ash Wednesday service should be getting out, we would start heading home and remember that we didn't have the proof of service, the ash cross. Since we all smoked cigarettes and the ashtray was always filled with ash, we would dip our fingers into the ashtray and make the sign of the cross on our forehead. We never told our dear mother about that deception; it would have broken her heart. Throughout our lives, when my Mom started to lose hope that her children would turn out ok, she would say to my Dad, "Where did we go wrong?" He would say, "Don't judge them until they are about forty!"

Chapter Four
Life on Turtle Lake

Looking back, I realize my self-worth came from worldly things that didn't matter, but those building blocks made me feel good about myself. The power of the dream was at work, molding me and guiding me on my life journey. I would excel in stuff I was interested in, like boxing; I would watch Muhammed Ali, study his art, and emulate him and other great boxers as time passed. I carried two sets of boxing gloves and asked kids, even kids older and bigger if they would like to box. I discovered that I was naturally fast with my hands and would usually be victorious.

The other talent I acquired was water skiing. The vacations on Turtle Lake opened my Mom up to the idea that our family should buy the resort and spend more time together. She had convinced my Dad that this was a good idea. So when I was twelve years old, we moved to Wisconsin, all ten of us, to run the resort. My Dad gave up ironworking, and we all rolled up our sleeves and went to work in the spring of 1969 as the new owners of the Crystal Bowl Resort.

Turtle Lake was small, only about a mile long and half a mile wide, and spring-fed, which made it very clean with excellent visibility. It was in-between two towns, Whitewater and Delavan. It had two resorts; ours was the biggest and the best. Schroeder Resort was on the other end; we didn't like going there because they were our rivals and competition, at least in this twelve-year-old's mind.

Turtle Lake was like a slice of heaven to me. I woke every morning to the sound of small outboard motors carrying the fisherman to their favorite fishing hole. I loved the smell of a freshwater lake, with hints of fresh algae rolling up on the beach from the fisherman's boat wakes. I was always excited about what the day would bring.

When this family of ten showed up as the new owners, with children of all ages, the local kids came out of the woodwork to see who the Carrolls were. We had immediate popularity. One of the first kids we met was Pete. He was very outgoing and likable and had a boat.

When we got to know Pete better, he offered to take my brother and me for a boat ride. It was a cool, rainy spring day, and we were appropriately dressed for it. Back then, the daily attire for lake living was cut-off jean shorts and bare feet. I noticed a pair of yellow skis when I climbed into his aluminum boat with a 16-horsepower Scott Atwater engine. Do you know how to water ski? I asked. "Of course I do." Could you teach me? He said, "Sure, let's do it." He gave me a crash course on how to put the skis on, my body position once in the water, and what to do with the rope.

I got the skis on and then floundered like a dying fish on the water's surface. The rope would tighten, and Pete would drag me through the water sideways; this would take a lot of work. Finally, after several attempts, I was able to stay facing forward. I would yell, hit it, and he would push the throttle forward. I could get myself out of the water, but I'd fall over once I tried to stand up.

We tried skiing from the water several times before Pete suggested we do a dock start; that way, you would be almost halfway out of the water before you got pulled up; this was a bad idea, too. I soon found out that this technique takes time and experience. After several dock start attempts and getting banged up from falling on the skis, I decided to try again from the water. On the 12th try, I came out of the water with straight skis. I waited patiently for enough speed for my skis to glide on top of the water, and I just stood up. I was skiing, and my brothers Pat and Pete started yelling and screaming for my success; learning to waterski helped me confirm that I was not a quitter.

There is widespread thinking that failing is bad. Like many others who have succeeded, I don't see it this way. We have failed at every corner, and through a great strength of character developed along the way, we rose, dusted ourselves off, and continued the pursuit of our dreams.

Just like your childhood, there was a failure that should have led you to success if you got up after you fell. If you take the time to look back on your life and identify the little wins that usually took place after that failure, you will find that those experiences nudged you along and put just a bit of wind under your wings. This lesson is the formula to use for the rest of your life. For me, winning a spelling bee (well, sort of) or even getting out of second grade can make you feel like a winner.

Looking back at your childhood, you see nothing but bad things and struggles. I believe God will give you the strength to overcome, be victorious, and show the world how great your God is with your testimony. Don't let your past struggles and failures keep you down; rise and use them to be victorious.

Chapter Five
Walking On Water

After I learned to waterski, I was always looking to see who I could talk into taking me out. We sold gas to the boat owners, so I would offer to fill their gas tank if they would take me skiing. (Thanks, Dad.) Skiing on two skis became easy; the next level would be dropping a ski and slalom skiing. Back in the early 70s, there were just a few excellent water skiers, at least on our little lake, from whom I could learn. So, I grabbed instructions wherever I could.

It seemed simple enough. Get on two skis and drop the ski from your less dominant foot. Since I was right-handed, I guessed I would drop my left ski. The next step was to loosen the ski binding from the left ski to make it easier to kick off. After several attempts and successfully kicking off the ski, I got used to balancing on a single ski and not overcompensating. You also had to figure out what to do with your trailing foot that didn't have a ski on it. Like anything, it takes time to learn how to master it. With some time, I soon cut back and forth, crossing the wake and making turns like somebody who knew what he was doing.

If you didn't have exposure to good skiers, you were limited to what you could accomplish independently, which is valid in all aspects of success. It's called the power of association. You become who you associate with. So I tried to find some books on the subject, but there were few. I did find one that someone at the American Water Skiing Association wrote. It showed basic instructions on how to learn to ski on two skis and then progress to slalom skiing. At the time, the highest level of skiing was on your bare feet. But, if you could ski on one ski, you were considered a good skier.

I found a poster of a guy named Mike Suyderhoud; he was skiing slalom and was making a turn around a buoy where his shoulder was almost touching the water. Coming off the ski was a huge rooster tail of water. That poster hung on my wall, where I looked at it daily. What Suyderhoud was doing would become my standard to strive for.

The money I earned from working at our resort would go towards ski equipment. To dream build, I frequented a local marina called Crummies in Whitewater, Wisconsin, about eleven miles from our lake. They had this beautiful mahogany O'Brien slalom water ski. That is when I learned the power of a dream. After saving enough money, I asked my Mom to drive me into town to buy the ski that went from the wish, want, need to get. I also purchased the protective vinyl case and the red O'Brien ski jacket to match. Looking back on that time, I was looking for something to set me apart. Skiing would become my identity. I had the equipment and the passion to become one of the best skiers. I was on my way to becoming a big fish in a small pond.

The beach was filled with kids laughing and screaming on top of a bed of 70's music blasting from outside speakers located on the boardwalk. Some days, a bunch of us would swim out to this raft, which was about 12-foot square and just big enough for about ten kids to hang out on. It was just out of sight of any parents trying to keep an eye on us. We would carry things like cigarettes and matches in a plastic bag over our heads as we swam. It was a great time and place to be growing up.

My Dad was always working on marketing the resort to bring more people. He hired a water ski show to perform. The buzz on the lake was that a team called the Rock Aqua Jays was coming. I had never been so excited wondering what kind of things they could do on skis. On the day of the show, the team showed up with all their cool ski boats rigged for unique ski acts. I sat on the beach and watched them prepare for the show; this was the first time I had seen that much ski equipment in one place: ski ropes, various types of skis, boats, and sound equipment. The Rock Jays had a major production.

The closer that show time came, the larger the crowd became. The Master of Ceremonies began right on schedule, "Ladies and gentleman, boys and girls. If you will look towards show center, here comes . . ." he began to describe the details of the ski boat, its color, type, and horsepower just as it roared its engine closer to the beach. Without warning, the driver pulled the power, cranked the wheel, and did a complete 360 without moving another foot toward the beach! Wow, and this was just the beginning!

That day, I saw people do things on skis that I hadn't thought possible. One act that grabbed my attention was barefoot skiing; I had seen it in a waterski book but never in real life, and that became my next goal. The other attraction was these two blonde-haired sisters, who were as good as the guys. Looking back, I realize this event significantly impacted my life's direction. I decided that day, I didn't know how, but one day, I would ski for the Rock Aqua Jays.

I had become a good slalom skier, but after watching the ski show that day, I realized I had a long way to go; there was so much more to learn. If I could learn to ski on my feet, that would put me at another level in the sport. But there was no one to teach me. I pulled out the AWSA (American Water Ski Association) book, found the procedure for successfully skiing on my feet, and started to familiarize myself.

Step 1. While skiing on a single ski, take your trail foot out of the back binding and get into the same position as skiing on two skis.

Step 2. Slowly place your foot on the water, heel first, with your toes pointed up.

Step 3. Carefully transfer your weight onto your foot in the water.

Step 4. When you feel stable on the foot in the water, take your foot out of the binding of the ski and place it on the water to balance the weight onto both feet.

Well, that seemed easy enough. Accomplishing this became my next goal, and I would begin at the first opportunity I had to ski again. Since we didn't have a boat, I had to wait for a weekend when some out-of-towers would be coming to the lake. The boat also had to meet some requirements. It had to be fast enough to support the surface area of my feet and hold me up; this would be trial and error, but mostly error.

That was easy to figure out. The first time I got to ski, I took my foot out of the back binding and followed the steps. I realized I needed more speed because my foot felt mushy when I put weight on it. There was no way this speed could support me skiing on my feet. But I still learned a few things that would benefit me, like taking my foot out of the back binding and getting into the crouching position to drop my ski.

There were a couple of times that I went for it, even knowing it was too slow and down I would go. I would have to get used to this; falling was part of the process, and the faster the boat went, the harder the falls became. I kept thinking, if it were easy, everybody would be doing it! I needed help finding somebody with a boat that was fast enough to learn the final steps and successfully barefoot water ski. Finally, these three guys came to the lake in their high-speed boats. The owner of the boat was Clint, a super nice guy. I told Clint what I was trying to do, and he said he would be happy to help.

He was going over to Whitewater Lake to do some skiing and told me I was welcome to come with him. So my brother Tom and I tagged along. It was a beautiful day for skiing, and the wind was calm, which was important. You needed water that wasn't rough from wind or boat wakes. So, we found a cove on the lake with some nice glassy water.

Clint said, "This looks good; you're up, Mike; let's see what you got." I put my O'Brien red ski vest on and asked Clint if we could get the boat to 42 mph. I was still determining the needed speed, but 42 would suit my weight. A minute later, I was in the water with my ski on, gave the command, and hit it. I was out and up faster than I had ever been. I knew this boat had all the power I needed; the rest was up to me.

Looking forward, I saw a nice, smooth patch of water ahead. Here goes nothing; I took my left foot out of the back binding, crouched down, knees bent, and left foot gliding on the water. I shift my weight to my left foot, heel down, toes up, feeling good. I start to take my right foot out. It has to be quick enough that your right foot is back on the water to support the left. The ski isn't coming off; it's too tight. Wham, down I go, that hurt. I'm seeing some stars. I've never fallen at 42 mph, but it turns out that the water gets harder at higher speeds. Who knew?

I raise my hand; this is the telltale sign to let the boat driver know you are okay. Clint races over, knowing that had to hurt. "Are you okay?" I told him I was fine but thought the front binding was too tight and that I couldn't get the ski off. He recommended removing the heel cup; I would have to slide it out. That made total sense, so we removed it. I was concerned that I couldn't get up on a slalom ski without it, but I was ready for my second attempt anyway. I was not too fond of how it felt falling at 42 mph, so I thought, don't fall. I just had to follow the steps.

Hit it! I came out of the water; my right foot stayed in the binding with no problem. The water looked good, so I gave Clint the thumbs up for speed; within seconds, we were back up to speed. I was just outside the wake in a trough that wasn't turbulent from the prop.

Everything felt right; I planted my left foot, crouched, transferred weight, pulled my foot out of the ski, planted my right foot, and went down. I need a helmet. That hurt worse than the last time. I raised my hand, the boat did a 180, and in an instant, he was there to assist if needed. "Are you alright?" Clint said, "You almost had it, Mike."

That was just enough encouragement; I needed to give it another try. Okay, let's do it again. Clint circled me, bringing the ski rope to my hand, and . . .hit it. Back up to speed, there it is; water looks good. Focus, Mike, there is a learning curve to this. You may not know it, but you now know what not to do and what to do, so do it! My left foot came out, planted, and transferred the weight a little towards the rear so as not to fall forward; it feels stable—right foot now, one motion, out and on the water. I can see everybody in the boat screaming, hands in the air, thumbs up; they had never seen anybody ski on their feet. I was smiling ear to ear and skiing on my feet! I was rock solid; I didn't want this to end, but my feet were starting to burn, a good burn, but it hurt. My feet had never been on the water at 42 mph; this would take some getting used to.

Learning to ski barefoot, as meaningless as it may seem, was one of those Moments in my life that opened a door in my mind to believe in the possibilities and the what-ifs. It was a defining Moment that separated me from the masses. It became my identity, who I was, and who I would become.

After that day, I knew I was now part of a small group of people that would call themselves "Footers." I didn't realize how small the group was since there were no internet or barefoot forums. I did subscribe to Water Ski magazine, but I never read any article or saw any photographs of barefoot skiers.

Along with my newly acquired skills that would continue to strengthen, I became a solid slalom skier and started to learn some tricks. These tricks were on short, fat skis that took little speed to

35

perform on. I could ski behind small fishing boats with just 10 HP, which was nice when nobody was around with their ski boats.

Occasionally, I would ask my Dad if we could get a ski boat, and he always had the same response: why would I buy a boat? Everything you boys touch turns to crap, but he didn't use the word crap. Looking back on all the things the three oldest boys had destroyed, he was probably right.

One day, my brother Pat and I were in the bar, and one of the locals came in to speak to my Dad. "Dave, I'm going out of town for a few weeks. Would you mind looking after my boat?" He threw the keys to my Dad, saying, "If your two boys would like to use it while I'm gone, that would be okay by me." My Dad told him that he didn't want to do that. But the man said that it would be fine. Dad laughed, "It's your boat," and hung the keys up. My brother and I took note of where they were hanging.

We would take the boat out for joy rides for the next week. We liked to chase down ducks. When we thought we could run one over, it would duck dive below the surface. When it resurfaced, we would start all over again. We played chase with the ducks daily; I'm sure they had as much fun as we did.

In the last week, before the boat owner returned, my brother and I drove the boat around the lake, and Pat decided to drive towards the beach at a slightly higher speed than usual. Right before hitting the beach, he would kill the engine, and I would pull up the motor before it hit the sand; this gave us an idea. We agreed to have a contest to see who could drive the boat to the beach the farthest. We got a measuring tape and measured each attempt to beat the other's distance. After taking turns several times, we gathered a crowd for our contest.

We kept moving closer to the beach on each attempt before cutting the engine and jumping out of the driver's seat to go to the stern and pick up the engine before hitting the beach to not damage the motor's lower unit. Each of us took turns with the other on the beach to measure. Pat had the winning distance, but it was my turn, and I was determined to win. I drove the boat about half the distance of the lake, lined it up, heading towards the beach. I hit the gas, and the boat lurched forward, racing closer to the beach. I was thinking, wait for it, not yet, wait for the last possible second to kill the engine. I had an idea: why shut the engine off? I just sat there smiling and hit the beach so hard that the boat almost hit a tree before it stopped. I jumped out of the boat and yelled, beat that!

I was the winner, and the crowd clapped and cheered; nobody had ever seen anybody drive a boat up the beach like that. We decided to get off the beach before Dad saw us, but the boat would not budge. It was high and dry and stuck. I started to panic; I knew we had to get this boat off the beach, so we recruited as many kids as possible to help push the boat back into the water. But it was too heavy; it just wouldn't move.

Suddenly, I see my Dad's car pull into the driveway. He parks and gets out of the car with a look only my Dad could give. He says, "You boys leave that boat right there, get away from it." Then walks off without another word. After about three days, the boat owner enters the resort and sees his boat sitting on the beach. He walked into the bar and asked my Dad why his boat was on the beach. My Dad looked at him and said, "I told you so!"

My Dad was wise, so we never owned a boat other than the rowboats we rented; it was hard to hurt those.

After learning to ski barefoot, I decided that it was time to get serious about trying to ski in a show. All I had to do was keep practicing and improving my skill level. There were few opportunities to practice barefooting, but I could continue working on other areas, which helped improve me. An idea came to me while working on my slalom skiing. I noticed that I could create a lot more speed when the boat was in a turn. As the boat started its turn, I could cross-cut from inside and cross the wake to the outside of the turn. I could reach maximum speed there and drop my ski barefoot for a few seconds before the speed diminished; this allowed me to work on dropping the ski, which was one of the most challenging steps of barefoot skiing.

I met some people visiting from Whitewater Lake, where I learned to ski barefoot. They invited me to ski with them; I jumped at the chance because they had a boat with plenty of speed to practice whatever I needed to work on. I learned later that they were members of the Whitewater Minneiska Ski Team, and their purpose for inviting me was to see if I was any good. After skiing and showing my skills, I was asked if I wanted to join their team. I couldn't believe it; it was a dream come true. My ultimate dream was to ski for the Rock Aqua Jays, but they weren't offering it, so this was the next best thing.

The show season had yet to start, and the team had a lot of work to do to prepare. Along with doing shows every Sunday in the late afternoons, we would compete with other show teams around the country. Our team didn't have a ski jump, so we were limited in what acts we could perform. I hadn't been exposed to a ski jump yet anyway, so I didn't know what I didn't know. We relied on the basics: the parade of flags the girls did, a triple stack pyramid, and some barefoot stunts.

The team was always trying to improve and increase the difficulties of the acts to increase their chances of placing in the tournaments. The show coordinator asked me if I had ever done the jump out of two skis to barefoot routine. I hadn't, but I was always willing to try anything. He explained that I would be skiing on two skis, and when I reached a speed in front of the show center, I would jump as high as I could into the air, out of the skis, and onto my feet. He said, "Mike, if you can do that, it will be a solo act for you."

I always had this drive to be the best of the best. I wanted to separate myself from the rest of the footers, and this was one more way to build up my identity. I needed to prove myself worthy. That second-grade failure was always simmering right under the surface, but the push it gave me was a blessing.

If you've ever seen modern-day barefoot water skiers, you will notice they wear padded wet suits to protect themselves from high-speed falls. The suits make it more comfortable to do tricks transitioning from water to feet and feet to water. In the 70s, there was no such thing. When the team presented my uniform, they handed me a red Speedo with white side stripes. Usually, my skiing attire was cut-off blue jeans, which had more protection than the Speedo. So this was a definite step down.

However, I accepted the challenge of learning the two ski-to-barefoot routines in my new team uniform and gave it a go. I launched off the dock with two skis, which, since learning to slalom, I hadn't done in ages. I had also never skied that fast to barefoot speed either. We circled and then started heading to the show center; I crouched down so my vertical jump was high and dramatic. At the show center, I jumped into the air, flying with nothing but a handle in my hand. And since what goes up must come down, I braced myself, knowing that my feet would contact the water. If I were two forward, I would go a_ _ over tea kettle. So, I knew that when I landed, I needed to be on my heels to keep that from happening. My feet made contact, and I crouched back to absorb the impact. I couldn't believe it. I was back on my feet and skiing. Everybody in the boat stood up, clapped, and cheered. It was a first-attempt success; hopefully, it wasn't beginner's luck.

After practicing all spring, the team was ready for the show season. I had never experienced performing in front of a crowd. Typically, a few friends rode in the boat, waiting for their turn to ski, but that was it. The Whitewater Minneiska Ski Show was a significant production, like a Broadway show, with costumes and props to entertain the audience. It brought me back a couple of years ago watching the Rock Aqua Jays getting ready when I was in the audience. Now, I was one of the performers who would wow the crowd with something new they hadn't seen before.

One of the opening acts was the girls skiing with the American flags, with the national anthem playing, which brought everybody to their feet with their hands over their hearts. It was a great way to start the show. After the first act, it moved quickly; while one act was on the water, the next would be ready and waiting on the dock, skis on, and prepared for the tow boat to come by. It was just slow enough for the dock handler to hand the lines to the driver. The boat's speed would take up the slack of the ropes; each skier was responsible for being ready for the jerk and to ski. If one skier fell and another could perform the act, one of the crew members would cut the rope loose from the boat and move on with the show. In competition, that would be a significant point reduction.

My first act for the show was the five-person barefoot routine. Five of us would launch off the dock while standing; with a single jerk, we would hit the water with our slalom skis. The boat would take us out of sight from the audience, where the waves created from the boat wake could subside and give us bare-footers cleaner water.

Spread out across the wake, all five skiers would be nearing the show center, crouching, barefoot planted in the water, and watching each other with peripheral vision to know when to drop the ski simultaneously. And there it is, ladies and gentlemen, the five-person barefoot team. We would all be barefoot skiing, passing the show center where the crowd was. Then, we held on through the turn to see who could hang in and keep skiing until the boat had brought us back to the center beach, where we would drop in a couple of feet of water and wave to the crowd without falling.

Waving was unlike any experience I'd ever had; I was a show performer, like in a circus. At first, I thought it was weird to wave to the crowd as they graciously clapped for your performance. After a couple of shows, you get used to it. Remember that how you conduct yourself as you ski and interact with the crowd will be judged during the competition. It helped me understand that it was like any performance in a competition; they didn't call it show skiing for nothing.

My next act would be a solo act; I was the only bare footer on the team who could jump out of two skis and onto my feet consistently. It made me feel special, one more thing that separated me from the masses. Standing out was a theme in my life; one more degree of separation from my second-grade failure and that "I'll show you" attitude was always lurking in my mind.

As the other skiers were performing, I was up next on deck. I grabbed the specific rope for my act. It was longer than the rest, 100 feet rather than 75; this was to place me farther behind the boat and keep me away from the turbulent water created by the propeller of the 350 HP engine. The HP was powerful enough to provide me with cleaner water away from the boat's wake.

I was ready with two skis sitting on the dock; the rope handler had the end of my line that he would hand to the boat driver as he went by. The boat takes me to the clear water parallel to the beach. I give him the thumbs up, telling him to increase his speed to 42 mph. I barely hear the announcer say my name and something about two skis. I am getting close now; I am crouched down and ready to spring out of my bindings into the air while leaning back just enough to absorb the impact of the high-speed water; my heels hit, oops, a little too far back.

I feel my rear end make contact with the water. Oh no, that didn't feel right. I'm still on my feet; I can hear the crowd cheer. I fight the turn; I am now back in front in a couple of feet of water. I let go of the rope and sank to the bottom on my feet. I smile and wave, but something doesn't feel right. With no protection from my Speedos, I believe I experienced a 42 MPH enema. As the crowd was distracted by the next act, I was hoping that the audience didn't notice me walking straight to the bathroom. From that day forward, I told the show coordinator that our barefoot uniforms would be blue jean cut-offs; he agreed that would be a good idea after I explained my situation.

The show season was going great; every Sunday afternoon, we would perform, and through the week, we would practice and work on being the best show team we could be. Throughout the summer, we would compete with some other show teams nationwide. Our Whitewater team was no match for the Rock Aqua Jays, but we would still always finish in the top three. If we work hard, we might be better contenders at the Nationals at the end of summer.

The National Water Ski Show Tournament is where the top water ski show teams compete against each other to see who is the best in the country. The contest would be held on the Rock River in Janesville, Wisconsin, the home of the Rock Aqua Jays.

Our team placed second behind the Rock Aqua Jays when all was said and done. We were delighted with the results. Our team performed well, and it was something to celebrate. We all returned to Whitewater Lake for a team celebration at the president's lakefront property for pizza and beer.

After several hours of celebrating, I was tired and ready to go home; it was about a ten-mile drive. I had borrowed my older brother Pat's VW convertible bug. I put the top up because it had begun to cool down. I jumped in and started my drive home. I was rocking out on my favorite radio station, WLS, out of Chicago, thinking about what a great day it was finishing 2nd in the Nationals. It had been a long day, and I began to feel the energy drain. I don't know if I dozed off or had just glanced away for a couple of seconds, but when I looked up, I was coming into a hairpin turn at a high rate of speed. I was going way too fast to make the turn, and there wasn't enough time to slow down. It was already getting dark, and I couldn't tell what was on the opposite side of the road. I tried to make the turn, but it was just too much for that little bug, which started to roll over and over like a yellow beach ball.

When the dust settled, I was disoriented and didn't know which way was up. I realized I was in the back of the car because I could see the light from the radio and could hear the music playing. I was afraid that the car would burst into flames, probably from watching too many movies, but I was trapped and didn't see any way out. The car was on its back, and I was lying on its roof. There was something in the middle of the window, a bar or maybe a doorpost.

I kept pushing on the post that was keeping me from my freedom and possibly holding me captive until this car burst into flames. I knew I had to do whatever it took to get out of this car. I hit what I thought was the window post as hard as I could with my forearm, and viola, it broke through. I crawled out of the window and got clear of the car. Once I found my bearings, I saw that I was actually in a cornfield, and thankfully, there were no flames or smoke. I also realized that I didn't have the strength to break the doorpost; it was actually a corn stalk holding me hostage.

I was excited to be free and probably in shock . . . so don't judge me. I jumped onto the chassis with its wheels rotating in the air. It reminded me of a turtle on its back, so I danced to the music from the radio happy to be alive.

My forearm and head were bleeding pretty good, so I jumped off the car and walked the ten minutes to a farmhouse up the road that had its porch light on. I arrived at the house and knocked on the front door. It opened, and an older couple was looking at me like I was some monster. With the porch light, I could now see there was blood all over my shirt, running down my arm and dripping onto the porch. I could feel the warmth of the blood running down my face. I must have looked pretty scary. The man said, "Wait here on the porch; we will call for help." Still, to this day, I was surprised that they didn't try to help me stop the bleeding, but I wasn't in their shoes. Twenty minutes later, the ambulance gave me a thorough assessment. With no life-threatening injuries, I went for an ambulance ride to the trauma center, where a nurse sutured up my cuts. When my Mom arrived, she was overjoyed to see that I wasn't seriously injured and was very caring and loving.

Pat, the owner of the cute little yellow VW bug, was not. When my brother woke me up the following day asking why I wasn't at football practice, I had to tell him I had wrecked his car. I could see he was enraged as soon as the words left my mouth. He turned around, ran upstairs, and yelled, "Mom, Mike wrecked my car last night!" My Mom said, "I know Pat; I picked him up at the hospital last night. Leave him be; let him rest."

Throughout my life, I carried the guilt of wrecking his cute little VW bug. It wasn't that long ago that he needed a golf cart for his river house, and I happened to have a nice one at my hanger at the airport. I told him that he could have mine. He asked me how much I wanted for it. I said nothing. Do you remember when I wrecked your bug? We're even. He just smiled and said, "Thanks, Mike!"

Chapter Six
Power of the Dream

The following spring, my Mom and Dad decided to move to Milton, Wisconsin, which was about 15 miles away from Whitewater. I had already finished two years of high school at Whitewater High; now, I would be the new kid in my junior year at Milton High. I don't remember being pessimistic about switching high schools. I didn't want to leave my friends, but I was okay with the thought of making new ones.

Not too long after moving into Milton, I was visiting the town of Janesville, and ran into a guy I knew from the Janesville Rock Aqua Jays. "Mike, what are you doing over in these parts?" I told him that we just moved into Milton. "Wow, that's great; since you are so close to Janesville, have you thought about coming out for the Jays?" I didn't tell him it was my lifelong dream to ski for the Jays. That would be great, I said. He took my number and promised to call as soon they organized tryouts. I walked away thinking dreams do come true. I wasn't happy about leaving my friends at Whitewater High, but this is becoming a God send.

A few weeks later, I got a call from the Jays show coordinator. "Mike. I heard you wanted to try out for the team?" I said, I sure do. He gave me the date and location of the auditions. I assured him that I'd be there. When I got home, I mentioned the auditions to my sister Maureen, who loved skiing. She might want to try out as one of the flag skiers.

The day finally came, and my sister and I drove down to Traxler Park on the Rock River in Janesville, Wisconsin. The Jays were very welcoming to us both. I recognized one of the guys, Duane Snow, even without his clown makeup. Snow had been with the team for a long time; his clown act with this crazy-looking boat called the Flivver was famous on the show circuit. He was very gracious and seemed happy I was trying out for the team. I wasn't sure how much of a tryout it would be since they had seen me ski in the tournaments, but I was ready.

After warming up with a slalom ski, I signaled the driver by pumping up my thumb, which told him to increase speed. I kicked the ski off. Now, on my feet, I was skiing with ease. It had been a long winter, and my feet felt the burn, so I was ready to let go after a couple of figure eights.

J.R. Wilson, the national champion boat driver, turned the boat back in my direction, and within seconds, I was crawling back on the swim step, feeling good about my performance. Duane Snow stuck out his hand and said, "Welcome to the Jays." Dreams do come true. My sister and I drove home, elated that we had made the team. What started as a negative with moving turned out to be a blessing and another turning point in my life.

After practicing throughout the spring, our team was ready for the prime-time show season. In the first year, I performed just the barefoot acts. I was always looking to improve and try new things, but during those early years, I was very limited in what I could do on my feet.

One of the senior members phasing himself out of the show came to me and told me that he had been thinking of a new act he wanted to try. "We have a big ramp for trick skiing and distance jumping. What if we built a ramp for barefooting? I'm leaving the team, but this act would be perfect for you. What do you think?" I'm game! I said.

A couple of weeks later, he pulled up in his truck with this ramp he had devised. It was a piece of plywood with a fiberglass layer, which made the surface slick. He mounted the ramp on a couple of 55-gallon drums. We unloaded it and plopped it in the water, and it automatically floated in the perfect position, like the ramp was meant to be there. We anchored in front of the show center. He wanted to give it a try to see how it worked.

Now, I was thinking. I will hit this ramp at 42 mph; this could be catastrophic. You just don't hit things with your feet going that fast, especially a ramp that will launch you into the air. What's the worst thing that could happen? Yikes. Let's do it. I launched off the dock with a slalom ski. We headed downriver; the boat made a 180-degree turn and started heading back towards the ramp. It floated in the water, waiting for me to hit it barefoot. The only protection I had was my ski jacket and jean shorts. I'm so glad I wasn't wearing my Speedo.

Mike's bare foot skiing jump

Off in the distance, I can see the ramp. I ski outside the wake, slip my left foot into the water, and start to crouch, now putting my total

47

weight on that foot. Feeling solid, I pull my right foot out of the ski, and now I am footing. The ramp is in full view. It looks tiny. It could damage my feet if I don't hit this ramp square.

I was lined up perfectly; the boat passed the ramp on the left side just close enough to spray it with water; it would be slippery. I'm hesitant about having my feet go out from underneath me and hitting my head. There are a lot of what-ifs involved. If I hit it at the right angle, I must prepare to lean back a little to land on my heels and not face plant.

It's happening. I hit the ramp. I feel my feet contact and fly through the air, maintaining my body position. My heels hit first, next my butt, and I am still on my feet. I couldn't believe it. It was the first time, at least, that's how I remember it, water ski barefooting off a ramp. Not only will this jump be a great crowd-pleaser, but it will also add points during the tournament.

I was right. The team had a great show season and was successful in the tournaments. After my first season with my dream team, I hated to see the summer come to an end. Now, I had to face the reality of starting my Junior year of high school in a different school, and it turned out that I was more apprehensive than I thought.

Chapter Seven
The Fighting Irish

I will take the liberty of going back in my history, which will break the chronological flow in this book and tell some stories to help you understand why we make the decisions in our lives that make us who we are. I did the things I did, not because I was self-aware and growing; I was doing what I did, because I was like any normal kid doing what I liked, and it seemed that I got good at what I liked.

As I tell you these stories, especially the ones that were very close to death experiences, one might ask how and why did you do that. Weren't you afraid? As I look back on my life, there was a lot that I was fearful of, but I was not scared enough to be crippled by it; I did it, and after, I wasn't afraid as much. Like many people, I throw caution to the wind and jump.

My environment growing up had something to do with it. I mentioned that my Dad was a WWII Navy guy. When I talk about him, I tell people he is like the actor John Wayne; he even looks and sounds like him. When I would play John Wayne movies, my kids would say "Grandpa," so it wasn't just me.

My two older brothers and I were entertained by our Dad's wonder years growing up and his WWII tales as a sailor. As a father, I learned from our pastor's teaching that one should not share his youthful indiscretions with his children. Looking back at my life and my brother's, I was sure my pastor was correct.

My mother was always trying to discourage my Dad from teaching us boys how to fight until this bully entered my older brother's life and tormented him to no end. So when my Mom had enough of my brother coming home crying from this bully's beatings, she asked my Dad to take Tom into the basement and teach him how to handle himself.

One day after school, my brother was walking home, and this bully started chasing my brother; just by coincidence, my Dad just happened to be pulling into our driveway and got out of the car and yelled, "Tom, what are you doing?" Hearing my Dad's encouraging voice, Tom turned on his feet, doing a 180-degree about-face, punched the bully in the face, and that was that; the bully never bothered my brother again. Being raised in a fighting Irish family, these stories became a common occurrence, especially with four brothers trying to out do each other.

Until this particular night, they were just my Dad's stories. This one night, I saw my Dad in his John Wayne alter ego. My Dad was bartending like most nights, and this man had been there for a while; needless to say, he was getting kinda hammered; finishing his beer, he said to my Dad, "Give me another beer." My Dad says, "I think you have had enough." The man repeated, "I said give me another beer." As he said this, he made a colossal mistake by reaching across the bar and grabbing my Dad's shirt. Anticipating this man's action, my Dad grabbed him by the shirt and pulled him into striking range, hit the man twice, and then dropped him to the floor. This event confirmed why we boys had a healthy fear of our Dad and why we never kept our hands in our pockets.

Chapter Eight
New Kid on The Block

Here I was at a new school and not knowing one soul; I knew from history that I could make friends, but I realized for the first time in my life that there would not be one sibling in the same school; this would be totally on me with no older brothers 'reputations to lean on. I didn't even have my twin sister Kathy, who was in her Senior year; she elected to stay at Whitewater High and graduate from the school she had attended for the past three years.

Going into a small school, everybody knew when a new kid arrived on campus. I could feel the judgment. Who are you, and where did you come from? I knew it was just a matter of time before somebody would test me. Well, the test came sooner than I thought. If I remember correctly, it had only been a couple of weeks when I was in metals class; this was before they had taken all the industrial classes out of most public schools, wood shops, auto mechanics, and metal shops where we would learn how to weld and make things out of metal.

I was a little bit of a class clown; it was just my nature and probably over-compensation for my lack of academic skills. I was trying my hardest to make an impression as the new kid. So, as the metals teacher was giving the class some instruction, I returned with an offhand comment that some of the class thought was funny, but the teacher's student assistant did not. This good-looking blond-haired senior football star wearing his letterman jacket walked up to me and, without a word, slapped me across the face. He said, "Don't you ever talk to Mr. McNeal like that again!" I couldn't believe what just happened. I immediately told him, "I will see you after class!" He nodded and said okay.

As I walked away red-faced and furious, this big kid named Tom Slowey approached me with a warning. He said, "You don't want to mess with him." I said, we will see. I had difficulty focusing on my project and couldn't wait until class ended. I was no stranger to conflict, and I was looking forward to seeing how my side hobby of boxing would pay off.

The bell rang, and I immediately walked outside; the metal shop was an extension building away from the central part of the school, so there was a nice grassy area for schoolboy brawls. There he was waiting for me; he was about to teach the new junior school kid what's up, or so he thought. We squared off, and I did what I always did, led with a left jab and made contact; he was shaken and surprised and had a look like where did that come from? This fight was one of those examples of the misuse of a God-given talent. I had speed, and it came naturally. I never started fights, but I had a dislike for bullies. This guy was a bully, and he was about to be delivered a life lesson the hard way: you have to watch out for the skinny kids; they've probably had to deal with bullies before.

He was relentless and did not want to lose to a new kid who was his junior, but what he didn't know was that second grade was the most brutal two years of my life. I started to feel sorry for him, though; I kept dropping my hands while I shook my head as if to say you've had enough. He was bleeding badly from the cuts on his cheekbones, nose, and mouth. Finally, the wood shop teacher appeared and stopped the fight. He marched us both down to the principal's office. Halfway down the hallway, his girlfriend appeared in her cheerleading outfit and started to scream when she saw her boyfriend's face. I began to feel guilty and thought this was not the first impression I was looking for.

The principal sent me home and suspended me from school for three days. For some reason, my Dad was home early; I told him what had happened and how it started, and he said, "Let's go." I asked where, and he told me we were going back to school. He wanted to have a word with the principal. We walked into the principal's office, and my Dad asked him why he suspended me from school for defending myself. I appreciated my Dad standing up for me, but I was still out.

With three days of suspension, I had some time to think about the impression I had made. I started to wonder if there would be retaliation. But, when my time was up, I returned to school, and everything I thought would happen did not. My newfound friend Tom Slowey had shared with everyone who inquired what had happened, so I was welcomed back and was no longer considered the new kid. I was the kid who stood up to a bully and was victorious. For the next two years, no one challenged me for a fight. It took some time, but even the girlfriend started to talk to me.

Tom Slowey asked me if I would teach him how to box. I told him to set up a speed bag and other boxing equipment at his house. We became good friends, and I gave him lessons. He turned out to be somebody not to mess with now that he had skills matching his size.

One other serendipitous event came from me standing up for myself that day. I had played football in my freshman year, but didn't like it. I was small in my first year and physically fulfilled from water skiing. At the end of my junior year, the head football coach came to me, "Carroll, you like to hit people; I could use a good nose guard on the football team." I said, okay, sounds good. So, in my senior year, I started as the nose guard on the Milton High School football team.

After the last game, the coach said he wished I had come to Milton earlier and thought I was pretty good.

Comments like that are the ones you carry with you. Those are valuable deposits in your life that compound over time and help you win in other endeavors. I know fighting is not the answer; as a matter of fact, I have analyzed the mentality of trying to find a solution through physical fighting. It was probably a self-image problem. I was angry from being made fun of and realized I was good at it. So when conflict came, my solution was, okay, let's fight. I want to tell you that I overcame that at a very young age, but I did not.

After graduation, I looked forward to spending my summer skiing with the team; this would be my third and final year with the Rock Aqua Jays. My time with them has remained one of the highlights of my life. However, as it was my last summer, I didn't work my job pumping gas and checking customers 'oil in their cars. The truth be told, I was fired because I couldn't count back their change after they paid their gas bill. When I go to a family-owned business, I am always impressed when the owner's child counts back the change from a larger bill. Most companies today have a computer register that does it for them.

Mike in the air

54

Being fired humbled my ego, but I was excited that I would not have to work so I could put all my intention into skiing. Several ski team members skied daily, working on new tricks for the show season. I learned a new one: I would jump from the big jump, doing helicopters (a 360-degree turn) in the air as another skier went underneath. I was doing five different acts in the show last summer; it was quite the confidence booster and proved helpful in my life's journey.

It was one of the most incredible summers before I would have to grow up and get on with my adult life.

Chapter Nine
Birds Of a Feather

My love for aviation came out of nowhere; like most kids, curiosity would cause me to look up and wonder where a plane was going when it flew overhead. My Dad would tell the story about his love for flying. He got his license to fly after the war and loved it. He met my Mom, fell in love, and decided to marry, but she had a bad experience with aviation; her fiancé was killed in an airplane accident, and she told my Dad she would not marry him unless he quit flying. Obviously, my Dad's love for my Mom was greater than for aviation.

Twenty-seven years later, during a trip to California on an ironworker job, my Dad met a man, named Bob, who had an airplane. My Dad must have had a conversation with my Mom. I don't know how that conversation went or if they even had it, but Dad started flying again. After raising eight kids, my Mom's attitude about flying had softened. A few months later, his license was current and up to date.

Bob planned to fly from California to Wisconsin to attend a big airshow. So he and his son flew the little Champ Citabria to Oshkosh and stayed with us. Bob asked my little brother Danny and me if we wanted to take a ride in his airplane, and we both enthusiastically said yes. We drove to the municipal airport near our house and pulled up to see this orange and black aircraft, one of those aerobatic planes that can fly upside down. Being a two-seat airplane, my brother and I would take turns. I was to be first, and I remember Bob had parachutes; I had never seen one before, and I thought, why do we need these? Bob helped me get into the parachute, he explained what to do if the airplane malfunctioned or the wing broke off. He said that all we needed to do was jump out of the plane and pull this silver handle on the chute, and everything would be ok. I wasn't afraid at all, in fact I was excited and hoped that I'd get a chance to pull the silver handle.

The airplane ride was absolutely beautiful, and I fell in love immediately; it was so graceful and smooth. I saw the countryside like never before. We flew over Turtle Lake, and I could see our resort; it looked so small, like everything did from a higher altitude.

After landing back at the airport and exiting that little two-seater airplane, I couldn't stop thinking about the possibility of learning how to fly. Little did I know of what was to come.

My Dad flew commercially back to California, and his friend Bob and his son took off for a long cross-country flight in the Citabria. It was about two weeks later that my Mom got a phone call from a man who asked her if it was the residence of David Carroll; she said yes, it was, and he said, "Well, tell him that he is the new owner of an airplane, a Piper J3 Cub." My Mom couldn't believe it, who wins an airplane? She had never heard of such a thing. She shared the news with us kids still at home, three boys and, two sisters. My brothers and I were over the top excited, but my sisters were not so excited. We couldn't wait for our Dad to come home and take delivery of our new airplane.

A couple of weeks after the news, my Dad finally came home to pick up his airplane; I don't think I had ever seen him so excited. My three brothers and I drove to the airport where the airplane was parked. We pulled into the airport parking, and there it was, sitting on the ramp, this little yellow airplane with a teddy bear painted on the tail. I could not believe it; we owned our very own airplane.

My Dad and a pilot experienced in the J3 Cub flew it to the airport that would be its new home close to where we lived. After the excitement wore off, my little brother Danny and I were the only ones of our eight siblings still interested in aviation. When my Dad felt comfortable and safe flying the little yellow bird, he offered to start teaching my brother and me how to fly. I couldn't believe my dream was coming true at fifteen years old especially so soon after that first flight with Bob. The three of us drove to the airport, and upon arrival, we pulled the hanger door open, and there she was. My Dad began the instruction on pre-flighting the airplane, checking all its controls, oil, and fuel, and draining fuel to see if there was water in the tanks; this would become standard practice before each flight.

As the oldest, I would go first; we climbed in the J3 Cub. Unlike most tandem aircraft, I would be in the front, and my Dad would fly from the back. My Dad did some final checks while a gentleman stood by waiting to hand prop the engine. The little 1943 Cub did not have an electrical system or an electric start. This was just like in the old black-and-white movies. My Dad gave him a nod and yelled, "Brakes on, switch on." The man grabbed hold of the prop and, with one sweeping motion, pulled the prop downward. The engine came to life. It only had forty horsepower so it sounded like a little tractor engine.

We taxied out to the runway, and after doing a 360-degree turn to make sure no one was landing, Dad put the throttle forward, and we were rolling down the runway; after a few seconds, we were airborne. Excited was an understatement; and fully confident in my Dad, I had no fear.

At first, we flew straight and level; it was so smooth. I enjoyed the feeling of flight, high above the landscape, on this beautiful morning. Suddenly, my Dad was pulling back on the stick, nose pitching up until it wouldn't go any higher, and then it was like the bottom fell out; he repeated this several times until I was not feeling very well. I couldn't believe it. I was about to throw up all over my Dad's new airplane. Trying to focus and not lose my cookies, my Dad repeated that stall maneuver. I could no longer suppress; I was vomiting all over his airplane. Immediately, my Dad pitched over and started heading back to the airport to land. Coming to a complete stop, I began to say how sorry I was about getting sick in his airplane. He just looked at me and said, "It happens." I'm sorry, but my love affair for aviation was lost that day, at least for now.

Chapter Ten
Anchors Away

As I was getting close to that age where a boy was growing into manhood, I had to start thinking about my future and what I would do with my life. As long as I could remember, my father would ask us boys if we wanted to be an ironworker like him building bridges and buildings. I always thought, no, I don't want to be an ironworker. I grew up enamored by the undersea world, with shows like Flipper and more importantly, Sea Hunt, a show about an underwater investigator. There was no such thing, but they built the show around it. Mike Nelson, played by Lloyd Bridges, was always underwater catching bad guys. I don't know what they were doing under the water, but there they were. Mike Nelson would swim up behind them with a knife and cut their air hose, rip their face mask off, then swim them to the surface, and the sheriff would take them off to jail.

So I told my Dad that I wanted to be like Mike Nelson from Sea Hunt. He said, "Mike, that's a TV show. If you want to be a diver so bad, you should join the Navy and be an underwater welder." That was a great idea. It's incredible how many people make one of the most critical life decisions through a comment, idea, TV show, or association.

Based on that conversation, a few years later, I found myself at the Navy recruiters station asking questions about being a Navy diver. After the recruiter gave me his best pitch and sat me down to take the (ASVAB) Armed Services Vocational Aptitude Battery Exam, it seemed that I was qualified to join the US Navy and be a diver. I told the recruiter I was going home to think about it and have a conversation with my best friend, Bob Earle, to convince him to join me.

Now, the recruiter told me I could be a Navy diver, but first, I would go to welding school, and halfway through, I should request dive school, and they would then send me to fulfill my childhood dream. Do you know how you can tell if a military recruiter is lying? Their lips are moving. No offense to all the military recruiters past, present, and future, but I have talked to quite a few, even in recent years, and they still exaggerate or embellish, admittedly so, but they need to fill the quotas.

My buddy, Bob agreed to join with me and after we swore in to defend our Country against all enemies, foreign and domestic, we had our ship date to start boot camp training in Orlando, Florida. On the eve of my departure to serve in the Navy, my two older brothers, twin sister, and a couple of friends decided that I needed to have one last hoorah as a civilian. We started in one of our favorite bars, Campbells, and started ordering beer, it wasn't long until one of my brothers yelled, "It looks like a nice night for a fight!" Well, you can't yell that in a bar in Wisconsin without having some takers; therefore, the fight was on. Fairing pretty well and knowing the police would show up soon, we decided to get out while we could. We decided on the next bar, and after a couple more beers, started another brawl. Then it was on to the 3rd.

Not aware that police were called to each bar, they started to put two and two together and realized when they got the 3rd call that it was the same guys starting the trouble. When the police drove up, we were rolling around the parking lot with the locals like something out of a Hollywood movie.

After spending the night in jail, the bailiff escorted us that next morning to the courtroom for our arraignment. The judge said,

"Michael Kelly Carroll, stand up. Is it true that you are supposed to depart for Navy boot camp today?" I said yes, sir; he replied, "You are free to go." My heart leapt with joy, but I couldn't help think about what would happen to my brothers and twin sister, but I had no time to think about it; I had a train to catch.

In September 1976, Bob and I were off to Navy boot camp in Orlando, FL. It was nine weeks there, then off to school where we would learn welding, firefighting, and damage control techniques, which make up the designation of a Navy Hull Tech. After remembering the recruiter's words, "Now halfway through Hull Tech school request dive school." At the halfway point, I asked to speak to the career counselor to make my request. He laughed when I started telling him what the recruiter had told me. He said, "You can't go to dive school; you must spend a couple of years in the fleet on a ship and pay some dues before you ever request dive school."

I remembered a presentation in boot camp about the Navy UDT/SEALS. I'd never heard of them but was curious. This colossal guy who was built like a brick house and wearing a starched green uniform was very impressive looking. He started his presentation with a movie called, Someone Special, a very intimidating film about the training that a frogman would go through to be the Navy's elite. Besides all the Superman stuff they were doing, what caught my eye was the diving. After the presentation, he asked if anybody would like to volunteer to take a physical screen test to see if one could qualify to get orders to BUD/S Basic Underwater Demolition/SEAL training.

Mike's Navy bootcamp company (Mike's holding the flag with the torch)

So, I asked the career counselor, those SEAL guys, they dive, right? He said, "Yes, but you would never make it; those guys are 7 feet tall and eat snakes for breakfast and people for lunch." Have you ever noticed that sometimes people judge their success on other people's failures and are quick to tell someone that they can't do something? Well, I would like to try, I said. Being stationed in San Diego at NTC Naval Training Center, I was told to head to Coronado Island, where BUD/S training occurred, so I grabbed the bus and headed on my way.

At the time, I was not in the best shape, although in boot camp, I led our company in PT, Physical Training, but had yet to do any PT since. I reported to the BUD/S command building, BUD/S stands for Basic Underwater Demolition, where we were put on another military bus to take us across the street to the base pool. The SEAL instructor told us what the test was going to entail. First, there was the 500-yard swim that needed to be completed in less than 12.5 minutes. Then, with no rest and in only 10 minutes to get dressed and make your way over to the training field, you needed to complete 50 pushups in under 2 minutes, 50 sit-ups in under 2 minutes, and 10 pull-ups in under 2 minutes, then run 1.5 miles in under 10.5 minutes. This is the current day Physical Screen Test, PST, it's similar to the one I took in 1977.

I gave the run everything I had and lost my breakfast just as I crossed the line right under the time limit. As I caught my breath, the instructor walked up to me and said, "Congratulations, you will hear from us."

I returned to the barracks at NTC Point Loma to continue my hull tech training, which would last another seven weeks, but I couldn't stop thinking about this SEAL training I qualified to attend. When I brought it up in conversation with my classmates, they made it sound like an impossible task that I couldn't endure. Doubt started to creep in, and I needed clarification about what to do.

It was only a short time after I had taken the screen test that my buddy Bob and I got our orders to our first Navy duty station; it was a ship, a sub tender called the USS Sperry, docked right there at Pt Loma, San Diego. We would be together as Hull Techs fixing and making things the ship needed to maintain its readiness. My mind started to take me down the path of least resistance. I should take the sure thing, not the unknown, and stay in my comfort zone. These negative thoughts were insidious, they just kept creeping in. I think this fear is where most dreams go to die.

I was excited when Graduation Day finally came after 14 weeks of training, we learned all the skill sets to become a Hull Tech in the United States Navy. My buddy Bob and I had our orders and would be together just like the recruiter had told us.

All dressed up in our dress blue uniforms, lined up in formation, ready to shake with our right hands and receive our certificates of completion with our left. One by one, the commander of the training center would step before each of us and congratulate us, shake our hands, and present the certificate.

As the line got shorter, I noticed my certificate package was thicker; standing in front of me, he presented his hand for me to shake while congratulating me, then said, "Fireman Carroll, your orders to SEAL training came in; you have two sets of orders, one for the USS Sperry and these, you need to choose, now!"

Wow, never in my life was I forced to make a life-altering decision in such a short time, but I guessed my subconscious had been working on this decision for the last seven weeks. I could see Bob out of the corner of my eye. He wondered what I would do, but was almost sure I would stay because we discussed the dream of being together on the ship. I took a moment and turned towards him and said, see you later, Bob. I boarded the bus with my sea bag in hand and was on my way to Coronado Island to report to the most demanding training program known in the world.

Chapter Eleven
Don't Ring The Bell

Stepping through the door of SEAL headquarters, still wearing my dress blues, I was greeted by this huge guy who looked over seven feet tall and was built like a brick house. He smiled, "Can I help you?" I replied yes, I'm checking in. "For what," he said. I'm checking in for SEAL training. Immediately, his smile disappeared, and he began to yell profanities, calling me names and commanding me to start doing pushups until he got tired.

As I was doing pushups, I immediately started to wonder if I made the wrong decision and started thinking very hard about whether I belonged here. Doubt started creeping in, and I hadn't even started training. At that moment, a BUD/S class entered the compound, dressed in green uniforms, bald, and tanned; they looked like sugar cookies covered in sand. I could hear them singing with a certain cadence in their march. At that moment, feeling very weak and ready to quit, I got this overwhelming feeling of renewed strength that I would be a Navy SEAL!

It wasn't long before this behemoth of a man got tired and bored watching me struggle to do pushups. He was yelling discouraging words like, you'll never make it, don't bother trying, and other expletives. He finished yelling and said something that I would hear all throughout training: "Recover, hit the surf." Recover meant that you could stop doing pushups and jump to your feet. Hit the surf meant precisely what it says; on that command, you would run to the beach (usually a time limit is put on the run to the beach and back) and proceed to jump into the ocean while making sure there wasn't a dry spot anywhere on your body from head to toe. It didn't matter what you were wearing, even my dress blues didn't have a chance.

Most people have an idea of what's involved in SEAL training based on what they've read or seen in a movie. There's a Discovery Channel production that allows the viewer to follow a SEAL class all the way through training, but I'm going to share it with you from my perspective.

In 1977, there wasn't anything written about training, so a BUD/S trainee did not know what to expect from day to day; every evolution and aspect of training was a mystery. Could you imagine reading the schedule for the week that was posted in the barracks but not knowing what it meant? It was like reading a foreign language. The one thing I understood about the schedule was breakfast, lunch, and dinner, and that's only because it was written in english. So, my resolution to make it through these six months of the unknown in hell was to make it to the next meal. If I could take this training one evolution at a time and make it to the next meal, I could make it!

Training is broken into 3 phases, and each phase is recognized by the color of the helmet the class wears. The First Phase was the weeding-out phase; the helmet color was green, it had your class number on each side and your name on the front.

Each phase was designed to identify those who could not make it into the final two training phases. The Second Phase, the dive phase, is the blue helmet. The Third Phase, the land warfare phase, is the red helmet. We started with an inspection and learned, after 1st Phase, that no matter how much we prepared for this inspection, we would not pass it. The instructors would find your barracks, rooms, and/or uniform unsatisfactory. In the end, we would do a lot of pushups, and the entire class would end up in the surf zone wearing our starched greens, spit-shined to a high gloss finish boots, and mirror-polished belt buckles.

Everyone knew that you had to play the game, and the instructors know if you actually played the game or not. If the class is rebellious, which would be the leader's fault, it would be reflected in the entire class, and we would pay the price.

The price was a Circus; this was done at the end of the day after a full day of training. The class never knew when or if the Circus was coming. At the end of the day, we would return from evening chow, expecting to retire to the barracks to prep for the next day. But when one of the instructors is standing outside the barracks waiting for the class to return, you think, oh crap.

The instructor calls the class leader front and center while the rest of the class stands at attention, waiting for instruction. After a short conversation, the leader says, "Class 94 fall out for Circus."

What is a Circus, you ask? A Circus is where the instructors are all in force to root out any rebellion, discipline, disrespect, or cockiness problems that the class may have. In other words, it's physical abuse, and only God knows how long it will last. It usually depends on how big the problem seems to be from the instructor's point of view. All the physical training used in BUD/S is implemented in the Circus.

It's jumping jacks, flutter kicks, burpees, pushups, leg raises, duck walks, bear crawls, leg raises, and so many others not worth mentioning. It is a harrowing lesson that the class must learn. The most painful part of the Circus is that nobody knows how long it will last. This is the most significant tool in the instructor's bag.

Not knowing how long something will last plays a long game in your mind. How long will you be in cold water, how many pushups will we do, how long is this run, how long is this abuse going to last? This tool of the unknown drove a lot of trainees to the bell.

Every part of SEAL training has its purpose; contrary to what we thought, it wasn't to punish and abuse at the instructor's whims. The entire structure of training had been passed down since before WWII. We were being trained for war, and you don't know how long the fight or battle will last, nor if the conditions will be unimaginable, you must keep fighting. There's a saying in SEAL Team, "Never out of the fight."

The most intimidating part of training was going to be Hell Week; at the time, it was the beginning of the 5th week of training. In the first four weeks, we're getting into better physical conditioning, running, swimming, and general calisthenics. Throughout these preliminary weeks to Hell Week, there were evolutions designed to find the weaknesses that would make you quit or panic, and that would be it; you are gone; the class size just got smaller and smaller.

One evolution that everybody learned to fear was called Drown Proofing. This is where your hands are tied behind your back and your feet tied together at the ankles. Then, you jump into the deep end of a pool and are instructed to do a series of exercises that would cause the average person to panic. First, you blow enough air out of your lungs to sink to the bottom, then push off the bottom to propel yourself 12 ' up to the surface and take a breath. Then repeat this 20 times. It seems simple enough, but when you're blowing out all of your air with your head below the surface of the water, it can mess with your mind, especially when it's taking longer to get to the bottom than you thought, the fear is getting stuck halfway down.

After completing that exercise, you're instructed to stay on the surface and bob. This involves putting your head in the water while staying afloat by using your lungs as a floatation device, then taking a breath and repeating it 20 times. Then, do a front flip and back flip without getting stuck in the middle, this tends to promote panic. After the flips, you swim to the bottom of the pool using a dolphin kick and pick up a face mask with your teeth. Then, successfully swim the length of the Olympic-sized pool using a dolphin kick.

As you can imagine, this evolution would pay dividends in weeding out the people prone to panic in the water. It seems harsh, and it is harsh, but the SEAL team does water operations, and if you can't take a beating in the water, then this isn't the place for you.

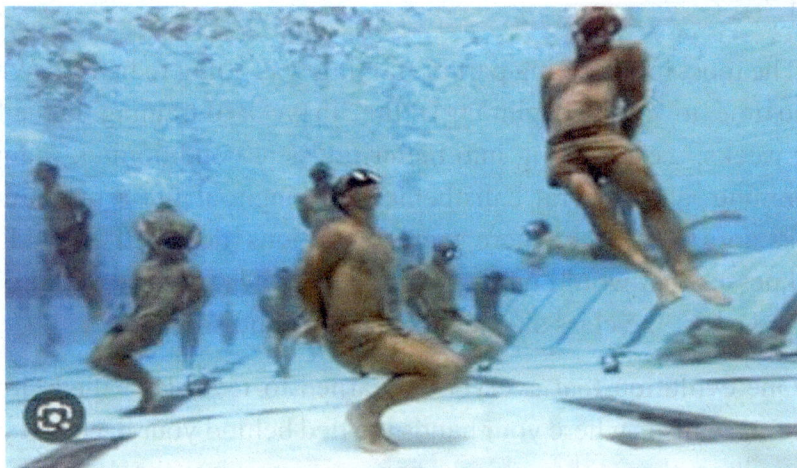

So the instructor's goal is to weed out as many trainees as possible, but keep in mind that the Navy always wants more SEALs. The hold up is that they need to acquire them without lowering the standards that make them who they are.

Class 94 started with 120 trainees and graduated 18. We lost people daily from the beginning of training, some from injuries and some from ringing the bell. There is a tradition in SEAL training: if a trainee wants to quit, they have to do it publicly by ringing a brass bell three times out so that everyone can hear them. During Hell Week, they have a bell mounted on a truck, so whenever a trainee has had enough, they don't have to wait or have time to think about it. Volunteer in, volunteer out.

After making it through Drown Proofing, there is only one obstacle left in the First Phase, the biggest one, which is where BUD/S loses more trainees than any other part of training. Hell Week!

The only intel you could get about Hell Week back in 1977 was by observing and listening to the rumblings from the class ahead of yours, but it was very limited. The most intimidating part was watching how they walked, like zombies, which is the best description I can think of; very slow and gingerly from the chafing they got from sand rubbing between their legs all week.

The entire base of NAB Coronado and most of the town knew when a class was going through Hell Week. Like the Loch Ness Monster, there would be sightings of this group of guys in wet green uniforms, which we called Greens, wearing bright orange life jackets (KPOC), running around with a giant rubber boat on their heads, looking like they were in extreme pain and misery.

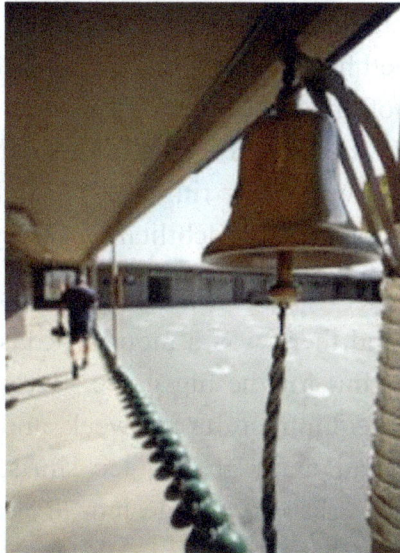

SEAL Training Infamous Bell

Class 94 knew their turn was just a few weeks away; but still, the unknown was concerning. You always wondered if you had what it took to get through it, and what it was that made all of those men ring that bell. We got a good look at all of the green helmets that were laid out like dead soldiers below the bell for us to fixate on. These helmets were from Class 93, the class that went through right before us. They had to ring that bell in public, in front of their classmates, instructors, and the entire command. Those near would hear the first ring of three and step out from their offices or barracks to see who'd had enough. I wondered what it took to suffer that kind of self-humiliation. Was it a weak moment regretted forever after the deed was done? Whatever it was, there was no turning back; once the bell was rung three times, it was over; you were going to the fleet to ride a ship.

Oddly enough, as an underclassman, I was tasked to polish this brass bell. I remember one morning, it was about 4:30 in the morning, and our class was doing their morning chores. It was very still; a light fog had surrounded the compound, and it seemed like it was just me and that bell. This bell has changed the course of thousands of young men's lives throughout history. I couldn't help it, but I whispered to the bell. I WILL NEVER RING YOU. I don't care if the instructors are about to eat me; I will never ring you! At that moment, all was settled in my soul: Outside of a debilitating injury, I would make it through Hell Week.

It was Sunday, and there was a mood in Class 94; it was like a team mentally preparing for the big game. Everybody was in their world preparing their equipment for the week, and this was primarily to ensure that you had extra greens, tee shirts, and socks if the instructors allowed the class to change into dry clothing throughout the week.

After approximately seven weeks together, we formed a very tight bond, a brotherhood for sure. Starting with 120, we were down to about half after injuries and bell ringers. Boat crews were formed early in training, but as the class was continually reduced, the crews were adjusted. Right before Hell Week began, we knew which crew of seven we would be with. The boat crews were arranged by height early in training; that way, there was an equalized weight distribution, which is important since you will be running all week with this heavy rubber boat on your head. As the week would go on and the loss of more trainees, sometimes the optimum of equal height couldn't be made, so you would sometimes see a shorter person in a crew and his head would not reach the bottom of the boat, he was hanging on along for the ride, sometimes it pays to be short.

I spent all day getting mentally ready, it was 4:00 pm (1600). Class 94 would run to the chow hall for dinner again without the IBS (Inflatable Boat Small) on our heads. We had yet to learn what it would be like to get food during Hell Week; some guys had stashed caches around different areas away from the base. This was based on the limited intel they had gotten from other trainees. I didn't see the point in trying to game the system; Hell Week would be Hell Week, so go with it!

Around midnight, all hell broke loose; Class 94 was sound asleep, awakened by crash grenades (hand grenades without the metal frag) exploding in a concrete cinderblock-built barracks, and machine gun fire. Smoke filling the rooms where we slept. Coming out of a deep sleep brought on by exhaustion from the previous weeks training, no one was exempt from the confusion, we must have been at war and under attack.

No, it was the start of Hell Week."Get dressed! Get dressed! Fall out! Fall out! Welcome to HELL, gentleman!" The instructions were getting lost in the midst of the yelling and M60 machine gun fire. They didn't care if we heard or not, and we would pay the price for missing the details.

Forming up on the grinder and standing at attention, the instructors swarmed us, automatic gunfire still blazing, and rubber hoses being shoved in our mouths, simulating a waterboarding effect while questions like, "Where is your other boot? Where is your UDT life jacket?" were screamed at us. The class would be punished for not paying attention to detail. We heard this phrase throughout training: "Pay attention to detail!"

"Class 94, dropdown and start pushing them out!" Our class leader would give the command, "Class 94 on my command, down!" That would start the pushups, which are all done as one body. We had no idea how many we would do; it was abusive filler, and the instructors knew the script and the agenda down to the minute. This would continue for five days and six nights. The instructors were on three shifts, and every eight hours, we had fresh, well-rested taskmasters who would see how many trainees they could get to ring the bell. All I was thinking about was making it to breakfast and following the game plan. It didn't matter what they did to us; I was not ringing the bell.

After what seemed like 100 pushups, our class leader was instructed to march us down to the beach, where the abuse continued. There's something about cold water; it penetrates down to the bone, and not knowing when relief will come takes a toll on your mindset and resolve. The Pacific Ocean off San Diego is at its coldest temps in February and April. Hell Week for Class 94 was in April. We were instructed to march into the surf zone as one unit, arm in arm, do an about face, and lock arms again."Take seats!" the instructor belted. Hitting the water, you felt the cold cut like a knife through every bone in your body.

One of the instructors was standing in the truck bed to which the bell was attached. He started to yell above the sound of the roaring surf crashing into us. The waves were throwing us around like dolls as we laid on our backs with just our faces out of the water. "All we want is one quitter; if we get one quitter, you can get out of this miserable cold water. We all started to sing as if on cue. We did this when things got tough; singing would lift our spirits every time. The instructors didn't want our spirits lifted; they wanted to weed out the weak, and that's what this week was all about. "Stop singing!" The instructor yelled. "Give me one quitter; if any of you quit, we will get you into a nice hot shower and back in your nice warm bed!"

After about 30 minutes, when our bodies were getting close to hypothermia, one of our classmates started to rise out of the water; we all knew what he was going to do; we began to yell. "Don't do it, don't quit! One of the instructors yelled, "Shut up, let him quit; if he quits now, he will quit on the battlefield!" He marched out of the surf zone right up to the bell mounted on the truck, grabbed the lanyard dangling from the bell, ding, ding, ding! Our first Hell Week casualty, that was it; his life just took another path from the one he was on. This happened forty more times before Hell Week ended the following Saturday morning.

There are different reasons why this week is called "Hell Week." First and foremost, the instructors keep the trainees wet and cold all week; there is something different from dry cold to wet cold. Wet cold cuts right to the bone. I remember being wet and cold as a kid; after swimming too long and getting out of the pool when the air was cool. I would shake uncontrollably, and my Mom would wrap a towel around me and warm me up.

Well, your Momma isn't with you here; she is replaced by a bad-to-the-bone sadistic instructor who wants to make sure that no one gets through Hell Week that doesn't belong in SEAL training. The instructors' mindset was a serious one. No one gets through that you couldn't trust with your life during wartime. This mindset isn't just with the First Phase instructors, but with the entire SEAL staff for all aspects of the training. Their goal was to find weaknesses, and these evolutions were specifically designed to reveal them.

Wet cold is one of the most powerful tools. I learned later as an instructor that the staff had hypothermic tables that told them how long trainees could stay in the water based on the temperature. The other tool was sleep deprivation. During this week of training, starting Sunday night at midnight and continuing to the following Saturday morning, the class was given approximately 3 hours of sleep. For harassment purposes, those hours were dispersed throughout the week. For example, the first hour of sleep would not be granted until Tuesday. From Sunday through Tuesday, we were wet and cold; the only warmth would come from our own bodies doing physical drills. Pushups were a constant during Hell Week; any mistake the class made was punished by pushups or getting wet. If no mistakes were made, the instructor would manufacture one.

While the class was standing at attention, shaking profusely on the verge of hypothermia. I overheard our instructor say something to our class leader about dry greens and sleep. I was wet and cold and had no sleep for almost three days, and to hear those words! Our class leader repeated the command and said, "Class 94 fall out." We couldn't run fast enough. Getting back to our rooms, we found a beautiful set of fresh, warm greens, removed from the dryer and placed on the foot of our beds by the underclassmen. Still shaking from being so cold, we stripped off the wet, nasty, and smelly uniforms that stunk from the mud flats (sewage runoff near the Mexican border) where we spent the night on Monday night, a dry, warm uniform never felt so good.

Sleep comes immediately when your head hits the pillow from 24/7 mental and physical abuse. We were already delusional from the last several days. Then, once again, out of nowhere, I heard the familiar sound of explosives and automatic gunfire. I thought it was part of a dream, but the sounds kept getting louder and closer until I realized that it wasn't. The instructors were swarming the rooms like locusts, yelling and screaming unintelligible commands through the explosions of crash grenades. Do you know how you feel right after waking from a deep sleep? Lazy and lethargic, it's a vulnerable period when one can be easily overtaken. This tool of choice was used to find more weak individuals who just might be on the verge of breaking.

It worked; the first command given to the class was to hit the surf after one hour of sleep. It was just enough to make the faint of heart, who were already hanging on by that thin thread of hope of being a Navy SEAL, to throw in the towel. Ring, ring, ring.

By Wednesday, the class was suffering from confusion and exhaustion. We were in zombie mode. While in ocean on long paddles, we would see things that weren't there: a stoplight, various water monsters, whatever our sleep-deprived minds could conjure up. The instructors could tell us anything, and we'd believed them. They told us that we had to do another week because we were such a bad class. This drew out a few more to quit and ring the bell and it wasn't even true.

Throughout the week, everything was a race, boat crew against boat crew. We heard during every evolution that, "It pays to be a winner." We had yet to learn the winner's reward but we could see the instructors keeping scores in their notebooks. The losers of each race paid the price immediately after losing by enduring more pushups and physical abuse. Watching them was the best motivation to compete to win.

Friday night, should have been the last night of Hell Week, but nobody was sure because of our mental state. We were led into a classroom, where we were briefed on an evolution called, Round the World. The instructions covered an entire dry eraser board, which was the width of the entire classroom. We couldn't believe our eyes. It was a scavenger hunt that brought us back to all of the areas we covered during the week. We were to run with our boats on our heads to multiple locations on the map, which was far more difficult now that each team was comprised of differing heights due to the loss of trainees. The instructors explained that this was a 12-hour race that would last all night, and, "By the way, it pays to be a winner."

Our boat crew was number six. We never thought there would be a prize for the winning boat crew; we just knew not to be the losers. On this particular race, each of the crews was sent to different locations, where you were met with an instructor who gave you a card with the next point on the map. When we arrived at our first point, the obstacle course, the instructor handed us our next point: the barracks. He told us that we were the winning boat crew and we could secure for the night.

At first, we thought it was a trick, but when he handed each of us a beer, we knew it had to be legit. The seven of us sat there with the instructor and drank beer with the biggest grins. We couldn't believe it; we were heading back to the barracks to put on a warm set of greens and get some sleep after being awake for five days. All we could think about was the rest of Class 94, who would be running and paddling all night while we were sleeping. Oh well, it paid to be a winner!

The following morning, we were awakened and told to fall into the grinder. I hadn't noticed before, I imagine, because I was out of my mind, but all the helmets from the trainees in our class, Class 94, were lined up underneath the bell. I couldn't believe how many there were. All I could think about was that I was still here after surviving the most challenging weeks of my entire life.

As our class formed up at attention, I couldn't help but notice how raggedy and exhausted the rest of our class looked. But then it dawned on me that as boat crew six was sleeping, the rest of the class was running and paddling all night. I felt a little guilty, but remembered that we were the winning boat crew; and honestly, it made the guilt subside just a little bit.

After a full head count and all were accounted for, we fell out into the classroom again. We took our seats, and the briefing started on the next evolution. We couldn't believe our eyes, it was another Round The World, except this one was longer. You could hear the grumbling coming from the class; at least boat crew six was well rested but very stiff from the week's toll on our bodies.

I could barely walk and couldn't open and close my hands; it was all I had to bend over and grab the handle of the boat. The command was given: "Up boat, march, forced march, march." This was a running march, and it took everything we had to keep up with the boat in front of us; this was a practice that had been reinforced by punishment. It kept the class in one tight formation as we moved from point A to point B. The starting line for this evolution was located on the beach behind our compound. The instructor commanded us to turn right and head north as we reached the beach. As we ran down the beach, you could hear noises that could only come from pain. At 100 yards in, the instructor gave the command, "Class halt, left turn!" Facing the ocean, we knew what was next. We would be running flat out with our boat, while the icy waters of the winter cut us to the bone. Anticipating that command, we heard, "Class 94 about face!" About face, what did he say? We were now facing the land instead of the ocean. The instructor looked us over, "Since your class is so STUPID and the WORST to come through training. Class 94, your Hell Week is secure! Fall out!"

Punch drunk and overjoyed, so we grabbed our boats and headed back over the sand berm towards the barracks. When we reached the top, we couldn't believe our eyes; the instructors were cooking hot dogs and hamburgers. Cases of beer were stacked up in celebration of

Class 94's completion of Hell Week and the First Phase of training. Hooyah, Class 94!

Chapter Twelve
No Bubbles, No Troubles

Before starting the Second Phase, which was the dive phase, we were given a week of recovery and were allowed to walk everywhere. Normally, you weren't allowed to walk ever. You had to run, seriously. As a matter of fact, if you get caught walking, you pay a price.

Class 94 was pumped that we survived Hell Week; we were a much tighter class, and had dwindled to 30 from 120. The camaraderie was intense; we all knew we had walked through the fire together and came out stronger; there was now a brotherhood that we didn't have before Hell Week. We still had two phases left, one-third down and two-thirds to go.

We spent the weekend preparing to start the dive phase and painting our helmet liners blue. As you remember, the First Phase was green. The instructor staff of the first Phase left all the quitters' green helmets on the grinder, right below the bell, so as to remind Class 95 what they were up against.

We, Class 94, were beyond excited to start the 2nd phase of training; I think I was more than most; as this is what I joined the Navy to do. Entering each phase was a formal process; all the instructors were introduced, this was important so we knew who would be the one to instruct and punish if we failed to "pay attention to detail." The dive phase was more dangerous than the First Phase, and the instructors were adamant that we pay attention to keep from getting seriously injured or killed.

First, we had to learn the basics of open circuit diving. It was basically the same training a civilian would go through if they wanted to get certified as a recreational diver, except with a twist. Inherent in our training, the instructors wanted to see if we could keep our cool under pressure during a possible life-death situation. The inability to breathe without a scuba tank was an easy way to find the panic button in most people who had one. If anyone in Class 94 had one, the 2nd Phase instructors would find it.

Dive training started pretty docile; the instructors seemed much more mellow and not wrapped as tight as First Phase instructors. This was likely because of the nature of the training; they wanted to create a relaxed atmosphere, so the ability to learn was increased in such a dangerous environment. It was also apparent that the instructors were treating us professionally. The fire of the First Phase tested us. They had more respect, but we were far from being their equals. It was a safe bet that a good percentage of us would be working with them soon, so their demeanors lightened up somewhat. But there would still be some trainees that wouldn't make it.

Around the third week of dive training came the test that everybody dreaded. We were taught most aspects of diving and breathing underwater with an open-circuit dive system. This was a scuba bottle that was filled with compressed air. It had a manifold with a 1st stage regulator that reduced the pressure from the scuba bottle. It also had a shut-off valve. When turned on, the air would flow through a rubber hose, which led to a 2nd stage regulator that regulated the air pressure into the mouthpiece. We were also schooled in dive physics, which taught us that if you panicked, you could die.

Pool Comp was the most feared challenge in the Second Phase; if you got through this and passed all of the other physical and academic standards, you would be moving forward to 3rd Phase. The problem was that dive training in UDT/SEAL was like drinking from a fire hose. We were diving every day and putting in hours of classroom time learning the academics of diving. We had two weeks of this compressed training to prepare us for Pool Competency.

When the day arrived Class 94 loaded all the dive equipment into a cattle car that they hauled us around in, and headed to the base pool. The class was very quiet. I wondered if this would be the day I would wash out. We were all worried about failing Pool Competency after making it all the way through First Phase and Hell Week. We were about to be tested in an area we had never been tested in before. No one was sure how to react to this test. Will we panic, or not follow procedure? There are so many details in Pool Comp that and if you make one wrong move, you'll be gone, literally and figuratively. What makes SEALs the best is that they are tested in every area and know how they will react to every situation; there is no question mark. They have a can-do attitude; they will succeed, and under no circumstances are they ever out of the fight.

We were instructed to enter the pool and descend to the bottom of the deep end, 12 feet deep. We would swim back and forth like sharks prey, waiting for the attack by one of the instructors swimming on the surface. In preparation for this test, we all used a double hose regulator, which can compress the hoses so the air will not flow in or out. This was the same regulator system that you would see in old diving movies or the TV show Sea Hunt, and it was designed to assist the instructors looking for that panic button in each of us.

The test would be progressive. Each instructor was told which trainee was theirs as we entered the water. This would be a surprise attack. The first phase would start gently; the instructor would dive down and rip your face mask off, reducing your visibility and increasing the chance of panic. The second attack takes one of your fins, leaving you swimming in circles. Then, the instructor grabs your twin tanks, rocking you back and forth to simulate being rolled around by the surf zone. It's easy to reach this point, but now it has started to escalate.

You can feel the attack coming, and suddenly, you can't breathe. What did he do? Did he squeeze my intake hose or shut my air off? Ok, I remember the steps, if you can't breathe, first check to see if there is a hand on your hose; if there is, tap the hand, and the instructor will release it. Ah, I can breathe again. Some trainees turn their air off, then confusion sets in, and then panic. Stay calm, Mike, and take your time; this is a test; follow procedures, and I will do fine. I continue to swim, and again, I can't breathe; I reach back to feel the hand, but there is no hand; he must have turned my air off, righty tighty, lefty loosey, except it's backward. Do what you practiced, turn the knob to the left, and viola, I'm breathing again. I'm doing good, but what's next?

I'm swimming, the attack is coming, wham, I get hit, I feel tugging and pulling, I can't breathe. Air is on; he must have tied a knot in my hose. I feel back, and sure enough, the hose is in a knot. Time to ditch, drop the weight belt, then pull the quick release on the chest strap, which is hidden under the life jacket; if you are not careful, you could waste a lot of time on this strap; too much time and panic can set in.

Ahh...there it is. Next, undo the belly strap, grab your manifold, and bring the twin 72 bottles over your head. Doing excellent, breath holding, and I've got plenty of time. Don't panic; almost there; the bottles are lying on the bottom of the pool; tidy up your straps, and place your weight belt on the bottles to keep them from floating. Turn the air off, and most critically, purse your lips and start blowing air out so as not to get an embolism in your lungs. Swim to the surface and yell, "I feel fine." The instructor comes over and says, "Well done, congratulations, you pass." Oh, what a feeling! I have one significant challenge down and many more to come!

I want to say that everybody passed the pool comp test, but they did not. Some panicked to the point where they passed out and had to be brought to the surface, and thank God they were resuscitated, but they were immediately dropped from the program. Others failed because of missteps and failing to follow procedures. If you failed for this reason you were given another opportunity for remediation training over the weekend, and given a chance to try again the following week. Some would pass, but others would be dropped from training after failing for the second time. It made me sad to see some of my classmates wearing the regular blue dungarees, blue shirts, and blue ball caps; this was the telltale sign that they were officially out of training and heading to a ship for the rest of their Navy career.

The rest of the Second Phase was learning a more complex diving, such as a closed circuit system, which meant no bubbles. This system was used for clandestine shallow diving for ship attacks. The Emerson, later replaced by the Draeger, was a pure oxygen system that when you exhaled the oxygen, it entered a scrubber canister that would scrub all of the CO_2, leaving the oxygen to be put back into the breathing bag, where you would inhale the same air you just exhaled. The other system was mixed gas, which allowed us to dive to deeper depths. Diving at night and doing sneak ship attacks was another major test before we would successfully finish the Second Phase.

Maritime operations are missions that separate us from other special operation forces. One of the duties that fall into that category is ship attacks. Since BUD/S stands for Basic Underwater Demolition SEAL training. Once you graduate from BUD/S, you move into Advanced SEAL training for another six months, where you learn more advanced techniques, such as neutralizing or taking down the ship while it sits in a harbor or underway.

Before finishing the dive phase, the class must be tested in a basic ship attack. The preparation for this training involves diving from a beach on San Diego Bay during the day. The class is paired up in two, and you're generally placed with your swim buddy, which you started with at the beginning of the second phase. While diving, you are connected by a 3-foot line that is snapped onto each of you. There is no way to separate yourselves while in the water; obviously, this is for safety reasons. If one gets into trouble, the dive buddy will no about it and can assist. Each dive pair has a compass board with a marine compass for navigation, a watch for timing, and a depth gauge.

We have a saying in SEAL team: crawl, walk, run. The crawling part is being able to depart the beach on a chosen heading straight out for a designated amount of time, then do a 180-degree turn, and if done correctly, the diving pair should surface back at the beach at the same spot they left. This works great if there are no variables like tide shift, which creates a current that can push the divers one way or another. Like skydiving, you must make corrections for wind; for navigation underwater, it's the current. One might think that you can make visible corrections. For one, there are no landmarks underwater, no horizon; it's similar to a desert. There is also the fact that you can barely see your hand in front of your face; visibility is zero.

Learning the art of navigation took time and a lot of practice. We spent hours of actual diving and running the basics before we attempted to navigate to a ship much smaller than a beach. Remember also that this is still SEAL training; when one dive pair missed their mark on the beach one time too many, we, as a class, would pay the price. One of the tools the instructors had at their disposal to punish and reinforce was to make us walk back to the base with all of our dive gear, including our scuba bottles and weight belt. On our feet were just neoprene dive booties with little support for walking several miles. After many dives of practice and negative reinforcement, we learned to hit our marks more accurately.

It was time to get comfortable with the night. Diving at night brings challenges primarily created in the mind. Everything is the same, except it's dark, and your imagination starts to work over time. Some people are not comfortable in the dark, especially underwater. After a few dives, I realized it wasn't different because you couldn't see anything underwater anyway. You had to rely on your compass and timer to navigate where you needed to go.

Once the instructors were pleased with our progression, it was time to test our skills with a ship attack. A basic ship attack was where the divers would enter the water approximately 500 yards away from the target ship. The goal was to arrive at the boat without surfacing (no peaking), and once the dive pair hit the side of the vessel, you would dive deeper, with your hand on the ship's hull until underneath it. You would know from the brief which way the vessel bow was facing, so you would turn towards the stern by following a weld seam that ran the ship's length. This would take you to the propulsion screw at the stern. You would then place a limpet mine on the strut where the screw was attached. Using an inert limpet mine would simulate the mine exploding and neutralize the ship from being able to get underway.

Lots of things could go wrong with an operation like this. You had to navigate to the ship without missing it, which is easier said than done because of how many ships were in the harbor at one time. Even though we were thoroughly briefed on the location and position of the ship, it was easy to pick the wrong one at night. You also had to be aware of suctions on the bottom of the ship that are used to bring in seawater to cool and run some of the systems. We are warned not to get too close because the suction is so strong that it can suck the diver to it to the point where you can't get off. The other important part of the ship attack is that the sailors have been briefed that SEAL trainees are attacking and to be on the lookout.

It can be challenging to keep your depth and not inadvertently surface and get compromised; in a real-world situation, the enemy would throw explosives in the water, which would be the end for you. We had to keep our depth shallow enough to hit the ship and not dive completely underneath and miss it. The noise coming from the boat had some advantages and disadvantages. One advantage was that you knew you were getting close to your target; it was like being blind, and you had to rely on other senses to find your way. In the pitch-black water, you are highly aware of any indicator that you are on track to your target. The disadvantage of sounds coming from a ship is that it's disturbing. It's eerie quiet down there, and other than the sounds of crackling that plankton gives off as you swim through it, this, combined with the sound of your breathing, is eerie.

This is all interrupted by this giant gray monster. The closer you get, the louder the sound, and you start to think there is danger in these sounds. You remember the suction portals, and you imagine that at any second, you're going to be sucked in and not be found until morning. Over time, you learn to block out these unproductive thoughts and use the noise to your advantage to guide you closer to the target.

Once you reach the ship, you stretch your arm out and start to feel; there it is; you feel the side of the ship on your hand; you face your buddy and give him a thumbs up, and he returns it with a big grin that you can barely make out from the luminescence emitting from the chemical light attached to the compass board. You start diving under the ship and find a weld seam; the bow is to the left, so we turn right towards the stern.

Swimming towards the back, keeping my hand on the weld seam, we move in the right direction. Awareness is high, and we are on time and on target by avoiding the suction portals. There it is, the ships screw. I had never seen one, and I couldn't believe how big it was. My buddy turned his back towards me to expose the limpet mine that was magnetically attached to his back. I pull it clear and place it on the strut, where the screw is attached. I draw the pin, which initiates the simulation of this mine. When the mission is complete, all there is to do is start the dive away from the ship and swim another 500 yards back to our extraction point, where the dive boat is waiting. After completing the ship attack, we proved that we were ready for the final phase of training: the Third Phase, land warfare.

Four months have passed since BUD/S training started; looking back, it's gone fast; looking forward, it is going slow. Our transition from the First Phase to the Second Phase began with painting our green helmets blue. It's hard to believe that after losing more trainees in the dive phase, that we were now down to 18 from the original 120, and I'm still here.

Chapter Thirteen
Ringing Out

Showing up for our final training phase with our blue helmets, now freshly painted red with Class 94 stenciled on the side, was a proud Moment. We had a huge celebration the weekend before, and I realized that the number 94 was something to revere and be proud of. We would be the 94th class since BUD/S training started in Coronado, California after President Kennedy called for increased special forces in January of 1962. Every SEAL knows and will always remember their class number. If somebody is pretending they were or are a Navy SEAL, all you have to ask is, what class you were in. If they aren't telling the truth, they'll start getting a little nervous at this point.

Entering the last training phase was like being a big kid on campus. As underclassmen with green helmets then blue, we always looked towards the red helmets as the pinnacle. All through training, you're wondering if you will make it to the third phase. There are so many hurdles and obstacles along the way, you could wash out or quit for a multitude of reasons in any of the phases, including making a dangerous mistake that could cost someone their life, or failing too many tests.

I was never strong in academics, so this was always a concern for me. I've always found it interesting that a failure early in life can stay with you for the rest of your life, if you let it. Because of my experience with the second grade, I had created this stigma that I was stupid. SEAL training made me realize that I wasn't. But, whenever we had to take a written test, I was filled with anxiety. I would study more than most to prepare. There was no way that I would wash out of training because I didn't study hard enough. I was always relieved when I would get my test results and find myself at the top of the class with my scores. Amazingly, I've found that the power of the dream and a strong work ethic can overcome any stigma created in one's youth.

Our instructors for the last phase of training were combat vets. These were bad-to-the-bone warriors who could recognize someone they'd want next to them in a battle just by observing us for a few days. They knew that our 18 guys would most likely graduate, and would be working with one of the UDT/SEAL teams. With all that said, they also knew, as did we, that graduation was not a sure thing for any of us.

In Phase Three, that concentrates on the aspects of land warfare we learned to become expert marksmen with long rifles and handguns, as well as all weapon systems used in combat as Navy SEALs. As a Special Operator, we were trained on small-unit tactics and how to move as small units.

There are the different phases of the missions that are given to SEALs. First, what is the target, where is the target, and how do you get to the target? Once there, what do you do on target, and how do you leave your target? SEAL, which stands for Sea, Air, and Land, means that we have to learn all aspects of sea, air, and land insertions and extractions; that is a lot of training to become experts in those elements.

We're also trained on how to take out different targets. There are different tools for each specific target because each target is different. Demolition by the use of explosives is used in a lot of different targets. So underwater and land demolition training is another part of land warfare. You can imagine that this type of training can be dangerous where attention to detail is stressed by the instructors every single day;

one slight miscalculation can end up being catastrophic. The instructors warned us that if we didn't follow instructions to the letter in every area that, they would hammer us as a class like we had never experienced in training thus far. Their threat was probably because, for the first time, the instructor staff was in as much danger as the students.

Using live ammunition while doing fire and maneuvers, is employed when ambushing, attacking, or assaulting a target; for instance, laying down weapon fire while another flanks the target from another direction.

Room clearing is when the team must strategically clear each room and remove the bad guys waiting for you behind closed doors. This starts with live simulation, or blank ammunition. The Crawl Phase is walking through the structure slowly with proper technique and saying, bang, bang, as each target is acquired.

After successfully clearing the rooms with no mistakes during the Crawl Phase, we moved to the Walking Phase. This is where we load our magazines with paintball ammunition rounds. Normally, it is not deadly but can cause severe damage if it strikes a target without protection. A member of the SEAL team was blinded in one eye by a sim round. In the amazing book Fearless, by Eric Blehm, you can read the story about this SEAL Team Six, hero, Adam Brown. We are going through the same steps of clearing each room, neutralizing targets using the sim round, and leaving a paint mark on the silhouette, which is a telltale of accuracy.

Next is the Run Phase, which can only advance when the Walk Phase with sim rounds is perfected. There is no room for error during the final phase, because our sim rounds are now replaced with live ammunition. Entering a building or an individual room is done using the same technique. Clearing can become very confusing at times. Each room can be a different size and shape and have hidden corners.

Also, there is the element of multilevel story structures, hallways, and stairwells, all of which have to be negotiated with other techniques. The last thing anybody wants is confusion when using live rounds.

When an element, which we call a train, lines up on a structure, each team member should know their job, especially when entering the structure. Without getting into the weeds of types of soft or hard entering tactics, I will talk about the basics. When the team is ready to enter, a shoulder squeeze comes from each member from the back to the front; this signals that everybody is prepared for entry. The door is opened using different breaching techniques. The team files into the room, taking their position and then acquiring and neutralizing each target. This is where it can be dangerous. First, the entry itself, everybody is amped up, even in training. Everybody carries a weapon with live ammo; every weapon has a trigger, and each member has to discipline themselves where that weapon is pointed, keeping their safety switch on until the target is acquired, then the safety switch is turned off, and the trigger is squeezed.

Also, remember the rooms can be small. When the team enters a room, there can be a lot of dudes in one area, all carrying weapons with live ammo. That live ammo is only being controlled by a muzzle and trigger discipline that keeps them from pointing their gun at another person when they're not supposed to. When and if there is confusion brought into the formula, it could lead to a deadly accident. This is why the three phases are implemented with the strict requirement that one must be patient and perfect in each phase before moving on to the next.

The Third Phase was divided into two parts: four weeks on the Silver Strand in Coronado, and three weeks at San Clemente Island. Class 94 was led to believe the reason for this remote training on an island was so the instructors could do whatever they wanted to do therefore, creating more fear and trepidation in all of us.

We were flown out to the island, and upon arrival, we unloaded our equipment and supplies needed for the final weeks of training. After settling into our new home, we filed over to the chow hall for dinner in our BUD/S camp, which was isolated from the rest of the Navy populace on the other side of the island. Before we could enter the chow hall, our class had to line up at the pull-up bar and do 20 pull-ups before we could eat.

The first meal on the island was delicious. It makes a difference when a cook is hired to feed 18-plus instructor staff rather than an entire base for thousands. The quality was at another level. We were lulled into thinking these last weeks of training would be a piece of cake. Class 94 was in for a rude awakening.

After dinner chow, it started to get dark, and we were told to fall into the classroom. The instructor entered the room, and our class leader yelled, "Ten-Hut." This command, which is a sign of respect, was given to alert us to stand up and pay attention every time an instructor entered the barracks or a classroom throughout training. The instructor started to brief us on our first evolution on the island. A night swim, one mile, beginning at the beach. We would be swimming to a buoy anchored at the half-mile mark, then back to the beach. This would be our very first night swim, and we were really concerned about sharks.

To make matters worse, the instructor had a movie projector set up and played the movie Jaws. The first 15 minutes where the naked girl is swimming, then the score starts, dun… dun… dun dun dun dun dun dun dun dun dun, you know how the rest goes. The projector is turned off, the lights return, and we all stare at the silver screen and are snapped back to reality." Ten Hut"; we jump to our feet, the instructor leaves, and our class leader instructs us to get our swim gear and fall out in front of the barracks. This was 1977 by the way, Jaws was only released two years earlier.

As we march down to the beach, we're all thinking about the last scene we just saw, that poor girl. After inspecting our gear for the swim, we wade out into the water, walking backward with our fins on until it was deep enough to start swimming. The class paired up with their usual swim buddy, now all lined up for the start. The instructor gives us the command, "On your mark, set, go!" It pays to be a winner.

With the thoughts of Jaws in our head, knowing he is lurking somewhere below in the cold dark ocean, picking out his target among these 18 strong, strapping young men, chomp, chomp. All I could think of was to swim as fast as I could and get out of the water as soon as possible. I'm sure every one of us was feeling the same. My swim buddy and I reached the turnaround point, half a mile down, half a mile to go. No sign of Jaws yet.

Swimming faster than we ever have, hoping we could swim faster than the slowest swim pair; maybe the shark will go after the last pair. We got to the beach in record time; our class had never swam so fast in all our training. Motivation is a powerful thing!

As the days ticked by on the island, I continued to get through the training and the academic tests, which seemed to be the biggest obstacles for me. It was obvious that I would graduate from BUD/S training, and the dream of becoming a Navy SEAL would become a reality. But, there was one final evolution, the grand finale, that our class had to get through; it was the most challenging in the final phase.

Chapter Fourteen
The Grand Finale

This mission dates back to World War II. It is broken into two phases; the first phase is a beach recon. Where the class members are dropped off from a fast-moving boat running parallel to the beach; each member is dropped off in 25-foot increments outside the surf zone. Each of us was outfitted with a mask, fins, a slate with a grease pen to write on, and a lead weight attached to a line.

The class swims towards the beach, staying in line with each other, stopping every 25 feet and unrolling their lead line until it hits the bottom of the ocean. The line has knots tied into it, indicating the depth where you take the sound. While taking the sound, each of us, with our head underwater, looks for objects or obstacles that would hinder the amphibious craft from landing on the beach. The obstacles could be mines, big rocks, or man-made barriers that had steel prongs protruding from a big concrete block, the enemy placed these to punch holes into the landing craft. You can see these in the movie "Saving Private Ryan" during the opening scene of the D-day invasion. We would mark these obstacles on our slate boards and make maps once we got back to the classroom.

We start our swim back to sea, where the boat returns to pick us up relatively fast. On line and still, 25 feet apart, we're kicking hard to get our bodies out of the water with our arms bent in the air, where a giant rubber hose loop grabs us and pulls us into a rubber boat tied broadside to the watercraft. After being successfully extracted from the water, we were taken back to the ship, where we would give our slates to the cartographer. Then, a map is made from this intel and distributed to the entire amphibious assault group.

In this training environment, we took the intel to the classroom, and a class member created the map. This would give us the information to conduct Phase Two of this mission.

Part of land warfare training was learning about explosives and detonators used underwater. These techniques would be used the same way that the Navy frogman, during WW2, used to blow up the obstacles on the beaches throughout the South Pacific.

One of the major reasons that UDT (Underwater Demolition Team) was formed in 1943 was that before these newly formed teams of frogman did the beach recons, the assault craft would hit the beach and land on a sandbar. The personnel would step off the landing craft into deep water and drown because of the weight of their equipment.

The other reason was to clear obstacles that would hinder the landing. This was done by tying a haversack of C4 explosives to each obstacle, then tying a trunk line of detonation cord, and connecting all the obstacles to simultaneously detonate them up into pieces. This would be done the following day before dawn.

Excited to complete and pass our final battle problem, our class woke after a few hours of sleep to the sound of the roaring ocean. We couldn't believe it; the surf was stronger than we had ever experienced in training. Because it was a training evolution, we would be inserted from the beach, not a boat. We would have to swim through the surf zone and load the obstacles with the haversacks, starting from the deepest to the ones exposed on the beach due to a low tide.

Very gung-ho but filled with fear, we started to swim, weighed down with explosives, trying to time the surf so we weren't pounded back to the beach to begin the process all over. Even with our can-do attitude and multiple attempts, you could see the concern of the instructor staff, fearful that the surf, with all of its force, would plunge us into the Japanese skullys (the name for obstacles built by the Japanese) and impale one of us trainees. At one point, as the class was lying all over the beach with the explosives, looking like a garage sale from the recent pounding of the surf, we could hear some instructors sharing their concerns with the OIC of the Third Phase.

"If this was wartime," that's all we had to hear; the OIC was not having us fail on our final mission before graduation. The order stands: get your a- - out there and load those obstacles. Knowing there was no compromise, we were determined to show the instructor staff that Class 94 could complete the job.

We started to make progress after finally getting out past the surf zone. Each obstacle had a three-man team to tie the haversack charge to each obstacle, taking turns breath-holding, swimming down to the bottom where it was sitting, and getting as much done as possible with a single breath, the next guy would dive down and repeat until all was secure and ready for the trunk line to be tied into the haversack for detonation.

After all the obstacles were loaded, the class swam into the beach filled with pride, mission complete. It was time for the last swim pair to pull the underwater detonator (UWD) to ignite the fuse. Having a 15-minute time fuse allowed the last pair to swim safely back to the beach and reach a safe distance with the rest of the class and instructor staff.

With about 10 seconds left on the clock before the charge would blow, we started a countdown: 10, 9, 8, 7, 6, 5, 4, 3, 2, 1, and all yelled, fire in the hole! A few seconds later, we saw the most beautiful water geyser shoot up into the sky about 150 feet in the air. That kind of stuff is one of the coolest parts of training, for sure.

After the water shot, we knew we had to pack up the next day and head back to Coronado. I couldn't help but think that this was the best decision I could have made up to that point in my life: to be a United States Navy SEAL!

Getting back to the Silver Strand after our final three weeks of training was awesome and finally stress free. We had been worrying for the last six months if we would fail or get kicked out of training, but this was now all behind us. Class 94 seemed to be floating, not running all over the base, with big smiles on our faces. All we had left to do was perform administrative duties before our families came into Coronado from all over the Country to watch their boys, now men, graduate from the most demanding military training in the world.

Chapter Fifteen
Graduation Day

I can hardly believe it; graduation day is finally here. Dad, Mom, and some siblings came in for the big show. I could tell my parents were so proud of me. I had never seen them act that way and smile that much! They didn't know what I had gone through, but they knew it was something big. None of us from our class looked the same; we all had put on 10-20 pounds of muscle and were all ripped. We were euphoric over completing such a hard program. I dreamt of this day for over eight months, and it was finally here. This was way-cooler than second grade.

As we were getting dressed in our dress blues, we could hear the military music playing as the guests were gathering. This was the same compound that so many great warriors from the past, spent the same hours being tortured that we did.

It was time, "Class 94, fall out! yelled our class leader. We walked this time; we didn't need to run. This was our day, and there was no instructor looking over our shoulder trying to find an excuse to make us do pushups or get wet. As a matter of fact, there were no instructors in sight. They were gathered in the compound, telling our families and friends what we had just endured and how proud they were of us. I found out from my time as an instructor many years later that it's nearly impossible to convey how proud we were of our class members in a few minutes of casual conversation.

We formed up as Class 94 for the last time. After this day, there would be no Class 94. Like all the other BUD/S classes before us, we would be disbanded. The class number had served its purpose of identifying the beginning of the 120 to the graduation of 18. After this day, we would become a part of the elite community of UDT/SEALS that had earned the reputation of being some of the most bad assed, feared human beings on the planet.

We were lined up perfectly in formation just like we learned to do back in bootcamp. From where we were standing we could see into the compound where the guests were seated. I remember some of the guys having girlfriends. I don't know how they had time for that during training, but they were obviously more efficient with their time than I was.

"Class 94, forward march." As we entered, in our dress blues, with our heads up, and chests out, you could hear a pin drop. All eyes were on us. It was as if everyone there understood the significance of what we had just gone through without knowing the details of how tough it actually was; we all felt a deep sense of pride and awe." Class 94, parade rest."

The commanding officer of the Naval Special Warfare Center (BUD/S) began the commencement presentation while various OICs (Officers in Charge) shared funny stories of our class from each training phase. In closing, the commanding officer gave us one last command. "Class 94, ring out!"

BUD/s class 94, Mike is fifth from left bottom row

Our class lined up a single file, and each one of us was able to grab the lanyard from that ominous brass bell and ring it as loudly as we wanted three times!!! What are the odds? Is this for real? Was it my birthday? Is anyone taping this?! This was the greatest thing ever, I got to Ring the HELL out of that BELL! The same bell that taunted us all through training. The same bell that offered to take us out of the misery we were going through if we would just ring it. Ring it three times, and your dream of being a Navy SEAL would disappear. Just one simple gesture: Poof! You and your dream were removed from this hollowed ground where all SEAL warriors had been put through the fire. But not today. Today, we rang that bell three times as loud as we could, and today, it was only for Class 94. The sound of victory! Hooyah, Class 94!

The graduation ceremony was concluded, and the guests were instructed to enter the classroom, where refreshments were served. We each found our family and friends and shared hugs and congratulations. Looking into my parent's eyes was one of the most significant rewards of my life. It was well worth the price I paid. Being post-WWII parents, they didn't have to say much; it was a look I understood; they were proud.

Once in the classroom, there was an announcement that they would shut the lights off to share a training film called, Someone Special, to give the guests an idea of what SEAL training was like. I had seen the film in boot camp, the diving in it inspired me to try out in the first place.

As the movie played, I looked at my Mom and Dad. My Mom was crying, and my Dad had this look, it was a combination of shock and awe. At the conclusion, I asked my Mom what she thought, and she replied, with tears, "I can not believe they put you through that." I said, Mom, that's nothing; that's just the recruiting film!

There were parties all over Coronado. It was a great time to introduce our classmates to our families and share stories. During the few days of exposure to the culture, our families better understood our trials and tribulations, but no one who hadn't gone through it could ever understand.

Chapter Sixteen
Discipline or Willpower

People think that you really need to be disciplined to make it through SEAL training. After thinking about it I realized it didn't take discipline, it took willpower. Discipline is doing something you don't feel like doing, but you do it anyway. No audience, no one clapping and cheering you on, you do it because it's the right thing to do for whatever your reason for doing it.

There are so many different aspects to which discipline applies. I use the gym analogy because that has been my world since I was a teenager. Discipline will apply to any goal that one wants to achieve, with no one to be accountable to but yourself. Take, for example, writing this book; when I got this idea, I asked Charrie if she thought it was a good premise, and she told me that it was and that I should write it. Then she said to write for an hour every morning and then send it to me.

It takes discipline to stay consistent in this project, but she made it easier because I felt accountable to her. I send her what I write, and she critiques it, suggests a few changes, and sends me either a cartoon toilet smoking a cigar or a gold star. I am proud to say I've received a lot of gold stars.

Having never written a book before, I was apprehensive to start. Charrie told me just to start and let my thoughts free flow, and we could clean it up later. So that's what I have done. It seems to be working. We shall see; you will be the judge!

Discipline becomes more challenging when you don't have to be accountable to anyone but yourself. This comes into play when you become bored with the activity. Take any athlete training for competition. Anything that you have to repeat, over and over again, in order to get better at can become boring. This is where discipline has to take over and be flexed.

You say to yourself, I don't care what you FEEL like doing. I have a goal; I told myself I am going to get in shape, I am going to write this book, I am going to be an Olympian, I am going to build my business, or I am going to get my degree. I am not going to give in to my feelings. Or you succumb to your feelings, stay on the couch, and feel guilty because you were weak, and you know it. This thought process is unhealthy for your self-image; the lack of discipline starts to spill over into all areas of your life. Discipline is like a muscle; you need to use it, or it atrophies.

Now, SEAL training doesn't take discipline; my goal was to be a SEAL, and I decided that I would get through training, without quitting, no matter what. Here is the difference: I have an audience, and I have the rest of Class 94; when I would fall out for training, I had a classmate on the left and one on the right. There is an instructor staff member who knows every one of us, and they are focused on our names written next to our scores on a board that measures our times for runs, swims, and obstacle courses. It doesn't take discipline; it takes willpower to keep showing up for the next piece of hell the instructors dish out. Class 94 and our instructors would know immediately that I quit, and the bell would announce my departure.

I've been asked why so few trainees make it through BUD/S training. First off, it is very competitive to get into the draft to have your name pulled out and even be given orders to try. So, if the cream of the crop is chosen for training, then why do only 18-22% graduate? I believe there is a correlation at work here. After being in business and studying the principle of success for the last 36 years, I've realized that a small percentage of people will succeed at anything; it is a matter of will and the power of the dream.

I've met and gotten to know so many people over the years with multiple gifts and talents, far more than I've ever had. The problem is that they didn't know they had them. There is so much wasted talent in this world. The good Lord has given us all certain gifts and talents, some more than others. It shouldn't be a question of how much but how one uses them. When I entered BUD/S training, I didn't know what SEALs did. I had yet to learn what their mission was. I believe the dream given to me as a child to be a diver of some sort blossomed in me, leading me to SEAL training, which opened up the doors and put me on my life journey, which brought me here.

Chapter Seventeen
Black Hats

After graduation, Class 94 would join the Ft. Benning Airborne Unit in Georgia, for three weeks learning the Army way of jumping out of an aircraft. Every class that had ever graduated from BUD/S, would tell you that as far as training goes, Army jump school left a lot to be desired. It was required that we graduate from jump school, but the Army way of doing things, well let's just say, we were not looking forward to it.

We had to accept that the Army had a job: to train the masses on how to jump out of an airplane. They take a class of about 500 students from every level of physical strength and intelligence and teach them, via repetition, how to be airborne qualified. And here we were, 18 guys who had just finished SEAL training. It was a shock to the system as it clashed with how we learned.

Needless to say, we had an attitude, and the Army instructors knew it. It turns out that the Army has had to put up with our attitude for years, and they disliked us as much as we disliked them.

The instructors at airborne training were called Black Hats because they wore Black Hats. Well, that made sense. The first morning at Ft. Benning, our class formed up with the other 500 men to start their training, SEAL Class 94 stood out like a sore thumb. Our expressions were soured and our camouflage uniforms were totally different than the Army's.

The Black Hats, spent three weeks trying to instruct and impart the historical value of our training on us by using the example of who had trained there before us. For instance, this was the same ground that the Army Airborne Rangers and Airborne Battalions trained on who had jumped behind enemy lines on D-day.

Well, not only was I 20 years old, but I was also someone who slept through all of their history classes, I'll admit it. I did not understand the historical magnitude of the training I was going through. All I could think about was that Class 94 had to put up with this archaic way of learning the simple act of leaping from an aircraft. Yes, we were cocky prima donnas, who thought they were all that and a bag of chips.

Now, the Black Hats had seen this movie before, and they were very familiar with our smug attitudes. You could see it in their eyes, they had nothing but contempt for us. There was nothing that the Black Hats would like better than to break us while they had the chance. We knew that it was never going to happen.

They swarmed us like bees while the entire airborne class was standing at attention. The senior Black Hat started the war by saying, "Look what we have here; we have some Navy in our presence." They had the same respect for us as we did for them, and that was zero. We took their actions as a frontal assault on who we were as SEALs and the training we came from; and it was game on.

It was us against them, and the other 500 men were the audience for the show. We had to fight respectfully though because we were in the military, however, it was imperative to show them that we couldn't be broken. The Black Hats had only one tool in their bag that had constraints, which was their mouth, and for discipline, they could drop us down to do pushups but only make us do ten at a time, and they had to have a reason.

Immediately, they were talking to us about our uniforms. If there was a loose thread, they called that an Irish pennant. The first one of us to be inspected by a Black Hat was called out, "Look what we have here, Navy; we have an Irish pennant, drop-down Navy, and give me ten." Class 94 looked at each other and dropped down together. One of our guys said, "Which arm?" The Black Hats took this as a sign of disrespect; and that's how we meant it. All 18 of us started our pushups as we did in SEAL training: down one, down two, down three, and so on to ten.

After doing ten easy pushups, we jumped to our feet and back to attention to start this exercise again—the next Black Hat standing before another classmate. "Navy, your boots are not shined to my liking. Drop down and give me ten." Our class dropped down together for ten more. After about an hour of our class doing 200 pushups, the battle between the Black Hats and Class 94 had to end. There was a training schedule to keep, and the Black Hats realized they wouldn't be breaking us today or any other day.

Later that morning, our class was called into the Marine liaison office. We were notified that every time a SEAL class showed up for jump training that the relationship between the Black Hats and the BUD/S class became problematic for all. We were asked to play nice, get through our three weeks of training, and return to our SEAL commands. We were also reminded that if we were thrown out of jump school, that we could possibly find ourselves on probation and not receive our our Trident emblems on schedule.

Our class agreed that we would play their game and not cause any more problems. You could tell that the Black Hat instructors had their talking to as well, as they showed us a little more respect. They knew that we didn't need any more training on discipline to learn how to jump out of an airplane; our previous six months of training took care of that.

The first part of our training was to learn how to land. We were all instructed on the proper PLF, Parachute Landing Fall, technique. The Army's way of training 500-plus men and women, as I mentioned earlier, was by repetition. This would ensure that the highest to the lowest IQ would build muscle memory through the act done over and over.This was done by climbing a platform about three feet off the ground, then jumping off and performing the PLF. This was done repeatedly, with critiques by the Black Hats, to ensure that it became automatic and was done to perfection.

The next phase of Army airborne training was simulating jumping from the side door of an aircraft. This took place 37 feet off the ground in what they called the 37-foot tower. This would have been a great Disney ride. We would climb the stairs to the top of the tower, the instructor would stand in the door and yell commands. You would then place your hands on each side of the door, looking straight with your body erect and feet placed as if you were getting ready for a foot race, and then propel yourself out as far as you can jump to clear the simulated aircraft. If you have ever watched an old war movie, this would give you an idea of the proper position the jumper would be in as they exited the door.

Once exiting the door, you were dangling from a cable about 50 yards long, which had you bouncing up and down as you counted, 1 one thousand, 2 one thousand, 3 one thousand, 4 one thousand. This was to simulate your count for the length of time that it took to get an open parachute; if not, this is when you would pull your reserve, which you had only a couple of seconds more until you hit the ground. This, too, was repeated over and over.

The final training phase before jumping out of the actual aircraft was the 250-foot tower. This phase would also make another great amusement park ride. There were three of these towers. When it was your turn, you would don a parachute harness attached to a parachute, that was connected to a cable that lifted you 250 feet above the ground. Then, when ready, your parachute was released, and you would float under the parachute and conduct the proper PLF.

This was the closest simulation to an actual parachute jump that you could get

250 Foot Tower

After completing the first two weeks of training, it was on to the last week, which was known as jump week. We would be making five actual parachute jumps. Other than the movies, I had never seen anyone jump from an aircraft. There is a possibility of the parachute failing, and the mental process of going through all of the emergency procedures when that happens is unnerving. It was a constant reminder of how dangerous jumping out of a plane really was.

Monday of this last week would be our first jump. We gathered in the staging area where all the parachute rigs were waiting for us to put on and load the C-130 aircraft. We would sing a song during BUD/S training. "C-130 rolling down the strip, taking the little froggies on a

111

trip, we're going to stand up, hook up, shuffle to the door, we're going to jump right out and count to four. If my main doesn't open, I use my reserve. If my reserve doesn't open wide, the little froggy is no more." It was only after the last two weeks of training, that I finally understood the song's words. But, we were all prepared; one thing you can say about Army Airborne training is that you knew from repetition what to do.

Once loaded and in our seats, the pilots started the engines, and we began to taxi out to the runway. It would take a little while to reach the jump altitude of 1250 feet. Jumping out of an airplane with a parachute has to be one of the most unnatural things to do. From 1250 feet, the distance to the earth looked short. You knew there wouldn't be much time before you hit the ground if the parachutes failed. These thoughts were just a few that were flooding my mind as the aircraft leveled off.

We knew it wouldn't be long after the side doors were open; the noise of the engines and wind created by the aircraft's airspeed was deafening. The jump master yelled, "Get ready, stand up, hook up." You would hook the static line attached to your parachute to a cable that ran the length of the aircraft above your head. Once hooked, you would pull on the static line, and the hook would close around the cable. You then placed a metal pin through the hook, while keeping the clasp from opening. The following commands were to check the equipment by checking the back of the jumper in front of you, making sure that everything looked right and the static line wasn't misrouted. Then, you would check the front of your own harness to ensure everything was rigged correctly.

Anticipating the next command, my heart started to race. The first man would stand in the doorway, and everybody else would be right behind the person in front of them, with no space between each other. "Shuffle to the door, 30 seconds, 15 seconds, stand in the door, stand by." Then it came, "GO!" Instinctively, you started to move towards the door, following the person in front of you. There was no thinking, just doing; awareness was low, and two weeks of repetitious training took over.

Hurling myself out the door into the wind blast, I instinctively went into the proper airborne body position. You are wrapped tight, legs straight, arms wrapped tightly around your reserve mounted on your chest, chin tucked, not giving the air blast any chance to misdirect your body from its proper exit position. If your chin wasn't tucked, it could cause your parachute to deploy irregularly and lead to a malfunction.

I counted to four and started to feel the parachute deploy immediately. I didn't get past three before I felt the jerk of the parachute fully deployed. I remember looking up at this beautiful round parachute. It seemed to be breathing as if it were fully blossoming. As you plummet towards Mother Earth, knowing that the only thing that will save you is the parachute on your back, when it does, it is a sight to behold.

Now, it's time to focus on the landing. These parachutes don't have much maneuverability and are at the mercy of the wind. The drop zone at Ft. Benning, Ga., was large enough to accommodate the airborne training that took place; thousands were trained, and 500 plus jumpers were put out at one time over this drop zone.

Face into the wind to slow your backward motion and slow the rate of descent, eyes looking straight to the horizon, feet and knees together, toes pointed towards the ground so the first point of contact will be the balls of your feet. Hands are on the steering toggles above your head. Relax; the ground is coming, don't look down, don't anticipate the landing, balls of your feet hit the ground, rag doll, hip is next, then shoulder, keep the Momentum, let the rest of your body follow. Ah, that wasn't bad; nice landing. First, jump down, and four more to go.

The next three jumps went pretty much the same; there would be one more jump before we graduate. This last jump would be at night. The thought of jumping out of an aircraft in the dark was even scarier. There would be new thoughts that weren't there during the daylight jumps. How could I tell if my parachute had malfunctioned? Can I see the reserve ripcord? Probably not. I would have to rely on feel and muscle memory from the repetitious training.

The other concern was landing. How can I tell if I was getting close to the ground so I could prepare for the PLF? I know I wasn't supposed to anticipate the landing, so I would be relaxed enough to be limp, so my body would fold like I was trained. It's easier said than done when you know the ground is coming up to meet you at about 20 feet per second. That's not a slow rate of descent; if the parachute landing fall is not done correctly, you can easily break something.

As the sun set, our class was in the staging area, donning our parachute systems. I could tell everybody was a little nervous by their less-than-pleasant selves. After our riggers check, the first of two checks were given by the Army jump masters before we boarded the aircraft to ensure we had donned our parachute system correctly. We loaded the aircraft, it was pretty much pitch black outside. Inside, the red lights illuminated the aircraft to preserve our night vision. This would be helpful when we exited the plane into the black hole of darkness. We were all loaded, and you could see the aircrew conducting their final checks before taking off.

Once in the air, we knew from the previous four jumps that it wouldn't be long before the jump master gave us the commands that would lead us to the doorway, to the unknown. All I could think about was getting through this last jump and returning to Coronado, our SEAL command, to return to the Navy way of doing things.

Completing this training would allow us to get more jumps to earn our gold Navy/Marine Corps Jump Wings. We would be presented the Army Jump wings after our last jump, which we would throw in a drawer and never wear. The gold jump wings represented that we had made at least ten parachute jumps.

Stand up, came the command, 30 seconds, stand by, stand in the door; the light above the door turned from red to green; go, yelled the jump master. The first man was out, and everybody behind was shuffling fast and tight, right behind the man in front. I was out the door and counting to four; at three, I felt my parachute giving that beautiful jerk from opening shock, which was the feeling you were waiting for a full parachute.

I could see the lights on the ground just enough to know where we were going to land. There wasn't enough light to see to prepare for landing; this would be done by looking at the horizon. Getting close and getting ready, toes pointed towards the ground, knees together, relax like a rag doll. I talked myself through the final steps before landing, but my body wasn't listening; it started to tense in anticipation of hitting the ground, which I couldn't see. I knew I was getting close, then wham, my feet hit the ground, and all I felt was this terrible pain in my ankle. Did I break it? I got to my feet, started to rigger roll my parachute, and stuffed it in the bag to carry it back to the trucks and load the bus to transport back to the base. My ankle hurt as I took each step, but I realized I had sprained it. I wouldn't be able to walk on it if it were broken.

As I approached the bus, I could see others limping; misery loves company. Even though my ankle hurt, this did not distract me from the thoughts of completing Army Airborne Training. Class 94 has completed the training and is heading back to our respective commands, some going to the West Coast and some heading east.

Basic training is replaced with advanced skillsets; working up together and going through this training, honing the skills that it takes to deploy somewhere in the world, and working together as a single unit brings another element of brotherhood, making a SEAL platoon a vast force multiplier on the battlefield.

After completing jump school, I went back to Coronado, CA. My orders were to report to one of the West Coast SEAL teams, where I would start my career. It was a little bit surreal starting my new journey with some of the most highly trained elite fighting forces in the free world and being a new guy in a team that was enriched with so much battle history, starting with the Raiders and then Underwater Demolition teams that served since 1943 during and before the D-day operation.

What an incredible job I have. I can't believe that I get paid to have this depth of camaraderie with people, as well as work out, jump out of airplanes, and train for all the operations that Navy SEALs perform during all environments, Sea Air Land, during insertion, extraction, and time on target, with all the tools of the trade to get it done, pretty darn cool!

Chapter Eighteen
Blue Skies, Black Death

Returning from Army jump school in Ft. Benning, Ga. I had decided I liked jumping out of airplanes but wanted to free-fall (skydive). At Army jump school, we spent three weeks learning how to exit an airplane in a body position most people have seen in a movie, depicting a military operation like D-day, with a mass amount of soldiers jumping behind enemy lines, and generally at a very low altitude to give the enemy less time to shoot at you while you are descending.

Free-falling was like it says: you exit the aircraft from a much higher altitude, fly out of the plane like your Superman, and have about 60 seconds to fly through the air doing anything imaginable. Most of you have seen some form of skydiving on YouTube or in a Hollywood movie or even had a chance to do a tandem jump yourself.

Back in 1977, we didn't have the internet, nor did you see any skydiving in a movie. During that time, skydiving was in its infancy stage, with a lot of pioneering still going on in the sport. Not long after returning from Army jump school, I was in one of our local SEAL bar hangouts, and I was exposed to a short skydiving film created with an old 8mm movie camera that someone had mounted on their helmet. It was a film about the Navy Parachute Team called the Leap Frogs; this team was made up exclusively of Navy SEALs. I didn't even know there was such a thing. As I watched these guys soar through the sky with smoke trailing from their feet, then join up and form a circle. It looked like these people were flying like aircraft, using their arms and legs as control surfaces to maneuver like birds in the air. It was incredible, I thought, I have to do that!

I started to inquire about learning how to free-fall. Most of the answers I got from my SEAL command were, "You're a new guy; you have to pay some dues before you can request free-fall school, and it's an Army school, and we only get so many slots a year, and they're not giving them to a new guy."

I wanted to pay my dues, but I didn't want to attend another school run by the Army to learn how to fly through the air like a bird. The more questions I asked, the more I found people with the answers. Back then, the skydiving community was small; not everyone felt like I did about jumping. Most SEALs didn't like jumping out of a perfect airplane. They would do it when they had to, for training or pay. By pay, I mean you had to jump out of a plane at least four times yearly to get your monthly jump pay of $55.00. These guys thought, why would you want to do more, and why would you want to go to free-fall school?

Then there were guys like me who couldn't do it enough; this was the minority in the teams. There was this camaraderie among skydivers, and when they met another person who thought like them, they wanted to help and foster their passion for the sport.

I was directed to Borderland in south San Diego, a civilian skydiving center. In April of 1978, I enrolled in the free-fall training course. It was a progression of jumps. First, you started by jumping a static line, as I had learned at Army jump school, but this training was getting you ready for free fall; the exit was different; it was done out of a tiny Cessna that held about six people. When it was your turn, the airplane would fly over the drop zone, and when you were close to the exit point, you were instructed to climb out of the airplane onto a little step that was no bigger than a dollar bill. Climbing carefully with your hands on the strut, facing forward into the prop blast, the forward aircraft speed was around 85 knots. Imagine you're riding a motorcycle, climbing up, and standing on the seat while holding onto the handlebars; you get the picture?

The jump master is now giving the pilot commands to make final adjustments; these corrections are to keep the aircraft on the right trajectory and to put the plane in the correct position upwind from the landing zone. The variables that change this exit position are based on upper and ground winds. The technique is to find the exit point where the jumper leaves the airplane. It's done with a streamer pass where the pilot climbs to the parachute opening altitude directly over the landing zone and throws out two rolls of cray paper, typically yellow, called streamers. The pilot circles the drop zone as the jump master observes the two streamers to see where they land. The exit point will be upwind, opposite the streamer's landing point.

As the aircraft takes off and climbs to altitude, it is the beginning of the pucker factor. This is where your blood runs through your veins rapidly, and your heart pumps and works over time. This is all controlled by thoughts: Why am I doing this? I could die; jumping out of a perfect airplane is not natural! All the thoughts of what can go wrong from all aspects of this jump activity. You could fall while exiting the aircraft and entangle yourself in the deploying parachute (that wouldn't be good), the parachute might not open, what if it malfunctions, I'd have to cut it away, what if I can't in time, what if the reserve doesn't open? These thoughts keep rushing through your brain.

The jump master and your instructor yell, "Jump run," then "30 seconds." My heart is pounding; this is stupid and wild. "Get ready, 15 seconds." Why am I doing this again? "Stand by, climb out," The brain goes numb. I follow the command; I place my left foot on the step while reaching for the aircraft strut with my right hand, and then my left and right legs dangle in the air. Go, the jump master yells. I

119

let go and started to count 1001, 1002, and 1003. I'm falling away from the aircraft, and I feel the deploying parachute leaving my back; there is a jolt, and then I look up, and there is this beautiful white, orange, brown, and green round parachute that just saved my life. It's the only time these colors, which were so beautiful, can be used in the same sentence.

I can feel my heart rate start to slow. I'm about 2000 feet above the ground; the view is spectacular; I can see the ocean as I face west. Focus, Mike, you need to land this parachute on the drop zone; if I don't, it could be a bad, broken leg, broken something. I am upwind; I turn my parachute towards the landing zone by pulling my toggle that turns the parachute to head downwind; even though there isn't much speed or maneuverability with a round parachute, it is enough to put you on or off the landing zone.

My altimeter placed on top of my belly-mounted reserve is reading 500 feet; looking good now, I have to pull this steering toggle and face into the wind. There is a wind sock that tells me which way the wind blows. Get ready to land; three weeks at Army jump school prepared me well for this phase of the jump: knees bent, both knees and feet together, balls of my feet will be the first point of contact with the ground, then the side of my hip, next shoulder, roll with it. Like a crash test, when a car hits the wall, an accordion-type action folds up the car to take the impact out of the crash.

Even though the PLF (parachute landing fall) is great in theory and works better than any other procedure one might come up with, it's hard to stay relaxed when you know this might hurt. Relax, Mike, looking straight ahead, not at the ground, don't anticipate, wait for it, wait for it, feet hit, hip, shoulder, legs are straight, the Momentum carries them over your body, not so bad that time. I'm alive; that was awesome; let's do it again!

I'd say that it was at least the first 100 jumps that, when climbing to altitude, my mind would take me through all the things that could go wrong; the fear was almost crippling until I climbed out on that step and focused on what to do. I want to tell you that the training progression would make me more comfortable, but it did not. It got worse.

You see, at each level of the training, you were required to do more than just let go of the strut and arch your back so as not to flop around like that rag doll. There was more to think about, so the anxiety and fear grew with each level. On the second jump, you had a ripcord handle that wasn't attached to anything, but you had to go through the procedure: look, reach, pull. Everything was the same as the first jump, except you had to demonstrate to your jump master that you could pull your rip cord, even though the static line was doing it for you; it was called the dummy ripcord pull.

After completing the dummy ripcord pull, it was time to do your first free-fall. It's going to get real now. Everything was the same, except there was no static line deploying your parachute; it's all you. Instead of a dummy ripcord, the rip cord is attached to the parachute system, and the only thing that will save your life is you pulling your rip cord. This sounds easy enough, but remember, when you leave the aircraft, you must maintain the correct body position of arching your back while looking down to find your ripcord. Remember where your eyes go; your body follows; if done wrong, you break your arch, and your body will start to roll over and flop out of control while searching for the handle to save your life.

Even if you find it in time, about seven seconds before you run out of airspace and ideas, your chute could wrap around your legs and malfunction. My hands are getting sweaty just writing this.

My first free fall was successful; it was time to move on to the following levels, and I advanced by doing five- and 10-second delays.

This meant you would jump from a higher altitude, allowing you to free-fall for those delays perspectively. The difference is that you are reaching terminal velocity, which is approximately 120 mph. During this phase, you have more time to get out of control by flat spinning or tumbling. Either one can be detrimental to deploying your chute incorrectly.

My fear and anxiety were to no avail; I completed all training levels and was signed off to start skydiving independently from the usual free-fall altitude of 12,500 feet, which gave the jumper about a 65-second free fall.

Like I said earlier, it took about 100 jumps to get rid of this fear and anxiety. Why 100? It took me this long to realize that these thoughts were nonproductive. I learned to block them out. Whenever my mind went down that rabbit hole, I would change the channel. I would begin to focus on the jump and the emergency procedures I practiced in my mind and through simulating each action required for each type of malfunction. But I would not let the fear or anxiety in while doing so.

Let's go back a bit; it was early in my free-fall training when we students were standing around, and a larger aircraft (DC-3) was on a jump run (12,500 feet and lining up over the drop zone). Our instructor told us to look up and keep our eyes on the airplane, preparing to spit out about ten jumpers. A Moment later, we saw all these people flying out the side door and joining in a big circle by flying towards each other like an aircraft. As they got closer to the ground, about 4,000 feet, they started flying away, separating into their airspace to safely deploy their parachutes so as not to run into each other. You could hear the sound of each canopy opening; imagine going from 120 mph to 0 mph with a rectangular nylon material, like a wing.

I noticed two things immediately: how fast these square parachutes moved through the sky, and one jumper had a color different from all the rest. The jumpsuit was powder blue with yellow stripes down the sides; the parachute was the same color. I thought to myself, those colors are strange, not very manly.

My eyes continued to follow this jumper; as he approached the ground, he seemed smaller. Then, on landing, the form seemed more feminine. After the landing, this person removed his helmet. My questions were answered: that is no guy; it was this beautiful brunette, and all I could think about was, Wow, what a woman! My thoughts of trying to meet her evaporated when I observed one of the skydivers walk over and kiss her. She was out of my league, anyway!

Robin was the sky queen, and I was sky trash. At the time, Robin was considered one of the few top female skydivers in the Country. I would see Robin and her boyfriend from time to time during my first year of skydiving. Learning the art of skydiving is not a fast learning curve; it takes hundreds of jumps to feel like you're becoming proficient in the sport.

I remember one beautiful summer day in that first year; I had just gotten to the ground after a skydive and was packing my parachute at the packing tables. A packing table was a long, narrow table about 35 - 40 feet long. It stretched out your round parachute system so you could adequately pack and stow it into the pack tray; this would ensure that your parachute would deploy without entanglements and twists, which could be costly if not done correctly.

While packing my parachute, I heard the jump plane overhead on a jump run. When you hear the sound of the engines pulling back to a lower rpm, this distinct sound tells you that jumpers will be exiting the plane, and all eyes on the ground look skyward. Like many times before, I see the jumpers exiting the airplane; the formation forms into a specific shape rehearsed on the ground. At break-off altitude, the jumpers start to track away from each other; this is where each jumper turns 180 degrees, folds their arms to their sides, and their legs straighten, taking the shape of a jet fighter where your vertical speed increases from 120 mph to 180 mph. This allows separation for each jumper to get into clear airspace to deploy their parachute.

All the parachutes seemed to deploy normally, but after scanning the sky and looking at each parachute, I noticed one did not look right. One jumper was experiencing a high-speed malfunction; this is where the parachute has opened very little to catch air. In this case, there is not much time before the jumper hits the ground and ends fatally. Now, all eyes are on this jumper. Every skydiver knows the procedure to use when experiencing this type of malfunction: to release the main parachute with a cutaway system; in the '70s and early '80s, there were multiple systems.

Everyone on the ground is thinking the same thing: cutaway. You can see the jumper trying to solve the problem, and then the main parachute separates. The next thing everyone is hoping for is the reserve parachute deployment, which is done by pulling a separate handle. Everyone on the ground is saying the same thing: pull, pull! Then, the white reserve parachute starts to show. Holding our breath as we watch it deploy, it seems to open, but all of a sudden, after the initial opening shock, oh no, it goes from an almost regular fully opened parachute to a streamer, where it collapses. Everybody watches in horror as the jumper tries to pull on whatever he can to right this canopy. The last 200 feet or so, the jumper, realizing what is about to happen, starts to scream. I can not believe what I'm witnessing. You could hear a pin drop. The worst part of this fatality, his wife and kids were there!

Everyone knows and thinks about the risk, but when you experience a fatality, it shakes you to the core. A parachutist magazine comes out monthly; in the back is the fatality report, with the background story on reasons. Every skydiver reads the report, putting themselves in those situations and maybe learning something that one can use to be a safer skydiver.

It was an eerie quiet all over the drop zone. Some ran towards the impact area, probably to see if there was anything they could do, and some because they had a morbid curiosity. I did not; I gathered my equipment, threw it into my car, and drove off. On the way home, I was giving a lot of thought to this dangerous sport. Witnessing an actual fatality in real time made me realize this wasn't something that happened that I read about in a magazine; this happened at my local drop zone here in San Diego.

What makes people do something that they know firsthand is inherently dangerous? Then I started thinking about my career choice; everything about my job was dangerous, and I liked it.

So, after much thought, I concluded that life is dangerous, and I can sit on the sidelines, worrying about what's dangerous or not. I can live a life playing it safe, or I can live my life without worry or fear. So the following weekend, I was at 12,500 feet, exiting a DC-3 with other skydivers who felt the same way I did.

That choice was made long before this unfortunate accident; it just brought it front and center. It made me realize who I was and why I am the way I am. A small percentage of the world's population lives their lives in the same way. The first responders come to mind, rushing towards danger when most people run from it. Let's examine all the dangerous sports and career choices some people enjoy. I believe they engage in these activities and careers because of the thrill and the adrenaline rush. It makes people feel alive. But I also think that this behavior is caused by people trying to fill a void with the pleasure-seeking feeling. It seemed that feeling guided my entire life. It started in my youth when I was always looking for something fun and exciting to do. What can I do to keep from feeling bored? The thrill of riding a bicycle, jumping off a roof with an umbrella, water skiing tricks that would give you the rush from trying the unknown, constantly pushing the envelope. From barefoot skiing off a ramp to doing 360-degree turns off the big ramp, we called those helicopters. It's like grabbing an electrical fence; why would somebody do that? You realize that the excitement of activity gets dull, so you must try something new, exciting, and risky, pushing it to another level; this is alright; it's not right or wrong; it's just different. We are all created differently, and some are born like me.

As you continue to follow my journey, there will likely be a particular path that you relate to. Or you might just think I'm crazy, along with all the other people who feel the way I think. There is a lesson in this story. So follow along, and we will come to the same conclusion: there is a plan and a purpose for every one of us in this life.

Chapter Nineteen
Piercing the Darkness

One of my first encounters with a near-death situation happened when I was on my first deployment. I was on a Westpac (Western Pacific) deployment with my first platoon as a SEAL. I would be a major participant in the training operations that were being planned since I was one of 4 qualified free-fallers in the platoon.

This was going to be a downed pilot extract mission; this is where a pilot is shot down behind enemy lines and is on the ground, evading the enemy until help comes to get the pilot out. So, the warning order was given, as well as the information needed to plan the mission, what, when, where, and equipment required for insertion, time on target, extraction, and everything in between.

We would insert four guys using a HALO jump, which stands for High Altitude Low Opening. This training mission would jump from 12,500 feet and open at 3,500 feet for safety margins. After landing, we would rendezvous at the rally point and patrol to the last known location of the pilot.

On the day of, we prepped the equipment needed for the operation. I was very comfortable with everything except the insertion part. This would be my first nighttime and first free-fall combat equipment jump. And since I would be the radio man, I would carry an extra load. I had no idea how stable I would be in free fall, carrying this extra weight on my butt in a pack.

After getting all my equipment ready and packed up, I spent the rest of my spare time packing my parachute. It usually would take me about a half hour to pack this particular round parachute system. Today, I will make sure each fold and line stowed is perfect. Whatever could be done, just short of ironing it, I did it.

After finishing, I spent the rest of the day thinking about my emergencies and visualizing the procedures. I wanted to make sure I was mentally ready. I was working myself up about this night jump. Naturally, I was very inexperienced since I only had about 45 jumps logged.

It was time to load the truck and head to the airfield, where we would load the C-130 aircraft. It was about a half hour before sunset, giving us enough time to get to altitude and jump out without detection. You could tell we were all nervous about the jump. We were quiet and continually going through all aspects of the jump. One thing that was concerning was landing in the ocean.It would be easy to miscalculate the upper winds that can push the jumpers while free-falling out of the target area.

Once at exit altitude, we could see, Herschel Davis, our Master Chief of the platoon, who was the most experienced of the four and was our jump master. A crew member of the aircraft opened the side door to see the ground and the drop zone, marked with a series of lights. The plane started its jump run, and Master Chief was shaking his head like he couldn't see the ground because of cloud cover; then he put his finger in the air and started to make the circle sign that meant go around, let's try again. He did this several times, which made it more disturbing. He was probably thinking that if he put us out and he couldn't see the drop zone, there was a good chance we could end up in the water. Of course, this is what was going through my mind.

After three go-arounds, the last jump run, I could see a smile across the Master Chiefs 'face; this was a good sign that he could see the drop zone. He gave us the one-minute warning; we were on our feet, marching towards the ramp that was now open. Check equipment he screams. Thirty seconds, stand by; the light changes from red to green, and he yells go.

In an instant, the four of us were out of the C-130 and in free- fall. Since it was a training jump, we had strobes attached to the tops of our helmets so we could see each other. After the exit, I never saw them again. I was buffeting like I had never felt before, probably from the extra weight I was not used to. I focused more on my altimeter to keep track of my altitude. At 4,000 feet, I started my wave-off to pull my rip cord and deploy my main parachute.

I felt the parachute deploying from my back, eventually bringing my body into the vertical position. The final opening sequence felt off; it sounded different, and I still fell through the air like the parachute was partially inflated. It was dark, so I couldn't tell what was wrong; all I knew was that something was wrong with the chute, and I needed to get rid of it.

The first part of the cutaway sequence is where you find the covers on the cape wells; this was where the risers from the parachute were attached. You pull the covers down to disconnect the risers from the harness, exposing the metal cable ring. You place your thumb in the ring and pull, the riser disconnects from the harness, and you are back in free-fall. Then, you pull the rip cord that is on your belly-mounted reserve.

The problem was when I went to grab the cape wells where they were on my shoulders, they weren't there. Now, I am starting to grope and panic. Everything works as it should when you're going through emergency procedures in your head and on the ground. But panic starts to set in when you do it to save your life, and it isn't working as it did in your head. You know that it's a matter of seconds before you hit the ground and die.

I kept groping, thinking they had to be there. All of a sudden, a voice in my head said, "If you keep panicking, you are going to die!" I stopped and then looked, which is the first part of the sequence to cut away. When I looked, they were extended about 4 inches off my shoulder because of the partial parachute tension. Immediately, I put both hands on each cape well cover and simultaneously pulled the covers down. Now, all I had to do was reach into the cable rings with my thumbs and pull. Instantly, I am back in free fall, falling back to earth. This put me in the perfect position to pull my reserve on my belly. I pulled the ripcord and saw this white flash before my face. The reserve parachute was open before I could take one breath. I saw this beautiful white parachute in the moonlight above my head.

A sigh of relief came over me like that was close. Now, I had to turn my attention to releasing this heavy pack so I wouldn't have to land with all this weight, which would increase my descent speed to the point of breaking a leg. When a red handle releases the pack, called the cherry, on the back, the pack drops 15 feet on a line to hit the ground first, and then the descent is slowed back to normal before the parachutist lands.

I am reaching for the cherry and suddenly see treetops. Not realizing I had opened that low, I realized there was no time to release this load. So I started to prepare for landing, thinking this would hurt. I then felt my body pass through this tree without hitting one branch, then the parachute caught a branch, and for about 2 seconds and about 2 feet off the ground, I was suspended in the air, which stopped the fast descent to the ground. Then my parachute was released from the branch and let me down softly.

I have to admit when I crawled out of my harness, my hands were shaking. I thought about this jump all day, prepping for this jump, loading the aircraft, riding to altitude, jumping out, and free-falling, and here I was on the ground. I realized I was petrified throughout this whole day until now, standing safely, unharmed on Green Beach. I knelt and kissed the ground; I do not know why; I just did.

The operation went as planned; the four of us rallied up, patrolled over to where the pilot was without detection, and patrolled to our extraction point. After returning to the base, the ground crew said they thought one of us had died; they witnessed four strobes get out of the aircraft. They then saw three strobes stop falling because of the opening of their parachutes, but they saw one strobe keep falling beyond the mountain; they thought that I had burned in. I would not have made it if I had been over the hill. Thank you, Lord, for saving me by telling me to stop panicking and look!

Chapter Twenty
Leap Frogs

My dream of learning how to skydive was to one day become a member of the Leap Frogs. I believed I would be one from the first time I saw the film. I was at the drop zone every weekend, spending all my money and time pursuing my dream of becoming more proficient in the sport. I got to know and became friends with some team members; they would give me direction and guide me toward fulfilling my dream. One thing I learned in pursuing dreams is that you need help from others to achieve. It's like the turtle sitting atop a fence post; it didn't get there alone.

As I said, the skydiving community was relatively small, especially in Naval Special Warfare. I was out at the drop zone, jumping out of airplanes every chance. Each jump was a learning experience. Like any community, the more you are exposed and people see you are committed to the sport, the more people want to help you. I started to meet a couple of the Navy parachute team members; once they learned I was a SEAL, they would show more interest in me as their brother.

There was a progression in the sport: when you hit a certain amount of jumps, you could move into more advanced equipment and parachutes. One of the first changes you could make was going from a belly-mounted reserve to a system with both a primary and reserve on your back. This tell-tale sign showed you were becoming more advanced as a skydiver. Wearing a belly-mounted reserve told everybody you were a beginner.

After reaching that number of jumps, which was around 50 or so, one of the members of the Leap Frogs asked me if I was interested in upgrading my equipment. I jumped at the chance to change my experience status, even if it was just by appearance. He helped me switch my parachutes to the new system. It fit perfectly, and I couldn't wait to try it out. It was very streamlined compared to my beginner rig, with everything on your back and nothing inhibiting you on the front: high speed, low drag. It was all packed up and ready to go, so I decided to head to the drop zone and give it a go.

Any time you change your equipment, especially that drastic of a change, the anxiety increases because your emergency procedures change. The rip cords are different, your release handles are in a different place, and when you have to make split-second decisions, if you are wrong because muscle memory kicks in from the prior system, it could cause death! We have a saying in skydiving: borrowed gear, borrowed death.

I arrived at the drop zone; it was quiet since it was a weekday, which was good; I could focus and not be interrupted by conversation. I went to the manifest to pay my money and get on the next aircraft load, that was going to altitude. Today would be a solo jump where I didn't jump with anyone else, so I could exit the airplane and get the feel of a parachute system with nothing on my front side. It changes the aerodynamics of your body, free-falling through the air. The plan was to exit the aircraft at 12,500 feet and free-fall for approximately 50 seconds. The thought was to open high for any needed compensation to take care of any malfunction or be able to take my time to pull the proper handle.

The jump went as planned and was uneventful. As I was descending, I thought, what a beautiful day! It was so clear I could see the ocean, and today's view was spectacular. I planned on making only one jump, but since I drove all this way and it was such a beautiful day, I decided to make one more jump.

After landing, I rigger rolled my parachute, and daisy chained my lines so as not to tangle them, which made it much easier to pack. I walked over to the packing tables. When packing the parachute, you stretch it from end to end and pull it tight, then you check the lines for continuity, that they weren't crisscrossed, which could cause a malfunction. Then, you flake each parachute panel so they are neatly folded into the container. The lines are folded into rubber bands and attached to the bag for a clean parachute deployment. I got everything in the bag and laid it into the pack tray; then, it dawned on me that I did not know how to close this rig. There are four flaps; these have to be closed in the correct sequence; if done wrong, it could be catastrophic when trying to deploy; you don't want to get this wrong.

I must have looked puzzled; I heard this female voice: "Do you need help?" I looked up, and there standing was that cute brunette that I saw on one of my first days in the drop zone. It was Sky Queen. I had never seen her up close; she was much prettier than I imagined.

I was confused about what to say; if I said yes, I do; this would tell her that I was sky trash and didn't even know how to pack my parachute. If I say no, she walks off, and that's it; I just blew my chance to get to know her, and worse yet, I would close my parachute system wrong, and then what? So I said yes; as a matter of fact, I do. I mumbled something about this being a new rig for me; before I could finish my sentence, she jumped up onto the table, like a little squirrel, and pulled out her closing cord, used to pull the loop through each flap in which the ripcord pin goes through, and within seconds she had it closed without even a question mark. She knew her stuff. She said, "There you go," and walked off just like that. Little did I know that was my future wife!

Chapter Twenty-One
This Little Froggy

One of the ways that I could increase my chances of making the parachute team was to show my enthusiasm for the sport and get to know the current team members, who would have a say in the decision process. When I returned from my first deployment, I was placed in the dive locker, where you would help maintain the dive equipment. This job was not time intensive, so I could follow my passion for skydiving if nothing was pressing. I did this by befriending a couple of the Leap Frog members who invited me to come out and jump with them. The team was always looking for new talent, as there was a turnover every year. It was a 2-3 year tour on the team.

Since free-falling was one of the SEAL tools used for insertion into a target, we were encouraged to follow our interest; this eventually would lead to some SEALs being the Subject Matter Experts (SMEs) in their field. This was applied to every aspect of our specialties; some were passionate about weapons, diving, sniper operations, demolition, boats, and more. My interest was always been in diving and air operations.

One day, I was jumping with the team, and I had just landed on the DZ and noticed something I hadn't seen before. Two of the members were flying their parachutes very close to each other, dangerously close, in my inexperienced opinion. It seemed they were trying to link up and fly their parachutes together. They tried several times, and suddenly, they were together. But something was wrong; their canopies started to twist and turn around each other. I could see that each of them was working to get the parachutes untangled, but after a few moments, I could see it was futile. They were getting closer to the ground, with so little of the parachute left open to slow their descent, it was obvious that they were going to slam into the ground. Sure enough, they hit with such force that when they impacted the ground, I could hear the thud, then the breaking of bones. I was standing approximately 30 feet from their impact.

We rushed over to them, not believing what just happened. Thank God they were both alive but in bad shape.

The ambulance came and rushed them both to the hospital. It turned out that they had both shattered their right femur; this could have ended much worse; gravity can be very unforgiving.

I found out later that these two members were trying something new to the sport called CRW, Canopy Relative Work. Whenever something new occurs in a highly inherent dangerous sport, there will be a higher risk until the latest is perfected.

In the skydiving world, most new techniques and equipment were being developed in the private sector, which was in reverse to the history of the parachuting world. Most of the history of parachuting came from the military. Parachutes were developed to save a pilot's life if his aircraft was disabled or shot out of the air. Later, they were used to insert large numbers of personnel behind enemy lines, such as on D-day. However, skydiving and high-speed square parachutes were developed in the private sector—another testament to the Free Enterprise System.

After the incident I witnessed, the parachute team leaders made it clear that there would be no CRW tried again; the risk was too high.

In the fall of 1979, I got my chance to try out for the team. The tryouts started in November and made their final cuts around January to finalize the team before the show season. I had a leg up because I had built relationships with some team members who made the decisions for the team. All I had to do was not make any stupid mistakes or do something dangerous, and I would make the team.

Some of our winter training was in Key West and Puerto Rico. I was on a three-week vacation in some of the most beautiful weather and landscapes one could imagine for skydiving. I was doing the one thing that I couldn't get enough of. We had two CH3 Navy helicopters tasked to fly us to altitude all day, like our own personal elevators. Flying twelve thousand, five hundred feet over beautiful turquoise blue water and huge white puffy clouds was amazing. Free-falling through cumulus clouds, it looked like you were flying through big balls of cotton. This was a life that I couldn't even imagine. I couldn't believe this was my job: Skydiving every day. Partying in the evenings to get up the following day. Doing it all again.

While we were in Key West, training was going well, with no incidents. We were jumping one day, and the winds started to pick up, so we had to exit the aircraft quite far from the DZ. After a beautiful skydive, I opened my parachute, and the DZ seemed a long distance away, even though I was now jumping a square parachute with much greater capability than a round one's speed and distance. I was upwind and flying towards the DZ, which was in a parking lot of the Green Beret unit stationed in the Keys.

I wasn't sure in my mind that I could make it back. Then, I spotted high-power electrical lines. Being a relatively inexperienced skydiver, not knowing the capacity of my parachute, I started to believe I could make it over these power lines and return to the DZ. After deciding to go for it, it didn't take long before I knew I had made the wrong decision. I realized I would fly right into these lines. At the last possible second, I straightened my legs and pointed my toes, hoping to possibly slip through two of the lines and keep them from physically touching simultaneously.

I felt my leg graze one of the lines, but the rest of my body passed through the power lines. A second later, I'm dangling in the air. I look up, and my parachute hangs in the power lines; it will be all over if my feet touch the ground. It would complete the circuit by touching the ground, and thousands of volts of electricity would flow through my body. A Moment later, my parachute was released from the power lines, and I fell three feet to the ground. My adrenaline was still pumping, and I realized how close that was to being my last day on earth. Thank you, God, for saving me!

The rest of our winter training was uneventful, and now it was time to get back to San Diego. When we got back, the team had a couple of days off, and then we would report to the Navy Parachute air loft, where we would work repairing our equipment and where everything was staged for all the shows. The team's new members, including me, knew they had made the team. Some candidates were sent home early for not meeting the standards they needed to meet while at winter training. One of them was my roommate. I felt sorry for him; he wanted to be a Leap Frog. Losing friends from not meeting the standards, getting injured, or quitting was common along my SEAL training journey, so you got used to the disappointment.

There was a team meeting called the first work day back that would make it official. The team leader called each new member up front and center to congratulate us individually. Welcome to the Navy Leap Frogs! I was fired up; I had the dream job of all dream jobs. For the next three years, my job is to skydive every day, weather permitting, and from April through October to travel all over the United States, jumping into airshows, rodeos, NFL football games, NASCAR, MLB games, Thunderbolt races, and any other event that would sponsor us to do a show for them.

For a sponsor to hire us for the show, generally done on weekends, they had to meet our standards; we required rental cars and A+ hotel accommodations, and a per diem for food and whatever we needed for the time away from our home base. In other words, we weren't slumming. We were treated with the utmost respect when we arrived in a town; it was a little bit humbling how the people acted towards us, almost like rock star status. Maybe it was because we had the identical flight suits that the Blue Angels wore.

We all knew skydiving was inherently dangerous, but our shows made it even more dangerous. Depending on the event, other than an airshow, which is performed at an airport, there is plenty of open space to place our drop zone. Which was on the edge of the crowd center, where the spectators could see us land. But most of the other shows we did had tiny areas where we had to land—especially rodeos. From the air, the rodeo arena looked like a postage stamp. There were wires and light poles to light up the arena at night, which was when we did our show for a rodeo. There was not a lot of room for error. In the movie "The Patriot," there is a scene where the father instructs his two youngest boys to "aim small, miss small" as they get ready to take out a troop of Red coats. That was a true statement; the tighter the DZ, the more accurate the team was. But that doesn't mean the pucker factor didn't increase with the tight DZs.

Not only were the landings into tiny DZ dangerous, but other aspects of the show. One of the acts that another team member and I were tasked with was something called the diamond track. Each act for the show was done separately, meaning that the act was done by itself, where the audience could focus on each act. By the time the members of each act had landed, another one was exiting the plane. Many members had smoke brackets attached to their boots; the smoke streaming from the jumpers added a dramatic effect and made it more visible from the ground.

The Diamond Track consisted of two jumpers exiting together from 12,500 feet, both with smoke; they would make a 180-degree turn and separate by tracking away from each other, holding a heading on the horizon. At around 7,000 feet, we would do another 180-degree turn, now heading towards each other with a closing speed of around 360 mph. Our distance was so great that all we could see was the smoke trail the other was leaving. As our distance closed, both would make minor corrections, making it more exciting for my friend, Harry and me, as well as the audience, when we crossed.

So imagine that from the ground, you would see two skydivers making a diamond shape with smoke. Unbeknownst to the audience, you would see them closing in on each other. We were carrying flare guns, and just as we crossed, we would raise our arms and fire the flare, and from the ground, it looked like we hit. It was a theatrical effect; this was a real crowd-pleaser. What made this one of the more dangerous acts in the show was that there was a chance that the jumpers would miscalculate and hit each other. This happened with the Army Golden Knights; one of the jumpers was killed, and the other lost his leg. We all knew the risk, which probably made it even more of a rush.

After we had returned from our winter training in Puerto Rico and Key West Florida, we were training in South San Diego, where most of the jumping was done on the west coast SEAL teams. I noticed someone was packing his parachute rig, whom I hadn't met before. He was packing a civilian parachute system, which told me he was an experienced civilian skydiver. I asked one of the team members who he was; he said he was our new OIC, the Officer In Charge of the parachute team.

A little background on the skydiving world and the Leap Frogs. A small percentage of the Leap Frogs were avid civilian jumpers; most enjoyed jumping and were trained by SEAL teams but didn't want to spend their money jumping out of airplanes. I was one of the guys who couldn't get enough and spent all my extra money and time in the civilian drop zone on weekends. By the time I arrived on the SEAL team, free-fall training had been halted and deferred to the Army, which owned all of the parachute training in the military.

This new OIC was civilian-trained and an avid jumper on weekends; I hadn't seen him before because we jumped at different skydiving centers, but he knew I was also a sport skydiver. We loaded the C-130 to climb to altitude, and he sat beside me. All he said to me was, "Have you ever done CRW?" I said, no, sir. He said, "Today is your day. I have a white parachute, find me, and get close, and I will do the rest." I nodded, and he just smiled.

All I could think about was "absolutely no CRW," which was the command that was reinforced every time we would jump. Now, the new OIC of the parachute team wants to teach me CRW. Didn't he get the memo?

I knew it was dangerous; I experienced the result firsthand when I watched two members slam into the ground. But I wasn't concerned about the danger; I was more concerned about staying on the team by disobeying a direct order. But I also thought this guy was the OIC, the head man in charge. I have a new order which supersedes the first.

After the free fall, I opened my parachute and started scanning the sky to find his white parachute, which should have been easy since ours was all blue and gold. I spotted it and started to head his way. This was all he needed to identify me because everyone else was keeping a safe distance not to get close to another parachute.

I thought his closing speed was breakneck; just as I thought we would collide, he made a quick turn right in front of me, and before I knew it, his feet were in my front lines at the top of my canopy. Then he did the unexpected: he started sliding down my lines, and when he reached my risers (all the lines are attached to the risers, which are connected to the harness). He said, "Hey there." I couldn't believe what just happened; he was connected to me, and we were flying around as if there was one single canopy.

He was in control, steering us back to the DZ to land. He then said, "We will land this together, flare your canopy like you normally do, and I will release you." I said, What! Are we going to land like this? "Don't worry, you will be fine," as if he knew what I was thinking.

I could tell this guy knew what he was doing; we were on final and ready to land on the T. The T is a large bright orange T used to orient for ground wind direction. We landed dead on the mark.

I couldn't believe what I just experienced; It was like jumping for the very first time, and the excitement of this experience was soon replaced by the feeling of, uh oh, I am in trouble! If looks could kill, I would have been a dead man. The senior members of the team who gave the order, "No CRW!" were defied by the most junior team members. No one said a word on the ride from the DZ back to the airport—the typical conversation of what a great skydive we just had was nonexistent.

I was not privy to the conversation back at parachute team headquarters, but I knew no word about my disobedience was spoken. I'm sure the discussion with the new OIC and the head shed (Top of the chain of command) was that I am the OIC of this parachute team, and we will all learn CRW, which will be part of our show! I don't know how that conversation went, but that is precisely what unfolded as the year went on.

It took a while before the unbelievers of CRW accepted this advanced technique of parachutes joining together, looking like a World War I biplane aircraft of the air. It seemed unnatural at the time that you could fly two parachutes together. After getting acclimated to two flying together, we thought, why not three?

Nobody on the airshow circuit had ever witnessed two parachutes flying together. After the team observed the recognition that the CRW biplane was getting and, without incident, slowly but surely, the rest of the team started to rethink their opposition to CRW. At one of the early airshows we were doing in early 1980, the Chief of the team, one of the biggest opponents of CRW, had started to warm up to this new technique, which was quite the crowd-pleaser. The OIC had noticed he became increasingly interested in getting in on the act.

The OIC pulled the Chief and myself together and said, "We would do a triplane tomorrow." A grin from ear to ear grew all over the Chief's face. The OIC gave us the instructions, and then we practiced on the ground by walking through each step called a dirt dive.

It was a beautiful day for the airshow; clear skies and light winds created the perfect conditions for our portion of the show. The crowd started to fill the stands facing what we called the show center. We started our preparation, rigging our smoke grenades onto the brackets that are mounted on our boots.

Approximately one hour before TOT, Time Over Target, our jump aircraft took off with our team aboard; this would give us enough time to conduct the streamer pass to provide us with our exit point over the airfield. The upper and ground winds, direction, and velocity would help us determine where to exit the aircraft. If this were calculated wrong, we would not be landing on our DZ in front of the crowd, which is embarrassing. This puts a lot of pressure on the designated team jumpmaster. And no excuse can be given to justify why the team could not land where we were supposed to.

The streamer passes completely, and the jump master quickly calculates on a slate with a grease pencil using a diagram with reference points on the ground. "Fifteen minutes," yells the jump master. The last equipment checks are done; we are ready. The

143

parachute team acts are conducted one at a time. A typical show would start with a first pass and flag jumper. One member jumps out, pulls high, and unfurls the American flag while the national anthem plays. The second pass would be four jumpers that join together in what we call a star formation with smoke, and at a certain altitude, they track away from each other, which looks like a starburst. The third pass would be the diamond track, and the last pass would be the slow, fast fall. This shows the crowd how much the body position can change the fall rate in free-fall; the show narrator would have the crowd counting after the fast faller jumper opened his canopy until the slow faller opened his, usually about 20 seconds difference.

During this show, the OIC, the Chief, and myself would be on the same pass on the starburst. Today, we would start our track to open a little higher to give us more time to build our triplane. Each show creates a certain amount of anxiety, from the stress and worry of screwing up, depending on how tight the DZ is. The anxiety today was not from that since it was an airshow on an airfield with plenty of room, but sometimes, this complacency caused some guys to land off target. Aim small, miss small became our motto, and this helped keep the guys focused.

Since the OIC would be on top of the triplane stack, he would have to pop smoke, with his leg hanging outside of the aircraft, to burn early so his smoke would burn out shortly after opening. He could then stow his smoke bracket into a heat-resistant bag. We could not dock on another parachute with burning smoke on our foot; this would burn and destroy your life-saving parachute from the heat.

We exited the aircraft, with the others pulling a lanyard connected to our smoke pins, which ignited our smoke. All good so far; we flew like eagles toward each other to form the star, all grinning from ear to ear and watching the smoke trail from each of our feet. As we enjoyed the free-fall and watched our altitude from our altimeters mounted on our wrists, after about 45 seconds, it was time to break off, do a 180-degree turn from each other, and then shape our bodies like a bullet, with our chins up, legs straight, arms to our sides and shooting across the sky to our opening altitude.

Going from 180 mph to 120 by flaring your body, like a bird getting ready to land, slows the speed down to deploy your parachute without hurting yourself or your parachute. You feel the welcome jerk as your body goes from 120 mph to almost 0 mph in seconds. Immediately, you reach above your head and grab the steering toggles, pulling them down to release your brakes and put your canopy full speed ahead. I spot the OIC and fly towards him; he immediately spots me and does the same. Closing speed is increased, and we are now in the perfect position for him to make the dock onto my parachute just as he slides down my lines to hook his feet into my risers.

I see the Chief closing in behind me. Within seconds, the front of his parachute hits me behind the knees; if the speed is too high, his parachute wraps around my body, collapsing his parachute, which creates what we call a wrap. This causes all parachutes to lose air and wrap the jumpers in a cocoon of nylon, which sometimes causes the jumpers to fall to their death.

Being an experienced skydiver, the Chief docks on my legs with perfect speed. I start descending his parachute lines and reach his risers; I hook my feet around his risers to secure the dock. After seeing we are locked together, the OIC starts heading the triplane towards the target. As we got closer, he set up his pattern like an aircraft setting up to land, downwind, base, and final. The Chief and I saw the OIC setting up to land perfectly; since we were along for the ride, any concerns the Chief and I had about landing on target were quickly put at ease. Landing this triplane would be the first time done in show history. The OIC starts his flare and releases me, and simultaneously, I do the same. The three of us landed successfully; the response we got from the crowd was almost deafening. This historical-making exhibit was a huge success.

Mike is on top

Our team woke up the following day to the local newspaper, which usually has the Blue Angels on the front page, but not this time. The entire front page, in full color, was the US Navy Leap Frog's first triplane ever. The Angels were staying in the same hotel, and maybe it was our imagination, but they could have been happier that we got top billing that morning. Come on, guys, be happy for us. It was the first and probably the last time. From then on, the rest of the team accepted that we would be the cutting-edge parachute team with the new show, which would have every team member connected to another member under a parachute using CRW.

Our OIC was with the Leap Frogs for two years. During that period, he transformed our team into one of the greatest skydiving demonstration teams in the Country. The Navy used our team to recruit for the Navy and UDT/SEAL teams. Looking back on that time made me realize that it was a very historical time when the sport of skydiving was evolving, to do things that most skydivers never believed possible. I was very fortunate to be an apprentice of such a forward-thinking officer.

Chapter Twenty-Two
That's No Bull

The parachute team brought us to many towns and cities across the Country for different events. One of the events that we did were state fairs. Sometimes, there would be sanctioned rodeo competitions at the state fair. We arrived in Sacramento, California, for one such as this. We were asked to jump into the rodeo arena in the evening right before the final event, bull riding.

Jumping into a rodeo arena was the smallest drop zone we would have to contend with. It would take tremendous focus and skills to land safely into this small area surrounded by bleachers filled with people; it was also dangerous for us and the audience. The first night was a huge success; we did our regular night routine: no free fall, just canopies, flags, and smoke. Landing in such a small area was exciting enough.

Imagine sitting in the bleachers with all the arena lights on; then suddenly, out of nowhere, these blue and gold parachutes are circling in the arena lights. As we got closer to the ground, our feet with colored smoke flew just a few feet above the heads of the crowd. It was a rush for us as much as the crowd. Most people have never experienced such a thing. Most people across the Country have never seen a skydiver in the air up close and personally like that.

After landing and waving to the crowd, we collected our parachutes and gear and stowed them in a van. The team had decided to stay and watch the bullriding competition. The crowd loved to watch that event; it was without question where a crazy cowboy would get hurt. Sure enough, the audience was not disappointed; two times, the ambulance came into the arena to give medical attention and whisk these poor boys off to the hospital, this did not deter the rest of these bull riders from riding.

During the event, the rodeo coordinator sat with our team to let us know how pleased she was that we were there and how much she enjoyed our show. She asked my friend Jim and me if we wanted to go out, have a couple of beers, and meet some of the cowboys. Jim and I said sure we would.

We all met up at the local watering hole. The bar was full of cowboys and cowgirls ready to party after a successful night of rodeoing; Jim and I were in the mood for the same. The coordinator had a table set for us with beers for all. We were thirsty, and the beers kept flowing. Our lips started to loosen after a couple of rounds, and the liquid courage grew. The subject of bull riding came up. I don't remember if it was Jim or me; maybe we were trying to impress this cowgirl, but one of us said, "Heck! We could ride them bulls!" The rodeo coordinator looked at us like we were both crazy. But, both Jim and I agreed that we could ride them bulls.

She leaned over the table and said, "If you two are serious, there are two extra bulls because those two cowboys carried out tonight won't be riding tomorrow night." We said, then set it up; it is settled; Jim and I will ride the bulls.

The following day, we were hungover and vaguely remembered something about offering to ride the bulls. Jim and I did not share our proposal with the rest of the team, hoping it was just a bad dream; if not a dream, she would forget about it. I mean, there is no way she could make that happen. Right?

Later that day, we prepped for the show, and I tried to get the thought of riding a bull out of my head. The show that evening went off without a hitch, just as successful as the previous night. After stowing our gear, we took our seats in the stands. Jim and I didn't say a word about the bull riding to each other. I think we were both feeling and hoping she would forget.

A few minutes later, she was walking towards us into the stands. She sits between us and tells us she has good and bad news. I had this massive sigh of relief that I didn't even think was building up, hoping that she would say, the good news was you two are off the hook. The bad news was that the Professional Rodeo Association (PRA) won't let you two inexperienced knuckleheads ride a bull.

But that was not what she said. She said the good news was she had it all set but only had one bull to ride. "Which one of you wants to ride it?" Immediately, I pointed at Jim and said, he will! Jim looked at me with a look that could kill. But, probably thinking we have a reputation to uphold, Jim would save our face and go. Go, Jim!

She then pointed at a cowboy waiting to give Jim a crash course on bull riding. I thought I had to see this, with a smirk on my face. The coordinator led us down to meet the cowboy, who we followed to where the bulls were kept. He instructed Jim on how to wrap up the hand he would hold on to for dear life. Jim was paying close attention, and all I could think about was Jim, you are certifiably crazy.

The thought of being off the hook from risking my life, with my big mouth filled with liquid courage, was abruptly interrupted when this cowboy came riding up on his horse. He asked where the other Leap Frog who wanted to ride the bull was. I half-heartedly raised my hand and said with a squeak, that would be me, sir. He said, "I have great news: we have another bull," my heart sank. I can't believe I got myself into this predicament. Life is hard enough, but it gets even more complex when you're stupid.

He said, "Follow me, and I'll introduce you to your bull." As we got closer, I could hear this bull snorting and throwing itself against the pen, which was closed up. He seemed very upset. The cowboy said, "Here he is. Give him a feel," I reached over the fence and felt his back, and he started to jump and get even crazier. The cowboy told me the order of the riders. He said, "Your buddy Jim would be first, and you would be clean up." At that Moment, I thought, if Jim gets hurt, I'm not riding.

Being the last night, the stands were packed and waiting with great anticipation for the bull riding to get underway. You could cut the excitement in the air with a knife. As I was asking myself, I wonder if the audience knows if two crazy Leap Frogs are riding the bulls tonight. I was snapped out of that thought when the rodeo announcer started to speak. "Ladies and gentlemen, boys and girls, we have an exceptional treat for you tonight. We have two Leap Frogs that parachuted into the arena tonight; they will ride the bulls!"

The crowd went wild, stomping onto the metal bleachers, hooting and hollering; it was deafening. Bloodthirsty, that's why they're here. The announcer announced, "First out of the gate from San Diego, CA. Representing the US Navy Leap Frogs, Jim Williams." The crowd went nuts and settled into almost a hush when they saw Jim raise his hand, knowing the chute was about to open. Jim nodded, and the bull lurched forward up in the air. A second later, Jim was on the ground, getting to his feet as fast as he could to keep the bull from killing him; the rodeo clowns were doing their best to keep that from happening.

I felt relief that Jim was not seriously hurt, but I also knew I had to go through with this insanity. I watched each bull rider do his thing, and I am happy to say that no one was hurt. One of the cowboys said, "You're coming up next, Mike, mount that bull." I climbed up the chute and lowered my legs over his back; the bull was upset that this greenhorn was anywhere near him. Bulls are very smart, and they can smell fear a mile away. I reeked of it. This bull was thinking: I'm gonna kill this little froggy.

I got seated as best I could, and the bull started to crash my legs into the side of the chute. I said out loud; he's going to break my legs before I get out of here. The cowboys were hanging all over my chute, and one of them said, "He does that; it's normal." I started to wrap the rope around my hand, and one of the guys said, "Don't wrap up too tight; you don't want to be hung up if you fall." I told you don't have to worry about that! "Just don't fall to the inside," he said, "He will trample you if you do." I'm thinking, now you tell me? The announcer let the crowd know, and last but not least, it was me. The crowd went wild again and then got quiet as if they knew this could be catastrophic.

The cowboy says, "Nod when you're ready." I froze, and he repeated, "Nod when you're ready." I thought I did. He said again, "Nod when you're ready." I don't know if I did, but that gate flung open, and that bull jumped up in the air and spun around. I couldn't believe how fast he moved. It was like he couldn't wait to get me off his back and stomp me for daring to try to ride him; he was a professional, and I was not.

Before I knew it, I was lying on the ground, knowing I had to get to my feet and run to the fence for safety; as I got to my feet and started to run, that bull kicked me right in the hip. I saw the clown trying to work his magic to keep him from kicking me again. I made it to the fence and was very happy that I was alive. Deep down, the crowd cheered and was hopefully pleased that the crazy Leap Frogs had survived.

Jim and I found each other to celebrate our survival and throw jabs at each other. He threw the first by saying, "Wow, Mike, that was quite a ride, all 2 seconds." I evaded by saying. Oh, you looked like a real rodeo star yourself. It was a way of saying to each other, great job, brother. Let's not ever do that again. We were the highlight of that night in more than one way.

We received a big envelope from the Rodeo Association a few weeks later. It was addressed to Jim and I. We opened it up to see two photos. The first was Jim falling off the bull, and the other was me, with my hand held high in the air, firmly seated on the bull, with snot pouring out of the snout of that beast. I looked at Jim and said that now we had Kodachrome proof of who the better bull rider was; we both laughed. We shared a memory that only a few people can share, especially from the parachute team.

Looking back on that night, I wondered why I was willing to risk my life by getting on that bull. After that crazy night, we went out again with the rodeo coordinator and the professional bull rider who doubled as the clown, whom we greatly appreciated for not letting the bull stomp us to death while we were on the ground. He shared with us that the bull that Jim had ridden had killed a young bull rider two weeks prior, and his mother was in the crowd. That put things in perspective on how dangerous it was for us.

At that point in my life, I might have been on a horse three times. So, no, I was not an experienced animal rider. I believe the same mindset was needed for skydiving, and all the other crazy stuff I was doing was probably the same as that of a bull rider. The problem with bull riding is that there is so much risk of getting seriously injured every time you get on that bull's back. What I was doing in the extreme sports world didn't have the same inherent risk; at least, in my mind, it didn't.

I feel like the culture of rodeoing, like skydiving or aviation, has to do with the environment in which one is raised. The risk-taking mindset is probably the same but is drawn to what you are exposed to. I was introduced to water skiing by being raised on a lake. But my risk-taking attitude took me to another level, more of the extreme in the sport. My environment on the SEAL team introduced me to skydiving and all the other extremes I was exposed to.

Chapter Twenty-Three
On Wings Like An Eagle

The OIC, Bill Woodruff, besides skydiving, had a passion for hang gliding. Because of my enthusiasm for CRW, he probably thought I would also be interested in learning to hang glide. He was right; I was introduced to hang gliding when one of our senior members of the Rock Aqua Jays water ski show team brought a hang glider routine to our show. The ski boat would tow him to an altitude of about 750 feet and then release him. He would then fly around the area like a bird. I thought then I would love to do that one day. Our OIC told me I was welcome to come to the training hill for an introduction. Being a pleasure-seeking fool, I jumped at the chance.

We drove about 30 minutes north to a place called Little Black Mountain. Upon arrival, he took the kite off his truck rack and showed me how to assemble the glider. It fascinated me; I had never gotten this close to one. After completing the assembly, he explained how to put the harness on; I thought he would give me my first lesson here. I became very excited that I would experience flight like never before.

He then instructed me to pick the glider up by putting the control bar on my shoulders and walking it up the hill. He started me low on the hill, where I wouldn't get that high off the ground, just enough to get the feel of maneuvering up, down, left turn, and right turn by pushing the bar in each direction to control the direction of flight.

As a pilot and an experienced skydiver, I understood the dynamic of flight and control. We reached the point of the hill where I would start my first lesson. He explained how to snap into the glider with a

155

carabiner; this would be my connection to the glider from which I would be suspended. Bill stressed the point that some hang gliding fatalities were caused by the pilot forgetting to hook in, then launching off a mountain with the inability to control the glider; you are now suspended from the control bar, hanging on for your life. The glider can not maintain level flight and would most likely stall and plummet to your death. I took a solid mental note to avoid making this fatal mistake.

Being hooked in and judging the direction of the wind, making sure it was blowing directly into my face, it was. He said, "Whenever you're ready." I picked up the glider with my shoulders, balancing and keeping the wing tips level, seeing that the glider was dancing in the wind as if to say, I'm ready if you are. I took my first step forward to initiate my run down the hill, and before I took three steps, I was flying. I could hear him yelling, you're doing great; keep your airspeed up. The thrill of flying a hang glider was incredible; I was flying this enormous kite carrying my weight, controlling with weight shift, and directing the control bar by pushing it in the opposite direction of the turn.

The flight was short but exhilarating, totally different from flying your body at 120 mph through the air with skydiving. It is so different from flying your parachute, using your steering toggles to pull down one side of the canopy in the direction of flight. I was hanging from a big kite and flying it like a bird.

He came running after me when he saw I conducted the perfect flare for landing. Bill smiled as if to say; I know exactly how you feel. I'm sure my big smile was saying, that was so cool, let's do it again.

After each flight, he would critique me to help me do better. I knew he was impressed with my progression because he would take me farther up the hill each time. Eventually, I was at the top, far from the landing area. So far, I was a hang glider pilot and started to feel very confident in my ability. Until now, all the flights were uneventful and the same, except each had a little more flying time.

After the first flight, Bill observed from the bottom of the hill; this left me alone to make sure I was hooked in properly and to launch when the wind was blowing directly up the hill into my face. There was a little wind sock at the top to help you decide when it was just right. Launching in a crosswind could lead to a fatal mistake, throwing you sideways into the side of the mountain before you could establish flight. Going from this small hill is less crucial, but you need to learn the basics on the training hill, which will keep you from making a mistake that could be fatal. One of the lessons in SEAL training that was driven home was attention to detail. This small lesson could keep you from making huge mistakes that kill you and, even worse, from killing others!

Everything looked perfect; I made one final check, looking up to ensure I was hooked into the top of the glider; the wind was in my face. I picked up the glider. The wind was more assertive this far up the hill. The glider weight was off my shoulders as the glider was already flying; all I had to do was take a couple of steps, and I was flying. Launching in the vertical position, now flying, I swung my body horizontally, laying streamline into the wind; this is incredible. The glider abruptly pitched up from the nose as I settled into the perfect position. It happened so fast that I didn't have time to react. The glider was stalling, and I didn't know what to do. I'm at full stall, and the glider is now turning to the right, and I can't control it because there is no airspeed. I am now looking at the ground; this is going to hurt. The first point of contact with the ground was the nose of the glider, then my face. Immediately, my chin and my nose started to hurt.

Bill comes running to me and yells, "Are you ok?" I am lying in a heap, moaning and groaning. I start to feel the blood running down my face. I began to move each of my limbs, and it seemed that I didn't break any bones. The glider control bar is bent on the right upright. As I am looking over the glider to make sure I didn't hurt his glider too severely, he says," It's all good, just a bent upright.

Conversely, you have some deep cuts, one above your nose and one on your chin. We need to get you to Balboa for some stitches." He handed me a handkerchief to put some pressure on the cuts while disassembling the glider.

After getting stitched up, we visited our favorite pizza place in Coronado, Pizza Galore. They are no longer there, but they had great pizza and cold beer. As we sat there eating pizza and having a cold one, I started to ask him what happened. He said, "Mike, as a pilot, airspeed is your friend. When you fly over the bump in the hill, it pitches you up because of the lift that bump in the slope creates. Whenever you get hit with a thermal or lift from the landscape that pitches your nose, immediately pull the control bar in to maintain your airspeed, keeping you from stalling." I knew that because of all the flight training and skydiving experience, flying a hang glider was so foreign to me that it caught me off guard. I thought, when you're dumb, you have to be tough.

Before we left Pizza Galore, Bill asked me if I wanted to try again; I said, heck yeah. He smiled, knowing he hadn't ruined me by advancing too fast. He knew I had the experience; I just made a mistake I would never make again. We arrived at Little Black the very next day. We assembled the glider, and I thought he would start me at the lower part of the hill for some refresher. I was wrong; he said, "Mike, go to the top, and let's try this again. Remember the conditions are the same; you will experience the same lift over that bump; remember to pull the control bar in, maintain airspeed, and you will fly right through it."

I was slightly nervous, knowing the same thing could happen again. Feeling the pain from my face that was just stitched up the night before, I was a little apprehensive. I climbed to the top of the hill and was now facing into the wind. I snapped in, making sure the carabiner was connected and locked. I thought, I don't need any more mistakes; it hurts too bad.

The wind was perfect; I picked up the glider, and almost immediately, I could tell it was ready to fly. The question was, was I? I knew I had to do this: I was reminded of my first bike ride as a kid when I went headfirst into the side of a house. My Mom told me to stay off my bike. Just like then, I knew I needed to get back on the horse, as the saying goes.

I took my first and second steps; I was committed, and there was no turning back; I was in flight. I transitioned to the horizontal position, feeling like a bird that just tucked in my legs after takeoff, and there it was: the nose started to pitch up. I thought, not this time. I started pulling the bar in, and I could hear Bill's voice: keep your airspeed up. I could tell by the wind in my face my airspeed was perfect, and I was flying. From the air, I could see Bill standing there like a proud coach, knowing his student did exactly what he was supposed to do.

Bill was with our team for two years, and during that time, I learned so much from him that he changed my future for the better. I had not heard the term mentor back then; at least in the Naval Special Warfare community, it wasn't common. But looking back, I know how important it is and what it means to be a mentor or be mentored. He was a mentor to me without me knowing it. That is the way it works sometimes. Someone with a particular skill set and is willing to share it finds somebody who is teachable, ready, and willing to take it to another level.

Michael ready to launch

But why did he pick me, one of the newest guys on the team? Why did he sit next to me on that C-130 that day? I believe some people can see things in people that we may not see in ourselves. He saw someone who was willing and eager to learn more. I will always be grateful for Bill taking me under his wing, no pun intended, and teaching me what he taught me during those two years. His belief in me at such a young, impressionable age greatly impacted the rest of my life. Learning something in the pioneering phase of the sport and being part of advancing his vision was a great confidence builder for me. That confidence helped me be a better SEAL; it helped me advance in rank faster. It gave me the foundation to be successful in future endeavors in all areas of my life.

I remember the day at the end of his final year on the team that brought his vision into reality. Our entire team had exited the aircraft over our training area; after a great skydive, we all opened up our parachutes, and I headed towards Bill for CRW; after we connected and started flying back to the target, we scanned the sky and every member of the team was doing CRW, there was not one single canopy flying in the air. I looked up at him, and he had the biggest smile, and he said to me, "My vision is complete." He had transformed a team that was absolutely against any form of Canopy Relative Work, CRW, and here we were two years later; every member was doing it!

Chapter Twenty-Four
No Time To Die

During my first two years, I became one of the SMEs (Subject Matter Experts) in the SEAL teams; I was now one of the primary trainers on the team. One of the progressions of an avid skydiver, especially one that does it for a living, jumping every day for one's job, is that you get pretty good at it. I was asked if I wanted to compete on the Navy 4-way team at the National tournament. The nationals in Muskogee, OK, hosted the 4 & 8-way team tournament yearly. Each team is scored based on how many predesignated formations are in 35 or 55 seconds. You get points for each based on how many formations you can build. There are YouTube videos that will give you a great visual of this. Of course, I said yes. So, for an entire year leading up to the nationals, the Leap Frogs allowed us to train to prepare for the National tournament.

While training during our first year as the Navy 4-way competition team, I noticed that one of our team members was noticeably faster at packing his parachute than the rest of us. The average time packing your main parachute was about 10 minutes. He was able to finish in about 7 minutes. After watching him to see how he could pack as fast as he did, I noticed he had removed his bag in which the parachute was S-folded. This phase of the packing was sometimes the most time-consuming. Without the bag, he could S fold his parachute and lines into the container itself. I asked him how it opened and if he had any problem with the opening sequence. He reassured me that he had been jumping it that way for the last 100 jumps and had no problem.

In the early 1980s, some pioneering was still ongoing, so trying something in the field to see if it could be improved wasn't uncommon. If I can save that much time, I'll try it. I removed the bag and coiled the lines on the bottom of the pack tray, and then S folded my parachute on top of the lines. It looked right and made sense that it would deploy in sequence properly.

I had success with my new way of packing and continued to jump it that way without incident for 50-plus jumps or so. Not giving my new way of packing much thought, I became very comfortable with it. Our four-way team was training one day, and we were on our third jump. We climbed to altitude, exited the aircraft, and successfully jumped. I had a device in my helmet that would beep at break-off altitude, meaning this is the altitude we would do a 180-degree turn away from each other, track away like speeding bullets, get separation into clear airspace to deploy our parachutes safely, without danger of running into each other.

After tracking away for a few seconds, flaring my body to slow my speed, waving my arms in a crisscross motion to signal anybody above me that I would deploy my parachute. This is standard for skydivers; it is called the wave-off. Robins's boyfriend was killed during this phase of a skydive, where an inexperienced parachutist hit him in free fall as he was deploying his parachute. She was banged up, but Dave was killed instantly. RIP Dave!

After waving off, I reached down to my leg, where my pilot chute was stowed in a pocket with what looked like a hockey sack sticking out the top connected to a small pilot chute. This acts like an anchor in the air; your body continues to fall, which deploys your parachute in proper sequence. I pulled it out, held it in the airstream, and let it go; usually, instantaneously, you start to feel the deployment, and a second later, you feel the parachute open with a major jerk from falling at 120 mph and going to almost 0 mph.

This time, I felt nothing. This can be very concerning to an experienced skydiver. You enter emergency mode when you anticipate that opening feeling you have experienced at least 1000 times before, and in one jump it doesn't. You have a few seconds to act and solve the problem. Immediately you try to asses; I looked over my shoulder, didn't see anything, then looked under my arm and saw the problem.

My parachute was in a ball of mess just falling alongside me; my heart sank; there were no options for a solution. When you have a main parachute that doesn't open properly, you try to clear it by shaking the risers above your head; if that doesn't work, you release it by pulling the cutaway handle. This gives you clear airspace to deploy your reserve. Many people have died by pulling their reserve into the malfunctioned main. This usually ends in a tragedy because the reserve entangles with the main, and nothing opens to save you from high-speed dirt!

I am still plummeting towards Mother Earth with a few seconds before I run out of airspace and ideas at the same time. I can not pull my reserve with this mess floating next to me. I had one chance. I reached out with my right arm and tried to gather this mess into my arm so I could deploy my reserve. Trying to hold onto a ball of nylon falling 120 mph was not working; it was just bellowing around my arm. I am going to give it one more try to deploy. The nylon ball was under my arm but trying to inflate, so I released it from my arm as fast as I could with enough force, hoping that whatever it was hung up on would release.

Within a second, it deployed. I looked up to see if the canopy had deployed correctly, and usually, if a square parachute doesn't deploy correctly, it is noticeable right away because it doesn't fly right. It was flying, and I started heading to the landing area. When you have a high-speed problem like I had just gone through, your mind slows

164

everything down to solve the problem. You don't have time to think about what if. But after everything returns to normal speed, your mind catches up and sends the signal, what if. I started to shake a bit to the landing. I thought, I almost burned in just seconds before. I can't believe I just lived through that.

These thoughts continued when I got to the ground. I found an empty lawn chair in the packing area and contemplated life, skydiving, and all the other crazy things I had done. My teammates came to me and said, what's wrong, Mike? I said I need a break. Let's get lunch. I didn't tell them what just happened; I don't know why. I sat there for about an hour, shaking off what almost happened. I decided to move on and block out the unproductive thoughts but held on to the solution. I walked out to my truck, retrieved my deployment bag, and put it back on. What a stupid thing to try; when you are dumb, you have to be tough! Thank you, Lord, for saving me once again.

After jumping as a four-way team, we believed we were ready. My first time attending the Nationals was quite the experience. Our team, for being first-year competitors, did ok. I'm sharing this story because it was another one of those times when my guardian angels were watching over me.

Our team was on the first early morning load a few days into the competition. The weather was a balmy 80 degrees that morning, and the weather conditions were perfect. Our team exited the aircraft and performed well. After our free fall, we opened our canopies and started for the designated landing zone. As I got closer to the ground, I decided to land in the middle of the large tented area where the teams would hang out and review videos of their performance. It would be my way of saying good morning to the Coors beer team we trained with at Perris Valley Skydive Center.

Because of the early sun's position, I did not see the high-tension electrical wires that hung across the tent area until it was too late. As soon as my body hit the wire, I thought, I'm a dead man. A second later, I was dangling three feet above the ground. As I looked around, all I could see were the faces with looks of unbelief. As I was hanging there, all I could think was that I couldn't touch the ground with my parachute hanging from the wire. Suddenly, I heard someone yell, don't touch him, knowing it could complete the circuit. At that moment, one of the Coors team members grabbed my legs to keep me from falling to the ground, a noble gesture that could have killed us both.

Thank the good Lord. I had knocked out the power when I hit the wire, so it was another one of God's saves, but I did not give him the credit then. Writing this book makes me think about all the times that God and my guardian angels were there for me, saving me for his purpose.

The Navy team was now in the limelight and on the crap list of the National organizer; because of my stunt, they had no power to run the ground-to-air videos for judging, therefor they had to bring a DC-3 aircraft full of 8-way teams back down from altitude, which cost them money for extra fuel. I had successfully, single-handedly put the Nationals on hold until they could fix the wire to bring back power. To add insult to injury, later in the competition, one of our members, Harry O'Connor, had a malfunction and cutaway his main, pulling his reserve. His main parachute floated down, landed on the same wire, and knocked out the power again. The powers that be got very close to sending the United States Navy competition team home. It could have been a better first impression for us. Our Navy team would go on to attend two more National competitions, and in 1987, we took home the silver medal in 8 ways, probably because the Army didn't come that year.

When I compare pleasure with purpose, I think back at my pleasure-seeking, foolish lifestyle compared to my purpose-driven life now. It was all about having fun for most of my life until October 1987. To be careful not to glamorize pleasure had its purpose in my life. For example, one of my passions was aviation. It helped fill the void of boredom. I believe that one who lives for pleasure hasn't found purpose in their life. Filling that void caused me to fill my time pursuing aviation ratings. Private license, commercial, helicopter, instrument, and multiple engines. Through that pleasure-seeking, I have enjoyed the freedom of flight.

Another essential part of my life happened because of my pleasure-seeking through skydiving. As I became more experienced in skydiving, I was recognized and respected in the Navy and as a professional skydiver. This respect brought more opportunities in the sport. I was asked to be part of world record attempts for the most significant formation for private sector and military records. One of them was the first 100-way ever done. It was done in British Columbia. There is no reason to get into details, and there are no near-death situations. That record has been beaten many times over; it's well over 400 today.

Chapter Twenty-Five
The Sky Queen

Along with respect in the skydiving community came better looks; let me explain. I first laid eyes on the cute little brunette in 1979, who was the sky queen of the sport at the time, and the pretty little brunette who jumped up on the packing table and helped close my rig. As I became more experienced in the sport, I became better looking to her. All kidding aside, she started to notice me more and acknowledge me. Even though she had a boyfriend, the three of us became friends, and through that friendship, we began to get to know each other as people, not just skydivers.

Tragically, as I mentioned earlier, her boyfriend was killed in a skydiving accident. It was a tough time, and she missed him dearly. After a year or so later, we started dating, and on 11 October 1986, Robin Lopez became my wife. The most important part of my life came from my passion for and pleasure in skydiving.

You see, God uses self-seeking pleasures to fulfill his purpose in our lives. As I mentioned, our God-given gifts and talents are used to nudge and guide us. Eventually, if we are open to his purpose, we fill the void that we have been trying to fill with pleasure our entire life, which is now filled with his purpose, which we were created for all along!

Pleasure is a good thing, and significant parts of your life can come from it because God always takes things, good or bad, and makes them better.

Michael's wife Robin balloon jump

Robin and I started dating in April of 1982; we enjoyed being together. Because we had so much in common we really enjoyed being together. We both liked skydiving and she loved to fly with me.

There was this crazy thing that we wanted to try in skydiving; it was called Mr. Bill (from the Gumby animation TV show) dive. I am still trying to understand why it was named that. The skydive required us to jump out of the aircraft, facing each other, with Robins's legs and arms wrapped tightly around my body as if she were hanging on for dear life. As we rolled out of the airplane as one, I deployed my parachute before hitting terminal velocity, which was about 120 mph. Robin was able to hold on during the opening sequence of the parachute. So now we are both flying around under my parachute. She would then climb up on top of my shoulders. Now, she and I are facing forward, and after doing that for a couple thousand feet, she would do a swan dive off my shoulders, free fall for a thousand feet or so, and then deploy her parachute. Robin was game for anything, and we had a ball trying new things together.

169

Robin was one of the skydivers that everybody wanted on their jump load. She was asked to be part of this team doing some pretty advanced maneuvers that hadn't been done before. They called them 16 ways. Obviously, 16 jumpers would create these different 16-way formations and break off in pieces, like four 4-person formations, fly the formations around, and then re-dock back into a 16-way. They were doing very cool stuff.

Whenever something interesting happened, everybody on the ground watched the performance in the air. On one particular jump, we were all watching, and the skydive was very successful after the sixteen-way tracked away from each other to get separation for the opening of their parachutes. I knew Robins's colors, so I could spot her falling through the air as she attempted to pull her parachute. I could tell she had a problem because she would never pull low. Everybody else has an open canopy, and she is still in free fall. Finally, I see the parachute start to open, except there is a problem: it is malfunctioning. Being already low with little room, she cuts the main away (releases the main with a handle) back in free fall, taking too long to pull her reserve.

Everybody on the ground was yelling, pull, pull; finally, at the last possible moment, her reserve deployed, with about 2 seconds before she would have hit the ground. That was the first time, and thank God, the last time I almost witnessed the love of my life die that day.

The Drop zone truck drove out to pick Robin up as she landed off the drop zone because of the malfunction. On return, she had the usual Robin Lopez smile as if she were happy to be here. After a couple of minutes reassuring her that she was ok, someone handed her another parachute system to get back on the plane to do another 16-way. She could not jump her rig because her reserve needed to be repacked, which had to be packed by a rigger. Her main parachute was in a twisted ball from falling to the ground after being released.

170

Remember the saying: borrowed gear borrowed death. Robin is now going back on the plane with borrowed gear after almost dying just a few minutes ago. Nerves of steel that girl had. But that was the mentality of a crazy skydiver. And the thing was, it didn't bother me either that she was going back up with borrowed gear.

Sometimes, pleasure can be insidious. You get to the point that you believe you're invincible. We had friends who met their demise because they kept pushing the envelope and pushed it a little too far.

I had a close friend I mentioned earlier; he was my partner on the diamond track and the guy who had a cutaway at the nationals that took out the power. Years after Harry O'Connor retired from the Navy, he became a Hollywood stuntman. He was working on the film XXX with Vin Diesel. During the stunt he was doing, Harry was killed after hitting the Pirogue bridge. I was told they had six good takes, but Harry wanted to do one more; he thought he could release it later to make it look better. The final take was his last; he hit the bridge upon releasing from the parasail too late.

I miss Harry, one of my close friends; we were inseparable while on the parachute team. Still, to this day, he was the only one in my life who threw me a surprise birthday party. Not that I want more surprise parties, but Harry, I will never forget that!

RIP Harry O'Connor!

Chapter Twenty-Six
The Path To Nowhere

Everyone is searching for what they were put on this earth for. The good Lord put purpose in every one of us, our purpose for his purpose. But I have discovered that most never find out why they are here. I hadn't figured out why; I wasn't trying to. I was a pleasure-seeking fool, and I was having fun. When I was bored, I would do and pursue things that kept me from being bored.

Many guys in our community were getting an education in their off hours. I decided to give that try. I found a local University that offered night classes so working people could work on getting a degree after they got off work. I found a degree that was right up my alley. It was a Bachelor of Science called Airway Science. Some of the requirements were pilot licenses, which I already had the ones that were required.

Like many others in our community, I decided to get a degree and transition into being an officer in the SEAL team. Why not? There is more money to be made and a higher retirement income. There were also the accolades that came with getting a degree, and throughout my entire life, growing up as long as I could remember, higher education was being pushed. So when I started down that road, it was like, this is what I am supposed to do, everyone agreed.

Since it was my choice, I took it seriously and realized that I could do well in school; I studied and got good grades, amazing what happens if you put the work in. I enjoyed the classes and felt I was doing something productive with my life rather than sitting home, wasting time, and being nonproductive.

I had a friend named Rico, whom I met in 1980, who was a member of the East Coast Navy parachute called the Chuting Stars; their team would cover all the shows east of the Mississippi. That team was disbanded in the '90s, and the Leap Frogs on the West Coast would cover the entire country.

Rico and I had a lot of things in common; he loved aviation and skydiving. He also was one of the members of our Navy 4-way competition team. He was the one that turned me on to the Airway Science degree. He went on to get his degree and became an officer in the SEAL team. He was one of the finest officers to serve. I never worked directly for him, but he was highly respected in the Navy Special Warfare community. On the other hand, I did not finish my degree; I came within nine classes of finishing, and the truth be known, they were the most challenging classes I was saving for last. The math classes were not my strongest suit.

God had other plans for me. I am jokingly going to blame Robin for not completing my degree. Because of the dynamics of our relationship, it was hard to keep focused during the challenging classes.

Chapter Twenty-Seven
Purpose

Robin and I had a love-hate relationship; we would have the most incredible times doing what we loved to do. After a day of skydiving, everybody would always hang out and celebrate the thrill of the day. Skydiving and drinking went hand in hand. When Robin and I drank, the fighting started. Our friends would describe their nights with us as Saturday nights at the fights with Mike and Robin.

After four years of dating and fighting, we decided to do something about it. We got married. We committed to each other on October 10th, 1986, and thought this should fix it. The definition of insanity is doing the same thing and expecting different results. We kept doing the same thing and getting the same results. Our relationship started to deteriorate after our marriage.

We bought a house together before we married; I also purchased that two-seater airplane I mentioned earlier. The one that was in pieces that I had flown in when I was 15 years old. I found out that one can get a great price on an aircraft when it's in pieces. So the airplane entered the garage, and Robins's new car entered the driveway, which made her happy.

After being on the parachute team for three and a half years and jumping every weekend since 1979, I started to get a little burned out and wanted to focus on my next pleasure tool, rebuilding the Champ Citabria, airbatic spelled backward. So, Robin and I lost the one thing we had in common that brought us together: skydiving. I would spend the weekends working on the airplane while Robin went to Perris Valley to skydive.

We were growing farther and farther apart. Being on the SEAL team did not help our marriage situation. The SEAL community had about a 75% divorce rate. It was common practice to share your marriage problems with your friends, and most times, they were going through similar issues. Misery always loves company, but with no solutions, plenty of commiserating didn't help Robin and me.

After taking the airplane project as far as I could, based on my discretionary income, I realized I was at a standstill until I found a way to make more money. In the 1980s, we did not have the opportunity that people have today to supplement their income—no Uber, Uber Eats, Lyft, etc. No internet, no cell phones. If you were looking for ideas, you would go to the Yellow Pages in the phone book. The new generations have yet to learn what I'm talking about.

I kept my ears and eyes open for an opportunity that would fund my newfound dream of putting my airplane in the air. One day on base, I ran into a retired SEAL commander selling life insurance; after some small talk and catching up, he pitched me something about Mother's Insurance. He called a couple of days later to set up a meeting with me and Robin. His approach was good enough for me to say yes to the meeting, at least hear him out. During the meeting, he laid out the hypothetical of what cost would accrue if the non-service member's spouse died, including child care, the funeral cost, and all the costs that would not be taken care of by the government like it would if something happened to the service member. He called it Mother's Insurance.

After his sales pitch, which made sense if you had children, Robin and I looked at each other, thinking the same thing; I said Dick, we don't have children. He said you were right; it probably would not be something you would need. He then offered me an opportunity and asked if I would like to make extra money selling life Insurance. Immediately, I said, heck yes. I had an airplane to put together.

Later that week, I met him at his office, and he gave me the tour and showed me where my desk would be. I started to get excited about the possibility of making extra money in my evening hours, taking my TV watching and couch potato time, and doing something to fund my airplane project. He set me up with a crash course over a weekend, preparing me to take the life insurance exam to be a certified California agent.

After receiving my license, I hit the ground running; the product made sense, and I believed in it. Due to the respect I had garnered in the community, I set up meetings and explained why this would benefit the qualified. Before I knew it, I was the part-time salesman of the month and stayed in that position from month to month. It was only a short time before I made a couple thousand a month in my part-time insurance business.

Soon after I started selling life insurance, I received orders to the Naval Special Warfare Center to be a BUD/S instructor. I was excited to be an instructor for several reasons. It was what we call shore duty orders. That meant I would not be deployed and could focus on life without going anywhere. I would have three years before my next set of orders back to a SEAL team. The other reason was that I got to be on the other side of SEAL training; instead of being the abused trainee, I got to be the abuser. The truth is, I was placed in the second phase (blue helmet) dive phase, which suited my personality, and I loved diving.

In the second phase, instructors had a different mission: to teach the trainees all the aspects of combat diving. The class proved they could endure whatever was thrown at them during the first phase. In the first phase, the instructor's mission was to weed out the ones who did not belong in the SEAL ranks.

Our attitude as second-phase instructors was that these men were now professionals, and we would treat them as such until they screwed up, then we would hammer them with all the tools that we were allowed to use.

I loved being an instructor right off the bat. First, I had to be instructor-qualified, so I had to attend Navy instructor training. It was a three-week course that was designed to teach you how to teach from a podium and be able to read lesson plans and follow the curriculum. For the first time, I had to get up and talk to people in the public classroom setting. I avoided all speaking and speech classes in high school at all costs. I believe they created a special class for people like me when I was a senior in high school. One of the requirements to graduate was speech class. I told the career counselor that I would not take the class. It could have been my imagination, but before my senior year, our school had created another class for me to fulfill the requirement. It was called Sport Lit. We would sit in class, read Sports Illustrated magazine, and then write a story about one of the articles. I remember one of the articles I wrote about Mohammad Ali; it went like this. "He floats like a butterfly and stings like a bee," and of course, it was double-spaced. Needless to say, this class did not prepare me for my next job in my Navy career.

After attending the instructor course, I could discuss anything at length if I knew the subject. It was all about preparation; if I knew the material inside and out, I could confidently teach it and do so effectively. After I graduated from Instructor training and am now a certified Navy instructor, I was put to work. The leaders of the second phase gave me two classes to teach from the podium, dive physics, and air dive tables. It took some time, but I knew the subjects well before my first class and could easily teach confidently. The last thing you wanted was to have SEAL trainees see weakness in the instructor, so you had to know your stuff, and if you didn't, it would look very poorly on you.

Learning my new job as an instructor during the day and selling life insurance in the evenings gave Robin and I limited time together. Robin was busy working in the man's world as a project coordinator for a large commercial construction company. Back then, women were not treated fairly, which wore on Robin. So, our marriage was under strain with my schedule and her job. During our first year of marriage, we were already talking about divorce. It wasn't looking good, and we had nowhere to turn for help, and back then, we weren't looking for it.

When couples grow apart, they look for the exit sign rather than the help sign. The relationship gets so volatile and resentful that you don't want help. The grass starts looking greener. I tell people today that if you go after greener grass, you will turn that brown, too!

Just before getting into the insurance business, I had a friend in the SEAL team that I had deployed with and was also a member of the Leap Frogs. He approached me one day about a business opportunity. I asked him what kind of business, and he said it was a business you could buy all this cool stuff at cost. He then invited me to a meeting in Riverside, California. I asked him when the meeting started, and he said 8 pm. I said Glay, that is 2 hours away; what time does it end, he told me about 10:30, and we wouldn't get home until about 1:00 am. I have to be at work at 5 am. No, thanks, I said.

I later learned he was involved in some direct selling soap business by talking to some other guys at BUD/S. I knew something about it because my aunt sold products to my Mom when I was about eight years old. I couldn't believe some Navy SEALs were doing what my aunt did. When I told my mentor in the insurance business what our SEAL brothers were up to, we both had a good laugh, even though I had no idea what they were doing, and I didn't want to know. Looking back on it, I wondered why people like myself laugh and make fun of something they don't understand. It's human nature; we are naturally pessimistic, so the easiest thing to do if you don't understand something is to criticize it.

When I saw these guys in the compound, I would throw out little innuendos, like hey soapy, hey bubbles. I thought I was all that and a bag of something. I was the big shot insurance agent, selling death and making real money. It wasn't long before I started getting disillusioned with the insurance thing. When you are around the culture long enough and get a peek behind the curtain, you begin to see the good, the bad, and the ugly. My mentor would also ask me to go out and drink after a meeting. Every time I went out, I didn't feel good about it. I hadn't seen Robin all day, and I was out drinking after a meeting when I could be home with her. And, of course, she could smell the beer on my breath when I got home, which caused more tension in our marriage.

One night, I had 24-hour duty at BUD/S as the Command Duty Officer (CDO). There was always a senior enlisted man on duty for 24 hours to ensure everything ran smoothly in the command. If anything came up throughout the day or night, there was one person to go to who could start putting out fires and make calls to solve whatever problem arose.

That evening, I turned into the bunk room for the night, and I was lying there staring at the ceiling when this voice entered my head; it wasn't audible, but it was very clear. "You are going to build that business." I thought, no way am I going to build that business. I had never seen it; all I knew was my aunt sold soap door to door, and I am a Navy SEAL; I am not my aunt. But I kept hearing, "You will build that business." I could not stop thinking about what I was being told. I lay there all night and could not get to sleep.

The following day, I got up and called Glay and said, hey, Glay, I want you to sign me up in that business. He said, "What?" Please sign me up in your business. I said Glay, I want you to sign me up this morning. He said, "I'm coming to work, I can't." I said I'm getting off work, he thought for a second and then told me that his wife Sharon was home and she would do it.

So I immediately drove to their house, and Sharon was ready. She had this business kit and the registration form all ready. She went through everything, and I signed the registration. As I left, she explained that I needed to go to a conference. I asked her what that was, and she explained that it was a big conference where this organization celebrates our economic system, Free Enterprise. I asked if I could bring Robin, and she said yes and recommended it. I said great, give me two tickets.

I went home and spread this sales kit all over the kitchen table, then went to sleep and waited for Robin to get off work. Knowing Robin, I knew this was going to be a battle. There was no way she was going to win this one. I had never been more convicted of something that I knew nothing about. I thought that doesn't even make sense!

Later that afternoon, Robin came home. I met her, and she stopped at the kitchen table. One thing about Robin is that she does not let anything go unnoticed; if there is anything out of place or something new, she will notice it right away. Ok, this is it; we will do this right now.

"What is this," Robin said. I said this is the answer to our financial problems. She took one look at it. "We're not doing this!" I said yes, we are, and she said, "Oh, no, we're not." We both repeated ourselves two more times. Then I said, listen, I will do this with or without you.

I want to tell you that I also said I would rather do it with you, my little sugar-plumb darling. But I did not. I said, I am going to do this with you or without you, and if you don't sign this registration form, where it says spouse. I will make a ton of money, and you won't see one red cent; this was the state of Robin and I's union. Robin looked at me and knew I was serious; she picked up the pen, signed her name, and walked away.

We were headed to Cancun, Mexico, for our first wedding anniversary trip the following week. Things had cooled down about our new business; Robin knew there wasn't anything that was going to change my mind. I still had not seen the sales and marketing plan, had not listened to an audio, and knew nothing about the business. Robins's sister and our brother-in-law had joined us on the trip to Cancun, and throughout the trip, I kept talking about how excited I was about this business. They both would say," How does it work?" I have no idea, but when I do, I will get back to you. I believe they thought I had lost my mind. Robin would explain to them that she thought I had sniffed too much glue working on my airplane. Robin did not share my excitement.

After returning home, the following weekend was this FED (Free Enterprise Day celebration weekend. I asked Robin to please attend with me. She agreed she would go on Friday evening, but she was going skydiving on Saturday and Sunday. One night is better than nothing, I thought.

I pulled out the best dress attire in my closet: a tan suit coat with a pink shirt and yellow tie. We arrived that Friday evening and walked through the door, and I knew immediately I was out of uniform; all the guys were wearing dark blue or black suits with white shirts. Being a Navy guy, I knew what it was like to be out of uniform, and I was definitely out of uniform.

I couldn't believe how many people there were; I heard later there were about 10,000 in attendance. That was impressive; I started to get the feeling that this was a huge deal. The evening was kicked off by a patriotic tribute to the military, with one of the best color guard ceremonies I had ever seen. Marching through the arena spotlighted while the national anthem was playing, everybody on their feet with their hands over their heart. Robin and I had never witnessed such a display of patriotism, and I had been in the Navy for 11 years. You have to remember I joined the military in 1976, just after the Vietnam War. There wasn't a lot of patriotism in our Country during that time. No one came to our boot camp graduations. Signs on people's yards surrounding the Navy bases said sailors and dogs stay off the lawn. It was not too long that when the military troops were coming home from the war, they were spat on and called baby killers. I believe it to be one of the most prominent black eyes our Country has received in its history. The same thing is happening to our police departments, like the military, that were following orders to defend the Constitution against all enemies, foreign and domestic. The Police are out there to defend, serve, and protect our way of life in our Country.

After the opening ceremony, the rest of Friday night's agenda was filled with couples speaking about how great our Country is and how it was built on the premise of freedom. It had been a long time since I heard these words spoken about the United States of America. I knew right away this was going to be home for me. I had never been so inspired in all my life; I heard things that evening that I had never heard before. Speakers spoke of personal freedom, which they were living firsthand. We live in a free Country, but most of its people are living in bondage. I was also reminded that our freedoms were being taken away little by little without notice by most. I started to look back on the freedoms that I had growing up and how some of those same freedoms were missing.

Sitting there that night, a cause was growing in my heart; I started to understand why I heard those words in my bed that night on duty, which brought me here to this celebration of our economic system, which is the catalyst of our freedom.

On the ride back to San Diego, I could hardly contain myself with excitement. Robin, on the other hand, was still a little skeptical. I asked her what she got out of the evening. She said she liked how the couples that spoke talked about their spouse the way they did, loving and edifying of each other, and you could tell it was real and not stage talk; it was from the heart.

What Robin heard that night gave me insight into how she felt about our marriage. It was something we needed more of. The rest of the drive was quiet. We finally pulled into our driveway at around 1:30 am. Our sponsor told me I should get there early to get in line and get a good seat. I immediately went to bed to get a few hours of sleep.

Early the following day, I was back on the road heading north, and even without much sleep, I was excited in anticipation of what I would experience that day. On arrival, I got in line as fast as possible and waited for the doors to open. Being introverted, I kept to myself and did not run into anybody I knew. The doors opened after a couple of hours, and we ran for the front-row seats. I was pleased with my seat and settled in for the function to start.

All day, I sat there, taking in every speaker and continuing to hear things I had never heard before. The longer I sat there, the more excited I got. I didn't want to go to the bathroom, afraid I would miss something I needed to hear. After sitting there all day, they said they would break for dinner. I welcomed it as I was hungry and badly needed a restroom run.

After the dinner break, there was a big celebration for six couples who were recognized for reaching the diamond level. I didn't know what this meant, but I knew it was a big deal. Listening to each couple reinforced what I was called to do. I didn't know what it would take, but I knew I would be a diamond one day.

It reminded me of seeing that BUD/S class running into the compound. That day, the instructor yelled at me while I was doing push-ups. I thought I had made the mistake of wanting to be a Navy SEAL. I decided right then and there that I was going to be one. It's incredible how the most minor thing can inspire someone. Six couples from different backgrounds had made a choice. One was a doctor, another a florist, a forest ranger. Then they recognized a couple; they introduced them as "The Return of the Champions." He was a school teacher; their names were Bill and Sandy Hawkins. I thought how great it would be to be friends with people like that.

Listening to them took away any excuse that might have been formulating in anybody's mind about how they couldn't do this business. I had no idea what to do, but I knew in my heart that I would not be denied.

After the celebration and recognition of the new diamonds, they introduced this man, Bill Britt. He danced out on stage to James Brown's music, "I Feel Good." This man was larger than life; he was funny and filled with energy like I had never seen before. When he spoke, truth and conviction flew from his mouth. The entire arena was filled with shock and awe. Everything he said made sense, common sense. The time he spoke flew by; before I knew it, it was after midnight. Bill exited the stage during a standing ovation; the crowd was electrified.

After the crowd had settled, the host made some closing announcements. He said if you liked Bill Britt, then you need to be here tomorrow morning for a non-denominational church service so you can hear Bill Britt talk about God's laws of success. I don't know what I heard, except Bill Britt is speaking about God's laws of success. But I will be there, and I will be early.

I didn't have a place to stay; I hadn't had time to find a hotel. I started driving south, looking for a hotel sign. Remember, we didn't have cell phones for a Google search. I finally saw a sign about an hour into the drive. The hotel was vacant, and I eventually got into bed at about 2 am. I'll be back up at 5 to get in line to get a front-row seat for Bill Britt. When I got to the arena, there was no line. I wondered why that was. After a while, some people started to show up, and the line grew, but nothing like it was Friday night or Saturday. When the doors opened, we all trickled in; it wasn't the mad dash I experienced on Saturday.

I found a seat in the first row right before the podium. As I was sitting there, I realized why there was no line. There was background Christian music playing. Then, it became apparent when the family music group called The Goads came out and started singing church music. I thought this was a church service. Oh well, as long as Bill Britt is speaking, it doesn't matter what it was, and I am on the front row.

After The Goads finished, the host introduced Bill Britt. He came out with that big smile just as the night before. He started warming up the crowd with some of the stories of his testimony, how he grew up with an alcoholic father, and how his mother never gave up on her husband and stayed with him despite his problem. He shared his story of his time in the Army. His testimony was through the trials and tribulations he experienced, and all his success in his life was a tribute to God's love and grace.

Then he let it rip, and he started to tell everyone in the audience if you are doing this or that; basically, he went down the list of sins that man falls from. I was taking note of all of them, saying to myself, I did that, yup, doing that, oh yeah, there is another one I'm guilty of. I sat there frozen in my seat as if everyone was staring at me like I had a sign over my head. I was convicted. He said, "I have a solution, and if you don't take the solution, you will need an asbestos suit because of where you are going." He said, "Here is the solution; get your butt up here, front and center, and accept Jesus into your heart, and you will be saved."

I was convicted; no fear would cause me not to be one of the first out of my seat; it was like this force had picked me up and brought me right in front, staring Bill Britt in the eyes and weeping like a baby. Here I was this rough, tough Navy SEAL: do anything, don't fear anything, tears rolling down my face. Bill Britt didn't move me; it was the Holy Spirit!

I accepted Jesus into my heart at that FED weekend, October of 1987, with Mr. Bill Britt delivering the message. I felt that my whole life had been orchestrated for this Moment; it was divine intervention from the beginning - my life had been spared on so many occasions. I was finally ready to listen and hear God's voice. I was at this FED listening to the truth for maybe the first time in my life. It was just all so strange how it worked out. When the student is ready, the teacher will appear.

Throughout the rest of Sunday, I couldn't wait to get home and tell Robin what I had experienced that morning. I became a visionary that morning. I knew before being introduced to this organization, that my marriage would not have lasted through the second quarter of our second year. I knew that morning that there was no back door to my marriage. Coming from a construction background, I was determined to weld that back door shut. I also believed that if I could fix my life and be fulfilled with purpose instead of pleasure, I could help others save their lives.

I became an eternal thinker instead of a temporal thinker. Because of the start of my spiritual walk and relationship with God, I started to keep life in perspective. I would dedicate my life to helping people have a great life here on earth, but help them build something that would not pass away on earth. The character that I would help them develop along with the people they would impact so they would have that same relationship I received that Sunday morning. As the great man Ron Puryear would say, "The only things you will take into heaven are your character and other people." After that weekend, I knew that's precisely what I would focus on from here on out.

Chapter Twenty-Eight
Mentor

When I got home, Robin waited for me to see how the rest of the weekend went. We were standing in the kitchen, and I explained what had happened to me that morning. Robin was raised in a Christian home and had that relationship with Jesus, but over time and bad association, she had drifted. She could see something different about me when she looked into my eyes. We hugged and cried together. We both knew at that point she and I would be ok.

I want to say that Robin believed in the business after that, but she needed more time. She wasn't negative, kind of neutral, which was better than the alternative. After a few days and decompressing from the life-changing weekend, our sponsor, Glay, asked me if I wanted to host a board plan, which is what they called a business presentation given in someone's home. He said our upline emerald Joe Foglio would be doing it. I had not met this Joe Foglio, but I had heard great things about him all that weekend. We agreed that the board plan would be in two weeks, giving me enough time to prepare and invite people to meet Joe Foglio and see the business.

I had been in the SEAL community for eleven years and had built a decent reputation. I also had a sphere of influence in the civilian skydiving world and had some respect there. So, I invited everyone I knew through phone calls and face-to-face. I did not understand the business but knew what I had experienced. They would ask me what kind of business opportunity it was. I would tell them it was a direct sales business. My enthusiasm was off the charts; I thought I could explain what I felt and experienced from that weekend, but I realized it was like trying to explain, from a woman's point of view, what it was like to have a baby.

After all the invites, I believed we would have a houseful. When the night finally arrived, I bought a new suit that put me in uniform with what a business builder would wear. Robin was supportive and looked great. Our house started to fill with people that I didn't know. Suddenly, I heard a buzz from the front door; it got really quiet, and I listened to this voice. I knew it had to be him. I walked to the front door, and this tall, dark, good-looking man was standing there, filled with boldness, humility, and confidence all at the same time, and he had the biggest smile I had ever seen. Joe was swarmed with people trying to get close and shake his hand, but he wasn't shaking hands; he was hugging everyone.

We had never met, but when we saw each other, we both knew. I introduced myself, and he said, "I know who you are." I shook his hand; I wasn't ready for a hug then; I still had the SEAL team posture going. We all took our seats since I didn't know how to do the introduction. My sponsor's sponsor, Carson, is someone I worked with as an instructor at BUD/S. He got up to introduce Joe. I was excited for Robin and me; this would be the first time we would see the sales and marketing plan. I was excited about the life changes I was going through, but I also wanted to know how the money was made. On the other hand, I was disappointed because only three out of all the people I had invited showed up. I learned later that it wasn't their fault; I didn't know what to say to raise enough curiosity to make them want to come.

That evening during the plan, I learned a few things: there was a lot of money to make, and I liked Joe Foglio. I thought now there was a man I could follow in life. I made a decision that night: I was going to be one of Joe's closest friends.

After the meeting, Joe stayed around shaking hands and hugging people. After everybody left and Joe was getting ready to go, I said Joe, you want to see something cool? "Of course, sure I do!" I led him out to the garage; my dream was the airplane. Joe looked at the aircraft and then at me; he looked excited, like he couldn't contain himself. Joe knew that this airplane project was important to me, and with all the enthusiasm he could muster, he showed me that if it was important to me, it was equally important to him. After that, I really loved Joe Foglio!

The next day, I grabbed Carson and said, hey, show me how to show this business plan. At lunchtime at work, we went into the BUD/S classroom, and he sat down with a legal pad of paper and drew out the plan. After he was done, I ripped out the page and said, ok, I got it. I knew I could build this business. I just had to show it. Deep down, I wanted to impress Joe Foglio and show him that I was someone who was going to build this and build it big. I was going to be worth his time.

I started listing names of people I thought might be looking. I started with everyone I invited to my house to see the plan. When I finished, I noticed that it was pretty long. I also had another list I called my chicken list. These were the guys I respected, and I cared about what they thought. I learned later that if you care so much about what people think, especially something you know is good for you and others, what does it matter what they believe? You will never have everybody agree with you, so why try? Joe would say, "You can't say the wrong thing to the right person, and you can't say the right thing to the wrong person. Caring about what people think is one of the major causes of failures in one's life."

It took me only a short time to fully commit to building the business. I knew Robin was watching me to see if I would falter. I proved to her right that it was just one more hair-brained idea that would wear off as soon as I realized this, and it wouldn't be easy. She was excited about my spiritual walk, though, but didn't know if I had what it took to change and give up my pleasure-seeking mentality.

I was committed; only I knew what had happened to me that FED weekend. I was transformed in a way that completely changed my outlook on life. I had become an eternal thinker. Let me explain. A temporal thinker is focused on their life here on earth. All decisions and actions are made to satisfy the temporal mindset. An eternal perspective is looking towards your impact on eternal life after you leave this life on earth. What effect did you have on other people's lives while you lived? Like the great man, Dave Severn would say, "Did the use of your life outlive your life?"

A pleasure seeker is all about how much fun I am having today and how much fun I will have tomorrow. It is not what impact I am going to have today. Based on that shift in my mind, I started to learn what I had to do daily to move in that direction.

I started to change the programming in my mind and heart. I read books and listened to audio. I gradually changed my association and decided who I would spend time with. I wanted to ensure that my time was helping me move forward in my vision. My vision was to be very successful in this business, knowing I would impact people's lives, their marriages, and families from that accomplishment. Helping people find a vision for their future would allow them to direct their lives purposefully. This change of thinking would help people have a generational impact. Now, that is a life worth living.

To make these changes, I knew I had to eliminate some things, such as pleasure-seeking toys. The first thing I knew I had to give up was my skeleton airplane, knowing it was the one thing that caused me to find this business. It was the power of that dream of one day flying that airplane, but now it was a distraction I didn't need anymore.

It helped me find my vision and purpose. It did what it was supposed to; now it was time to focus.

I called my little brother Danny, who also flew in the same airplane when he was nine. Danny was a SEAL at his point and was heavily into aviation. He had grown up with my Dad after our first six kids were all grown up and on with our adult lives. Danny was influenced by my Dad and adopted his love of aviation. He was happy to buy the airplane from me.

I knew I would own other airplanes, which would be something other than projects in my garage. I had lots of dreams that kept me focused on doing the work. Most underestimate the power of a dream. Our flesh has desires; even though I had a vision to impact the earth, while I was here, I learned to cultivate a dream that would move me when I didn't feel like moving.

Look at the story of King David when the Philistine Army was taunting the Israelites to fight their giant Goliath. David is sent to the frontline to bring his brothers some food. While there, he hears the taunting and the prize for the person who can defeat the giant, who would marry the king's daughter and have free land. He overheard this the first time, then inquired twice to make sure.

David understood the eternal impact, and his flesh desired the temporal. You have to have a clear vision of your purpose, but you also have the power of the dream that motivates you to do things for your purpose when you don't feel like doing them.

After Robin observed my choices and how I replaced my bad habits with new good ones, she believed I would never give up. She realized that I was changing for the better. One of the significant changes she noticed was how I started treating her. I give credit to my mentor, Joe Foglio.

Chapter Twenty-Nine
Running Mate

After some time had passed, I was able to spend some more time with Joe. I became comfortable with him and would share stories about Robin. These weren't positive ones. He would look at me like a third eye was growing out of my head. "What?" Joe would say, "I can't believe you talk about Robin that way."

I could always share the negative about Robin at work with my SEAL team brothers; we would commiserate about our wives. We would all agree that we shouldn't have gotten married, and if we were meant to be married, the Navy would have issued us a wife. No wonder there was such a high divorce rate in the SEAL team.

Joe would say, "The one thing I have learned is that 99% of the time, if there is a marriage problem, it is the guy's fault." I told Joe, well, you are looking at the 1% right here, Joe. He doubted it and handed me a book called If Only He Knew because Joe knew I didn't know. I started to read that book, and about the 3rd page, I realized it was my fault. It didn't happen overnight, but I began to change. The truth will set you free, and knowledge is power.

The other noticeable change was my language. I was convicted of my words since that Sunday morning experience at FED. It wasn't a conscious decision to change; it just happened. In the SEAL team, we have our own language, comprised of four-letter words; one in particular is used more than most. If you are talking and when there is a place in the sentence where that word should be placed, and you replace that word with something else, you are looked at like, what is wrong with you? As time went on, my SEAL team brothers started to swear less when they were around me. I never reacted or judged them; they respected it for not hearing it from me.

Being a BUD/S instructor allowed me to spend my off hours building our business. Other than when we had night dive operations, I was usually home by 5 pm. Robin would get home from her project manager job about the same time. She would prepare dinner, and after we ate, I would put my business casual uniform on and get out to see who I could meet. Early in the business, I learned I had to improve my communication and connecting skills. The only way to do that was to get out and start conversations with strangers. This was so foreign to me; it wasn't something I had ever done.

I could communicate with somebody who was placed in my world, in whatever part of my world it was at the time: SEAL team, skydiving, aviation, or my parachute team world. I had no skill in placing myself in some stranger's world and starting a conversation. I knew this had to be an acquired skill set; all it would take was training. Every night I went out, I told myself this is training: crawl, walk, run.

Robin wasn't engaged in the business; she was observing from the sidelines to see if I would stick with it. After hearing her complaints about her construction job and how much she hated it. I asked her if she would consider quitting if we no longer needed the money. She said in a New York second she would stop. When would you want to do that? She asked how about my birthday, which was about nine months away. I said that was a great goal for me. I will work hard to get you out of your job. I was focused and consistent. My head was on a swivel, searching for people I could share this business with. We started to get some traction and began to see some Momentum building.

My relationship with Joe Foglio started to blossom; he knew I was serious about my vision and was always there to help me in any way he could. I would sit down with him at least every month with a counsel sheet; he would guide and inspire me to keep doing what I was doing. He also counseled me about finances, where I could budget better and pay off some debts. Robin and I were debt-free from his counsel within several months of starting the business. We didn't owe any money other than the mortgage on our house.

We were looking good financially with the extra money we were making from the business and less overhead from being out of debt. One day, about seven months into the business in 1988, I came home early. On Friday, April 1st, Robin was lying on the couch. I said what are you doing home so early? She said, "Do you remember when I told you I wanted to come home on my birthday?" I said yes. "Well, April Fools, I quit today." I was surprised but excited that Robin did not have to return to a job she was unhappy with. Since then, Robin has not had to work outside the home since.

Robin started to become a believer in me and the business, and slowly but surely, she began to engage more and help me in any way she could. Shortly after she quit her job, I convinced her to take a road trip to Portland, Oregon, where the Puryear Family Reunion was being held. This would be her first major function since Friday at FED, which we both attended. I told her we could drive through the Redwoods and stop at a bed and breakfast, and it would be great. I convinced her to come to this event by packaging it with the promise of a vacation.

We did stop at a bed and breakfast and had a great time traveling through the Redwoods. If Robin could sit through this function, seeing the success of our business and realizing that I was in this for the long haul, she would catch my vision. After sitting there and taking it all in, I could tell she was getting increasingly excited about building the business with me. Once again, when the student is ready, the teacher will appear.

Our drive home was much different from the one going to Portland. We both could not contain our excitement. I remember on the journey home, we ran into some fog, and after driving straight through after a weekend with little sleep, we were a little bit on the crazy side. We both rolled down the windows to see if we could see the road better, and we started yelling outside the windows, "We are going, Ruby!" Ruby was at a particular level in the business that would create a significant amount of income. I had never experienced that emotion from Robin in all the time I had known her; she was indeed fired up about her future, which was with me and our business.

From then on, Robin was on my team and ready to run, doing whatever she could to help me build our business. It was the best time in our relationship that we had ever experienced, even over the times when we skydived every weekend together. This was the first time we lived for purpose, not just pleasure.

Robin's belief in me and the business gave me a more profound conviction, and now there was no stopping me. How could I go wrong with Robin by my side and Joe Foglio coaching and mentoring? It was going to be a win-win!

Since I was working down the Silver Strand at the Naval Special Warfare Center instructing, I was very close to Joe and his wife Norma's home in Coronado. I would call him some mornings and ask him what he was doing for lunch. He would say, "Having lunch with you, come on," was his reply. I would pick him up, and we would drive down to Imperial Beach and eat at our favorite place, Jalisco's. We would have the usual; Joe would order albondigas soup, and I would have the flying saucer with chicken.

Mike And Joe Foglio

Joe was always available for me; he knew I was serious and was doing the work to earn his time. He also knew I loved him; we had an extraordinary bond. He would always ask, "Mike, who loves you like you love me?" One day, he called me and said, "You want to go to Mexico with me?" It would be a short trip since we were just on the other side of the border. I loved spending time with Joe; I felt I was 10 feet tall and bulletproof after each outing. So I was looking forward to the time and seeing where he had worked before he got free from his job. Before construction, he sold homes in a resort called Bajamar just south of the border in Rosarito, Mexico.

When we got down there, we drove around to this house under construction, and Joe was drawing out windows and doors on a pad of paper. I asked him what he was doing, and he said, "I'm selling alarm systems to these people that are having these houses built; I have Security Systems that would be perfect for all of these houses. His mind was always working to find a way to help their upline Jim and Judy Head go Diamond, and he and Jimmy's other Platinum, Al, and Kathy Gallo, were competing to see who could get there first.

On the way home, we stopped at this little cantina that Joe knew about for lunch. The waitress came over to take our order, and Joe asked me if I wanted a Corona; I said yes immediately. It caught me off guard because I hadn't heard anyone talk about or seen anybody drink an alcoholic beverage. As a SEAL and a skydiver, Joe knew that I liked beer. After we drank that beer, I asked him, one more? Joe said, "Nope, just one!" There was a lesson there.

I got to see things and experience life with Joe that many people did not. Joe trusted me, and I trusted him. The relationship with Joe was something special; I don't think I have ever had that kind of relationship with another man, and I have not since. Joe was one of a kind, and anybody who got a chance to meet him knew he was someone extraordinary from just one meeting. The people fortunate enough to spend time with him got something extra special they will never forget.

After being in the business for about a year, we hit a wall after going through our sphere of influence. We succeeded, but I knew I had to take it to the next level. I sat down with Joe for guidance on how to do that. I told him, Joe, I am dead in the water here. I told him I'm always out working and meeting people but come home most nights with my tail between my legs.

Sometimes, I lay in bed staring at the ceiling, praying and asking God if this business will work for me, with tears rolling down my face; the answer is always, keep doing what you are doing; I have you!

Joe knew what I was going through; he had been there and knew the answer. He challenged me by asking if I could share this business with 20 people in a month. Knowing he was challenging me to push myself like I had never done, as far as being able to communicate and connect with strangers, I said, of course! He then asked me if I could do it for three months in a row. Again, I said, yes. I walked away after that meeting, wondering how I would share this with 20 people in a month and repeat it for two more months.

I knew it didn't have to be pretty; I just had to do it. Something happened; it was like a switch that was flipped. I started conversations with anybody that came within three feet of me. There was no overthinking; I began conversing with anybody who stood still long enough. It didn't matter if it was for kids or older people; there was no qualifying. I had to leave my comfort zone and learn how to connect with anybody from any walk of life. It didn't matter their background, educational level, or occupation; it just didn't matter.

I was no longer intimidated by anyone. Through this new mindset, I knew nobody was better than me, and I wasn't better than them.

I started to love myself down to the ground, truly. Therefore, I could love other people; you see, you can't give out what you don't have for yourself. Ron Puryear called this putting music into your words. "Tell people you love them with your eyes."

Communicating and connecting became more accessible and easier for me, but that didn't mean sharing my business with 20 people in a month made it any easier. After that meeting with Joe, I put a legal pad of paper on my mirror and wrote 1-20 for three months. Now, I had to fill in those 60 spaces with names. I had to get creative. If anyone would sit still long enough, I would show them what we call a napkin plan. It was a show of concept; if they were interested after showing them how the business worked, I would set up a meeting and show them the entire plan, or I would get them in front of Joe at a board plan he was doing.

When I neared the end of the month and needed to show more plans, I got a little more creative and crazier. I remember driving around and looking for someone to show the plan to. I spotted an older woman sitting at the bus stop waiting for the bus. I pulled up, parked, and sat down next to her. I asked her how long before the bus arrived, and she said about 10 minutes. I said perfect, can I show you something? I pulled out a piece of paper and explained the business. Afterward, I asked her name and told her I hoped she had a lovely rest of her day.

When I told that story, most people thought I was crazy for doing things like that. But it was something I had to do. Joe challenged me, and I would not be denied. There was no way I would go back to Joe and tell him I couldn't meet his challenge. After and during that exercise, I felt fearless. I could talk to anyone, carry on a conversation, and connect. I humbled myself and removed the chip on my shoulder, which I probably had since my second-grade failure.

That chip got me through many years and caused me to excel in different things in my life. It was that chip that motivated me through SEAL training. I had something to prove to my siblings and parents. I would show them that I wasn't a second-grade failure.

But I discovered that the I'll show you attitude wouldn't work in this business. Before the business, it was all about me; now, it had to be all about others. How could I help them? How could I introduce them to a greater association? How could I help them have a better life and marriage? Change the direction of their life drastically. Help them build a legacy. Build something so great that it would outlive their life?

The difference between this business and everything else I had done was this business was an inside job. I had to change from the inside out. This was filleting me open and making me take a good, hard look into who I was. This couldn't be about me; it had to be about others. I had to take my eyes off myself and focus on them. That's easier said than done.

So many people come into this business, like myself, thinking that this is all about my dream: what I can get. Some can't get past that, and then after a while, if they don't transition into what I have to offer others, they quit and say to themselves the business doesn't work.

After three months, I could tell Joe that I had succeeded in the sixty plans. He was very proud of me for overcoming, moving forward, and past the wall I had encountered. I believe that my willingness to grow and change from the inside was the one thing that catapulted Robin into the success we achieved. I believed that God was watching my heart change for his people. He knew he could trust me and started putting good people before us.

After two years, Robin and I hit a landmark of success in our business, Platinum, but we still needed to find someone to work as hard as we were willing to work. After being an instructor at BUD/S training, I was called into the office of one of the officers at the training center. He said he was tasked to assemble a basic and advanced parachuting school curriculum for the first time in Naval history, including an instruction manual with lesson plans that would be sent to Washington for approval. He then asked me if I would be willing to help write it. I told him I was honored to be asked, then I said, who else would be helping me write this? He said, Frank Radford. I knew Frank well; we were close friends on the Navy 4-way competition team. He also became a partner in the airplane project I sold to my brother.

So Frank and I were set up in an office with two desks facing each other, and for the next six months, we would be hammering out this schoolhouse curriculum. During this time, we had a lot of face-to-face time. I learned that Frank was going to be retiring in 18 months. I asked him what he would do after retirement from the Navy. His reply was always, "I don't know." Every day, I would ask him what he wanted out of life, what he would do if money weren't an issue, and what he would buy. I started to dream build with him.

One evening, I got a call from a prospect that I would show the plan; he called to cancel. So, I removed my name list, and Frank was at the top. I told Robin I would call Frank and show him the plan. Robin knew Frank before I did; they were skydiving friends a couple of years before I had met Frank as one of my trainers for the initial parachute team training.

Robin said, "You don't want to show Frank," she said, "Frank doesn't have the right personality." Frank was rough around the edges and not a people person. But through the years, I had an opportunity to see his heart. Frank was loyal and possessed integrity like nobody I had ever met, and he loved his Country.

I called Frank and asked him what he was doing that night; he said, "Nothing, and why?" I said I have something I want to show you. He paused and said, "I'll be right over." He arrived about 30 minutes later. I started to show him the plan; he was leaning back on two legs of the chair and seemed uninterested. I looked up and said, Frank, are you catching any of this? He said, "I'm getting it."

After showing him the plan, he was about to leave; I handed him an information box that looked like a Girl Scout cookie box filled with products and said, Frank, I don't know what you heard tonight. Still, I am working with some men who love their Country as much as you and I do. They don't like its direction, and they're doing something about it. You need to meet them.

The next day, Frank and I were back in the office working, and neither of us said anything about the business. Later in the day, he approached me and said, "I think I want to do this." I was dumbfounded; I said, you do? That's great. He asked what he should do next. I told him there was a meeting that night; Bill Britt is coming to town, and you don't want to miss it.

The next night, I met Frank at the meeting. We were sitting next to each other, and all through the meeting, Bill Britt, in his usual fashion, brought his fire, conviction, and truth. Frank was eating it up, loving what Bill was sharing. I could tell that he was getting what I got two years prior. There is nothing like the experience of finding somebody who gets it like you do.

After the meeting, Frank asked me what was next. I explained to him that we had a major function the following Friday, called FED, and he said, "That's like in two days," I said, I know, and it will blow your mind." Where's it at?" he asked. It's in Fresno; he said, "Let's do it." I told him we were driving up and he was welcome to ride with us. Frank, who likes to be in control, said," I'll drive."

So, Friday morning, we departed for Fresno; six hours later, we checked into our hotel and got ready for the Friday evening opening ceremonies. We got there early, so we got some seats right in front. The arena filled up quickly to total capacity. The place was buzzing with excitement. Like myself, two years prior, I could tell Frank had never experienced that feeling; the evening opened with the color guard and a tribute to America and the military. We had both been to many events where they opened up with the national anthem, Frank also being on the parachute team years before me. This tribute was different, though; you could feel the patriotism in this arena so thick you could cut it with a knife. The people here weren't just going through the motions in anticipation of the ball game to start. Most had attended this FED the weekend before and were educated about America. They had become true patriots.

Chapter Thirty
Patriot

I had served 11 years in the elite of the U.S. Military Force before I had experienced my first FED. I never considered myself a patriot in those 11 years. Of course, I followed orders and would go into battle. I would fight for my brothers on the left, right, behind, and before me. I was post-Viet Nam, and service people like me weren't feeling very patriotic. I joined the Navy to be an underwater welder. Not to fight for my Country.

Was I raised by parents who taught me to love my Country? Absolutely! But somewhere along the way, I lost that patriotic feeling because of events in my life. Vietnam was one of them, even during boot camp, and my training since then was not filled with patriotism.

I believe that the same mindset still exists and even more so today. As a society, we are more removed from the most patriotic time we have experienced as a Country. World War II was that time in our Country. Americans were unified; they pulled together and sacrificed for the greater good. During and after the war, the people were together. Thus, the Greatest Generation was coined.

The more time that has passed since that war, the more divided we have become as a nation. We got a glimpse of what that felt like right after 9/11. The American flags were flying everywhere; however, slowly but surely, patriotism turned into finger-pointing and playing the blame game. The War on Terror was weaponized into a political tool.

The military is filled with unpatriotic people; I was one of them. There are several reasons why people join the military today. Some are patriotic, a tiny percentage. Others participate because they seek a paycheck every two weeks, a roof over their head, and three meals daily. That is a huge percentage for the latter. Then there is the percentage of people who serve because it's a great way to get a paycheck and all the other perks I mentioned, including going to college on the G.I. bill.

It wasn't until FED 1987 that I became a patriot. When I heard the truth from Bill Britt at that Sunday service and accepted that truth, my patriotic journey finally started. I learned that America was God's plan to show the rest of the world that if you put him first, sew his way into the DNA of your constitution, and practice his economic system, Free Enterprise. Your Country will prosper and be blessed.

From the start, our foundation was built on Judeo-Christian principles. Our founding fathers fought for religious freedom. The Revolutionary War was fought and won, even though we were out-manned and out-gunned by the most formidable Army in the world at that time. I ignored this history when I was in school; I slept through all of it. But when I became a Christian, I became a patriot! When you become a patriot for the right reason, you understand what the founding fathers meant when discussing fighting for a just cause.

Our freedoms are under attack; the reason is if our freedoms can be taken from us, then we don't have a free Country to fight for. If we lose this battle being fought for our Country's freedom, we lose the beacon on the hill shining so brightly for the rest of the world to see.

I was starting to buy into this insidious movement, even though I was not raised that way. My military training was not promoting patriotism. It was my job, and I received a paycheck every two weeks. I was being taken care of by the government. I liked my job and would have continued down the same path until retirement. Then, I would have engaged in contract work or continued to work for Naval Special Warfare as a civilian.

But God had another plan for me. My purpose came to light as it came to Franks's life two years later on the same FED weekend. As I watched Frank throughout the weekend, I could tell he was getting it. I saw myself in him. I saw the blinders on his eyes slowly removed from speaker after speaker. One speaker in particular, Jimmy Head, got his attention. When Jimmy came on stage, the crowd went wild.

Every time he spoke, the crowd was stomping, yelling, and screaming at the top of their voices. Jimmy finally realized that they weren't going to stop. Seeing and hearing that the crowd had been so moved by truth all weekend was fantastic. I don't remember what he said, but all it took was one keyword that ignited the crowd like an out-of-control wildfire.

An American flag was on its stand, as it is at all functions. Jimmy marched over, grabbed the flag by its pole, and proceeded back and forth on the stage. The crowd went crazy; it was so loud that most thought the roof was coming down. Nobody had experienced such an out-of-control crowd before that FED, nor has anyone since. It was a Moment in history that happened, and anybody there will never forget it.

After Jimmy Head had walked off the stage and the crowd had settled, I asked Frank if he wanted to meet him. He said, "You can make that happen?" and I said I could. I led Frank backstage and introduced him to Jimmy; I told Frank, this is your upline, Jimmy Head. Frank was like a little kid that just got introduced to Mickey Mouse. Frank shook his hand, and we returned to our seats after a few minutes. Frank said I will never wash my hands again; at the time, I thought he meant it.

Frank had experienced what I had at my first FED weekend. His life was changed and never to be the same. I now had a running mate that got this business as much as I did. On returning home from that weekend, Frank talked about how excited he was; he wanted to put this together fast. He had 18 months before he retired from the Navy, and he did not want to get another job. This was his why! I told him what it would take, and some of that direction was don't do what Robin and I did. It took us two years to hit the platinum level. If you want to do it in 6 months, you must do this.

Frank went to work and did everything he was told and more. He reached that Platinum level in six months, then went to Ruby a few months later. It took us four years to go to Emerald, and it took him about 18 months. We had a two-year head start, and he caught us. I always joke when I say a prayer: please, God, help me find someone like me that I can run with. Frank was the answer to my prayers. After Frank caught us, and it looked like he would pass us, I said another prayer: God, make him stop.

I told Frank that there wasn't anything left that I could teach you; you needed to start counseling with Joe Foglio. Until then, I had the most favor from Joe; now, I must share that position with Frank. I remember when it looked like Frank was going diamond, and we weren't. I started to get these feelings of jealousy. We were at an all expense trip in Orlando for Independent Business Owners that qualify), and we were all hanging out one night at the Jacuzzi; I was sitting across from Joe when Frank walked up, and Joe got this big smile on his face and motioned to Frank, patting the seat with his hand next to him, he said: "Hey Frank, sit here." I got so mad I jumped into this cold pool, sunk to the bottom, and screamed with all my lungs could release, knowing no one could hear me.

Afterward, I returned to the room and told Robin what I felt. I told her that I was embarrassed and angry for Joe and Frank. I had no idea that was in me. Robin then said we needed to pray. We dropped to our knees and asked God to take this anger and jealousy from me. I can tell you after that prayer, it was gone. After the anger and jealousy were gone, I realized how stupid it was and why Frank was going diamond and we weren't. God revealed something that I didn't know was in me. How could I be a leader of people when I would be jealous of their growth?

Frank went diamond in 1993, and Robin and I were blessed to host them for our local FED. Robin and I were recognized as new diamonds the following year, and all was right. God knew what I needed to change. Sometimes, we have blindspots in ourselves, which must be revealed by adversity. Going through something now helps me remember all the great lessons I've learned from the valleys of life, not just the mountaintops.

Chapter Thirty-One
Freedom

1989 Robin and I were blessed by our first child, Kaitlin. Being new parents, we were leaning on what we learned from our parents growing up, some good, some not so good. Knowing that our parents did the best job with what they knew. Having the association of the support group, we had some great examples that had gone before us. We also had some great resources that had been written as well. We had the Lord in our lives and a vision that kept us from making significant mistakes. We learned the best we could was to show our children that their Mom and Dad loved each other and neither of us was going anywhere.

Since Robin was able to be a full-time Mom, it gave me great peace knowing no one could watch over our daughter like her Mommy. I was still working as a BUD/S instructor and working our business, so I was busy and sometimes didn't understand why I had to share childcare duties.

When I got home from work, Robin would have dinner ready. I would eat and then put on my business uniform, a suit. When we thought a suit and tie was a good look for meeting people, I felt ten feet tall and bulletproof. Dressing for success gave me an edge, at least in my mind, it did. Today's culture doesn't fit. We dress up, but it's more business casual unless it's for a business meeting. Nobody looked sharper in a suit than Joe Foglio. He was always dressed a cut above wherever he went, and for whatever he was doing, the man always looked crisp and sharp.

After being out and coming home with my tail between my legs, I would strike out with no meaningful conversations after being out for several hours. It was late, and I was tired and had to get up early for work. At about 3 am, Kaitlin would start to cry. Not being a very understanding husband and not realizing that Robin was exhausted from the day of caring for our daughter. Robin would say, "It's your turn!" My turn? That is what was going through my selfish pea brain head; I have to get up in 2 hours.

I would get up, pick Kaitlin out of her crib, and get a whiff of what the problem was. I would put her on the changing table. She would look up at me with big blue eyes and almost say, thank you, Daddy! I was looking at her, enjoying that precious memory of this time in our lives when it won't be long before she won't need me to change her. At that Moment, I was resolute; I would never verbally complain of losing sleep while caring for Kaitlin. It was a blessing that it would no longer be available one day.

Time passes so fast, and children are markers of time. I learned to enjoy the journey; attitude is your altitude. So fly as high as you can in this lifetime. There are no do-overs, no dress rehearsals. We have one shot in this lifetime; do it as right as possible. When it's over, it's over. No, looking back, no regrets!

In 1992, I was back at SEAL Team Five, still in Coronado, CA., where BUD/S training and all our odd number SEAL teams are stationed. I was brought back to the team as the Operations Chief Petty Officer, an administrative job handling the schools our guys needed to attend. These programs were for their development to help build their skill sets to be more effective SEAL operators. This was a job that nobody wanted, but it was fine with me because I wouldn't be deployed, and I could focus on building our business and being home for Kaitlin and Robin.

During that time, I sat down with my coach and mentor, Joe, for one of our monthly counsel sessions with my counsel sheet. As he looked it over, he said Mike, you have a great business. I don't know your plans, but if you ever decide to be free, you have the business to do it. At that time, I never thought of leaving the Navy four years before retiring. My job allowed me to stay home and focus on building our business while caring for my family. It didn't seem like anything was on the horizon to upset that apple cart.

It was still during the Cold War, so not much was happening. At this point in our business, we made about three times what I made as an E-8 in the Navy. So, financially, we were feeling very secure. Around this time, my little brother received orders to SEAL Team Five. He had just graduated from BUD/S about nine years after I did. I was happy to have him with me but knew we wouldn't work together in a platoon because of my admin job. Being a new guy, he would join a platoon and work up to deploy.

One day, we crossed each other's path on the grinder; he stopped me and said, "Wouldn't it be cool if they put us together in the same platoon? Could you be our Chief?" I said no! I didn't tell him that I had other plans. I knew he wouldn't understand.

Danny has always had a way with people; he convinces anybody to do anything. A couple of days later, I was told by a few people that they had seen my name listed as Platoon Chief! I thought there was no way after walking into the Operations office, where the platoon planning board was, sure enough. There it was: Michael Kelly Carroll, on the board as the Chief, and my little brother, who was at the bottom as the E, nothing. Still, to this day, I don't know how that conversation between my little brother and the Captain went.

Robin was pregnant with our second child, Michael; he was due in about six months. The last thing I wanted to do was work up (train), be gone for months, and then deploy for six during peacetime, training indigenous personnel from other countries.

At that time, we had a new POTUS, and he was cutting the military budget and asking/forcing people to leave, but none of those were SEALs. They called it a RIF, Reduction In Force. I had never experienced one in my 16 years, but I started researching and found it in the BUPERS manual; it's like the bible for the Navy. I looked it up, and it said. I'm paraphrasing; if any service member would like to leave their obligated service during an RIF that is not mission critical to their command and can financially take care of themselves, the Commanding Officer of that command, by request, can authorize the member to be released from military service.

So, being prepared and armed with the BUPERS manual. I walked into the Captain's office. Captain, do you have a minute? He said, "Sure, what's up?" I see you have me slated for a platoon. "Yes, it was your brother's idea." I thought so. Well, here is the thing: I have a three-year-old daughter and a son who will be born soon, and I don't want to deploy now. He said he understood, "Mike, but the needs of the Navy." So I said, in that case, I would like to leave the Navy. He looked at me with this puzzled look on his face, "Are you crazy? You have 16 years in, you are a Senior Chief, and you just went up for Master Chief, and you want to walk away; you could stand on your head for four more years and retire as an E-9 with all your benefits."

He then asked me what I wanted him to do. I hoped you could message Washington, tell them you don't need me anymore, and reference this chapter in the BUPERS manual. He looked at the RIF chapter and said, "If I send this, you will be out in two weeks." That's awesome; I didn't know it could happen that fast. He said, "Okay, it's your career."

The following day, I checked the message board, and the message went out. Every day, I would check the board to see if there was any message regarding my request. One week, two weeks, and then a month passed with no answer. Finally, after the sixth month, there it was. It said, Senior Chief Michael Carroll, your services are no longer required after October 15, 1992! I couldn't believe it; I was a free man. I never intended to leave the Navy, especially after 16 years as an E-8. After the message traffic was seen by most of the commands, they asked me why. It was simple: my priorities changed. Then people would ask me when I found time to build a business that replaced my Navy pay threefold; I said, while you were sleeping.

At 35 years old, I became a full-time Dad and husband; on October 15, 1992, I drove across the Coronado Bridge and headed home after 16 years of serving in the Navy. It is the only world I have known since graduating high school.

Being a free Dad and husband was quite the adjustment. I would wake up and look at the clock, thinking I was late for work, then I'd remember that I didn't have to go to the base. I would sigh with relief but still feel guilty that I wasn't getting up to go to work. It was a bizarre feeling.

People would ask me what it felt like to be free. I would tell them it was like getting out of school for the summer, waking up with no schedule, and feeling like you could do whatever you wanted. If it was sunny and warm, you could go water skiing or surfing or play whatever outdoor sport you wanted to. My childhood summers were filled with things that I loved. But then, as the summer came closer and closer to ending, I would get this sick feeling that I had to return to something I hated and get up every morning.

Freedom as an adult was very similar; I could get up and do whatever I wanted, play with my daughter Kaitlin, put her in her bike carrier seat, and go mountain biking with her and Robin. Or saddle up the horses and go for a long trail ride. Whatever we wanted to do, we didn't need permission to do it. We could sit by the fireplace, make some comfort food, and watch a movie if it was cold and rainy.

The biggest difference between getting out for summer vacation and having to return was that we didn't have to experience that sick feeling that it was ending. Oh, what a feeling.

We were getting close to Michael's birth. I am very excited to bring him into the world and have a lifetime of joy raising my namesake. We were getting late into the pregnancy, and at our last appointment, the doctor told us to stay aware of his movements; he called it the ten-kick, and Robin should feel him kick ten times within two hours or so. The concern was that he might be running out of amniotic fluid. A few evenings later, Robin woke up in a panic and said she was bleeding and she hadn't felt Michael kick. We loaded up the car and headed to the hospital. I got Robin checked in, and they took her right away. After checking on her, I went to the hallway to make my first and only phone call. I said Joe, something is wrong with the baby; we are at the hospital. Joe said, "I will be right there; everything will be okay." Immediately, I had peace come over me.

About twenty minutes later, Joe walked into the hospital room; he looked like he had just gotten done showing the plan; he was dressed in his usual first-class fashion. I know I woke him because it was about 3 am when I called. Robin and baby Michael were both doing great. The sonogram confirmed that everything was okay, and he had another week to cook before he would arrive.

Joe's wife, Norma, later told us that Joe jumped from their bed and said I have to get to the hospital; while Joe was dressing, Norma was blow-drying his hair. I could picture Joe trying to put on his pants and Norma saying, Joe, stand still. You have a hair out of place. Nobody like Joe; he was always available; it didn't matter the time of night or day; he was always there when you needed him. God Bless you, Joe Foglio!

Two years later, our business reached the diamond level; we'd been renting a home in Rancho Bernardo. It was a lovely community but an excellent time to buy a house. We were living below our means and putting away money. Robin had started to ride horses in a town southeast of us called Alpine, which was up in the foothills of San Diego. We thought of being out of the hustle and bustle of the city and decided Alpine had what we were looking for. It reminded me of a Mayberry but with horses, like the T.V. show Andy Griffith.

We were looking at this one home, and after penciling it out, we thought we could afford it. We sat down with Joe and asked him if it would be wise to buy it. After the meeting, he said that we could go ahead and put in an offer. Robin and I walked away very excited about purchasing the home.

Early the following day, the phone rang; it was Joe. He said, "Mike, I couldn't sleep all night thinking about the home you want to buy." He said, "I don't have peace about it; I don't think you should buy it." I was relieved to hear that. I thought it was too much house for that time in our lives. I told Robin what Joe had said; I knew she was disappointed, but she knew it too deep down.

I called the realtor and told her we were not moving forward; she told us that it was okay and that she had another house to show us that she thought we would like. We told Joe about it, and he agreed to meet us there. As we drove up to this beautiful country home, surrounded by gorgeous oak trees, I felt like this was it. As we walked through it, it was evident that this would be our home. It had a horse corral with two paddocks and a tack barn that matched the house. The best part was that it was less than half the price of the home we had turned down.

Robin was pleased with the home and asked if we could make some changes; I said, Honey, for that price, we can make all the changes you want. I then asked Joe what he thought. He returned with one of his favorite lines, "If you don't buy it, I will." I bought cars I wish I never had because Joe said that, but I was glad he said it about this house. This became our house for 17 years, where we raised our kids.

Chapter Thirty-Two
Dead Stick

Along the journey of building our business, we sponsored my twin sister and her husband; they were the third leg of our emerald business. It was an excellent opportunity to return home to Wisconsin, where my Mom and Dad still lived, in the same house where I graduated from high school.

One evening, my brother-in-law and I jumped into a rental airplane; it was the same make and model airplane that I owned back in San Diego, so I was very familiar with the capability of this Champ Citabria two-seater tandem aircraft. We took off from Southern Wisconsin and headed north for a business meeting. It was in the middle of the winter, and the ground was blanketed with snow. From the sky, the landscape on the ground looked layered with cotton. We arrived safely and had a great meeting. After the meeting, we shook hands and ate the cookies. We got a ride to the airport. My brother-in-law and I jumped into the airplane, took off, and headed south back to Janesville.

The air was smooth with low luminescence; it was around 11:30 at night, and we were 20 minutes from landing, but something wasn't right; the engine started to run a little rough. Thinking it might be carburetor ice, I pulled the carb heat nob to melt any ice that might be accumulating. It didn't help, so I started to look for a possible place to land the plane if it quit. All I could see was the snow-covered ground where you have no idea what lurks below the snow.

Off in the distance, I spotted a freeway; it seemed to have low traffic on it. I dropped down to a lower altitude and headed for a better view. Suddenly, it got dead quiet; the engine just quit. Without experience with airplanes and thinking when the engine quits, the aircraft falls out of the sky like a rock. My brother-in-law said, "Oh crap," he didn't use the word crap, though. "Are we going to die?" I assured him that we weren't.

I then saw two police cars just past an overpass where they had someone pulled over. I thought, what a great place to land if I needed assistance. I aimed the plane right at the overpass, knowing this would be my major obstacle to avoid. My brother-in-law did not know what I was thinking, and he said, "Do you see that bridge?" I got it, I said. I ensured my glide slope was right on the bridge to turn my airspeed into lift and pop right over it in the last second.

As we got closer, my second concern started to reveal itself. I was starting to overrun the traffic; I needed to time it to carry enough airspeed to lift us over the bridge, but not too much so that I would run into a car. The other concern was a car not seeing us after landing and hitting us from behind.

As we closed on the bridge, I knew I had enough altitude and speed to land where I wanted. I picked up the nose, cleared the bridge, and sat down about 50 feet past the police cars. The landing was perfect, and there was an off-ramp right after I rolled out; I pulled onto the off-ramp just in time, and the cars behind me didn't run into us.

Rolling to a stop, the police car came roaring up to us as we were getting out of the plane. The police officer laughed; he said, "I have been doing this for 20 years and have never seen anything like that before. What's the problem?" By this time, I had realized it wasn't carb ice but a fuel issue. In cold weather, the engine produces more power and uses more fuel; I flew the same aircraft, the same distance, but in San Diego. Yes, a miscalculation on my part.

I told the police officer that I could be on my way if he could get a fuel truck here. He said, "That shouldn't be a problem." About that time, the other police car pulled up. The first police officer told him what was happening; the second officer said we have to check with the Federal Aviation Administration to see if you can take off from the freeway. Now I'm thinking they are not going to let me. I will have a truck come and have the airplane dismantled and trucked to an airport; this could be a long night. About ten minutes later, the police returned and said, "FAA says it's okay if the airplane is airworthy." I was thanking God for this happening in Wisconsin. The fuel truck pulled up and fueled the aircraft a few minutes later.

The police officer asked me, "Can you take off between that bridge and the next one," I assured him I could. He said, "Start your engine, and we will shut down the freeway and lead you back to the overpass bridge." I fired it up, and I looked up. The highway was lined with fire trucks, ambulances, and police cars; I wish I had had a smartphone with a camera back then. I followed two squad cars and taxied back to the bridge I had flown over. Getting to my takeoff point, I saluted the police officers, spun the aircraft doing a 180 and put the coals to it, picked up speed, and lifted off to look down at all the pretty red and blue lights; what a sight to behold. Thank you, Lord, for saving me once again!

I left Wisconsin and headed for northern Minnesota for the annual Snowmobile Extravaganza hosted by Bill Hawkins. This has been going on for 34 years; my first one started in 1995 after Joe Foglio built the bridge for some of the greatest associations I have ever experienced. Bill Hawkins, Brad Duncan, Bob Kummer, and Glenn Baker. It was one of Joe and I's favorite trips of the year. We would ride hard all day, and into the evening, we would hang out at one of the local establishments and play a dice game called 4,5,6. On this particular trip, I was feeling pretty good that I had escaped near death when the engine quit on the airplane and landed on the freeway without incident.

After playing some dice with our bellies full of fresh walleye, one of Minnesota's favorite fish, We took off from the Old Milwaukee Club, excited to return to Bill's place to play gin rummy and have some excellent ole belly laughs until our sides hurt. We were on the trail back and doing our usual competitive riding, racing with each other and jockeying for the number one poll position. I found myself in the lead and feeling the pressure from behind me, which, at the time, I thought was Brad Duncan.

I was riding on the edge of my limitations when suddenly there was a hairpin turn to the left; being caught off guard, I went to brake but missed the brake handle, which cost me a fraction of a second. It was too late to recover; the lost time caused me to get my outside ski off the trail and head into the woods at high speed. The front of the sled took out one small tree and then hit a large tree head-on. This launched me into the tree, with my shoulder taking the entire force. The riders behind me didn't see the accident; they rode past me until they realized I had disappeared. They did a 180 on the trail to backtrack on the trail. When they returned, all they saw was a light shining into the woods. When they reached my sled, I was nowhere to be seen until they saw me lying in front of the sled and the tree. I was lying there, moaning in pain. I wasn't sure what injuries I had, but my shoulder was killing me. The sled was severely damaged, but once again, I was happy that I didn't hit the tree with my head and was glad to be alive.

After I determined that the injury was probably just my shoulder, and not wanting to interrupt the Extravaganza, I decided not to get it checked. The worst part of the accident was my ego and pride were damaged. Bill has a plaque hanging with all the others for the Extravaganza. There is one award that no one likes to have: it hangs on the Wall of Shame. Anybody with more than $2500 damage gets their name on that plaque. To date, my name has been on there three times. When I think about that week of my life, having two events that could have been catastrophic: landing a plane on the freeway and running head-on into a tree on a snowmobile at high speed, I feel that my angels needed a vacation after watching over me during that week. Thank you, Lord!

Years later, I was doing my final physical from the Navy; they were taking the whole body X-rays to see if there were any old broken bones and whatever else they could see with the scans. After the results, they sat me down and asked me when I had broken my collarbone. The memory of hitting that tree came flooding back in. Knowing they wouldn't understand, I said I was unsure; it must have been a training accident. In a way, it was; I was training to be a better snowmobile rider. Like I said before, when you're dumb, you have to be tough.

Chapter Thirty-Three
God's Greatest Blessings

One of the greatest serendipities of being a full-time Dad and husband was that there was a quantity of time, which led to quality time. A part-time parent cannot say, "Hey, kids, let's have quality time; I have about fifteen minutes." It doesn't work that way. So many incredible memories happen; it's spontaneous. If you're not around, you miss many of those funny Moments that your kids do when they are just being kids.

The spiritual advisor of our support group, Paul Tsika, says that you have to build a bridge with trust; trust comes from being part of people's lives where there are opportunities to build that relationship of trust. If you're not building the bridge with that trust, it collapses when it's time to drive over it with a truck full of truth. Sometimes, children won't listen to their parents because, at different ages, children believe that they know more than their parents. But as they get older, because you built that bridge of trust, they will listen when they need you.

Robin and I had the great fortune to see and get this incredible opportunity. It has given us the life that most people have never imagined. I certainly never imagined that I could have this life, being able to experience each of our three children the way we have. Kaitlin was born in 1989, and I was still working at the SEAL team for her first three years. Even though I wasn't a full-time Dad to Kaitlin, my mindset and priorities shifted. I learned that my life wasn't about just me anymore. I stopped being a pleasure-seeking fool. I turned my life from pleasure to purpose. I knew that raising children would be one of the most significant responsibilities I would ever have. This was the next generation, and it was up to Robin and I to make sure we did our part with the contribution to this world.

Trust me, though, when I say we made many mistakes, our children would be the first to tell you. We had never raised a child before our first; nobody has. So we go on to the examples of our parents or lack thereof. Until you are given tools and see examples from people who have done it successfully, you are doing what you know, which isn't always the right way. Joe Foglio always told me, "Mike, check the fruit on the tree before you follow somebody else in any endeavor."

Kaitlin was a lot like me, strong-willed and sometimes non-compliant. She wanted to do things her way. Kaitlin and I had some great times together; unbeknownst to me, she was a Daddy's girl. Kaitlin did not like sharing her parents with her baby brother, Michael, when he was born in 1992. She was physically and mentally upset. As long as I can remember, from Michael's birth, they did not get along.

One pleasant summer day, they played outside, and Kaitlin had filled a bucket with water. She had it up in the rainbow play system and then coaxed Michael to come up the slide to play with her. Michael was around two and Kaitlin five; Michael was still trusting and gullible with his sister. When Michael was halfway up the slide, Kaitlin unleashed this bucket full of water on Michael's head. This was the beginning of their sibling war.

No matter how many heartfelt talks I had with Kaitlin, she believed I had more favor over Michael than she did. It probably didn't help that Michael wanted to spend all his time with his Dad; maybe it was his diabolical plan to make his sister's life miserable. No, that couldn't be.

Michael was a month and a half old when I left the Navy to become a full-time Dad. He was an adorable baby and seemed to be very compliant. He learned early that everybody thought he was cute, which he was. He had a sweet, tender spirit about him, but he used these God-given gifts to his advantage along the way. Michael could talk his way out of anything. I was of the disciplined way of thinking; If I believed my child was being rebellious and it took a little more than talking and a time out, I brought out the wooden spoon for a little more reinforcement. I worked hard not to spank out of anger but with love but not with tenderness. Tenderness and spanking don't go together.

He had a way of convincing me that we should talk about his indiscretion; he would learn from me just talking. He would say, "Dad, can we talk about this?" Believe it or not, he would convince me that, in this particular case, talking would be fine. He was very convincing.

Very early in Michael's life, he had this gift of gab. He was about three when he was over at the neighbors playing, and they had this old antique Mercedes pedal car. The father came over and told us that Michael had taken a hammer and beat this metal car into submission, putting dents all over it. I wasn't home then, so Robin told the neighbor she would take care of this. Michael proceeded to explain that he had nothing to do with this accusation. He was utterly innocent, with tears rolling down his face, swearing that he had not done this heinous act. Michael was convinced that Robin had gone next door and told the neighbor there was no way that Michael could have done such a thing. The neighbor looked Robin right in the eye and said, "Robin, I watched him do it." From that point on, we had Michael's number. He had a gift that needed to be groomed and guided.

I said in the preface that I didn't know how the public would perceive this manuscript, but as I write, this will be great to be passed down to my children and children's children. They're gonna love this chapter, or maybe not.

Mike and Robin's children, Kaitlin, Michael, and Christian

Our third and last child came to us in 1996. Christian was born June 17; he was the quietest of the three unless Michael picked on him, and then he became quite vocal. Christian liked to take things apart to see how they worked. When he was about four years old, I remember seeing him on the driveway with a wrench, taking his training wheels off. A few minutes later, he was riding down the driveway successfully with no training wheels. Now Christian is 26 years old and still very handy with his hands.

It is still amazing that the same parents can raise three children in the same home, and all of them can be different. They will differ in many ways but perceive what they hear differently. It's like that game, Telephone, when you whisper a simple message into someone's ear, and they are to repeat it into the next person's ear; after ten people or so, hearing supposedly the same thing, the message is different.

I have found this to be true: raising three children, Kaitlin, Michael, and Christian, are all different. They are all adults. During this writing, Michael has become a great man, utilizing his God-given talents for good. He is married to a wonderful woman, Toni. She is a great wife, and the mother of our first grandchild, and his name is Michael Kelly Carroll. It is the same as mine if you didn't notice it on the front cover. If your son can convince his wife to name their first child after his Dad, I feel I did something right. To me, that is saying something, just saying.

Chapter Thirty-Four
Tower of Terror

Do you remember what you were doing and how you learned about 9/11? I do. I had just woken up and made coffee like I did every morning. While waiting for it to brew, I checked my voicemail, and Joe's voice came on. All I could hear was, "Oh my God, oh my God! Turn on your T.V." The only one I had at the time was a little portable Sony with a pull-out antenna, no bigger than a small radio. I had to find it first; it was shoved into one of the cabinets. I pulled it out, plugged it in, turned it on, and about that time, the second aircraft was flying into the second twin tower.

The entire country knew it was a terrorist attack on our nation, and all I felt was anger. I couldn't believe what my eyes were seeing. Never in my lifetime had I witnessed an attack on our soil, especially from an enemy without a face or country. I felt helpless and knew I needed to return to the SEAL team and help however I could. I had been out of the Navy for nine years. Without saying anything to Robin, I went down to the local Navy recruiting office and started the process of re-enlisting. I was 44 but still in good shape, or so I thought.

After starting the process, I realized that it would be a long shot to be taken back, and even more so, I knew that I was wrong about not wanting to say anything to Robin; I didn't want to worry her about the slight possibility of getting back in and going to war. But all I could think about was that I wanted to get in this fight.

The process landed me in front of the same Naval Special Warfare doctor who was in place the day I left the military. So we knew each other. He said, "Mike, I see you had a problem with your left hip when you left." He was right, and it was progressively getting worse; I couldn't do anything requiring a lateral movement, and when I walked, I looked like a 100-year-old man. When I walked into his office initially, I put on my best game face and walked as straight as I could, hoping I could mask my eroding hip.

I lied. I told him it was a nerve acting up, but it was all good now. He said, "Let me see you do some duck walking around the room." Duck walking is when you squat down and then move around without getting up. I couldn't do it, and my hip hurt too badly. He said," Mike, we would love to have you, but you would be a liability. Thanks for trying, though."

I went home defeated, thinking this was not meant to be. I learned from being a Christian that before deciding to do or not do something, I should ask God: if you want me to do this, open the door; if you don't, close the door and leave no doubt. Well, God shut the door, and there was no doubt.

For the next couple of years, my hip continued to get worse. When my friends would see me walk, they grimaced at the look of pain on my face. They asked if there was anything the doctors could do to fix my hip. My doctors told me that I was too young to have a replacement, especially in that replacements only last about 10-15 years, and then what? So I continued to grin and bear it.

I watched my Mom suffer from back pain my whole life; she had polio when she was pregnant with my sister and me. My Mom was a great example of grit, especially raising eight kids and dealing with her pain the way she did, never complaining. Well. she put that grit in me!

In 2004, I was sitting in a coffee shop and checking my voicemails when I got one from a business associate. He started by saying, "Hey

Mike, I am reading this article in this Men's Journal magazine, and there is this article about this 40-plus-year-old guy who had some procedure done on his hip called hip resurfacing; there is a picture of him dropping into this half pipe on a skateboard. You should pick the magazine up; it's a good read." I was next door to a Barnes and Noble, so I found the magazine, read the article, I called 1-800 to fix me, and set an appointment in January 2004.

I drove to Los Angeles to meet with a doctor from The Joint Resurfacing Institute. After X-rays, I was led into an examining room to wait for the ortho. A few minutes later, this tall doctor, about 6 ft 5, walked in. He said, "I am Dr Schmalzried. Mike, I have some good news and bad; which would you like first?" I said give me the bad. "Mike, you have two bad hips; the good news is I can fix you. Let's schedule your left one, which is the worst one, in March, then six months later, we can do the right one."

That's like going through surgery and recovery twice. He then told me that insurance did not cover the operations because they were still considered experimental. He said, "I'll give you a twofer—forty thousand for both." I inquired about performing both surgeries at once. "You were a Navy SEAL? In that case, you could handle it."

As I drove back down to San Diego that day, I was filled with hope that I could be normal and pain-free. There is nothing like living with chronic pain. The human body and mind are amazing in adapting and continuing even when you live with the pain, day in and day out.

I was scheduled for surgery on March 22, 2004. I had to make the down payment to schedule the surgery; it was $13,000, so the balance was $27k. I had the money, but 40 grand is still 40 grand, especially when I had insurance that wouldn't cover the procedure. The hospital told me to appeal the denial, which I did to no avail. Then, they suggested that I appeal to the California Board of Insurance. So, I wrote a friendly letter talking about my young family and how I was inhibited from my hips to give my family the quality of life they deserve.

On March 22, as the nurses were prepping me for surgery, they brought up the unpaid balance. I told Robin to give the nurse our Southwest Airlines credit card. I had to get on the phone to approve the transaction. After I paid in full, they rolled me in, seven hours of surgery, and then recovery. I woke up in my hospital room and immediately had to test these new hips. There was one simple thing I couldn't do before the surgery. I could not put my knees together because there was no cartilage, and my hips did not have that range. I put my knees together easily; I couldn't believe it. I started to cry; even after seven hours of surgery, I felt no significant pain. I had a morphine pump that allowed me to push the button if the pain became unbearable; I didn't need it. I hadn't felt pain-free in years.

The next day, I woke up to a phone call from the California Board of Insurance. "Is this Michael Kelly Carroll? We are informing you that your insurance company's decision not to insure you for your surgery has been overturned. They will pay for the entire procedure and all associated bills." Not only did I have two brand new hips, but I was 40,000 dollars richer and had another 27,000 air miles. Oh, happy day!

After six weeks on crutches, I could resume all physical activity. After discussing my limitations with the doctor, he said there were no restrictions and that I should train before I ran or rode a long race. I couldn't believe the improvement in my quality of life. I was out in the front playing football with my kids. After all those years of not even being able to play a game of HORSE basketball, I was now sprinting around on grass barefoot like a teenager.

I continued to train and work for the next two years like I always did. I hadn't thought of returning to the Navy since I was turned down after 9/11. The War on Terror had continued, and I was curious to hear what the boys were doing down range in the last five years.

In July of 2006, I attended a SEAL Reunion. Every year, they have a reunion on both the East and West coasts to get all the old Frogs and SEALs together for a big gathering; it lasts all weekend long, with different events each day. On Saturday morning, they have a briefing to let all the guys know what their active brothers are doing down range fighting the War on Terror. After sitting there and listening, the same feeling I got on 9/11 raised its head again. I walked out of that briefing thinking again, I want to get in this fight. As you read this, I'm sure many of you warriors thought the same.

I knew it was a long shot, but I had to give it one more try. My hips worked great, but they were still metal prostheses, and I would turn fifty years old on my next birthday. I went to the same recruiting office and asked one of the recruiters what kind of a chance I had. He said, "Not much, but let's give it a go." He completed the paperwork and set up the physical at the MEPs station, where the military provides the candidates with their qualifying physicals.

I reported to the station and went from one room to the next for each type of exam. First was a comprehensive physical to see if I would be a liability, forcing the government to pay for it in the future. When you qualify and swear in, you are the property of the U.S. government and are now their responsibility. After going through each department, I was stamped "disqualified" unless authorized by the signature of some higher authority. Each department head would say, "Man, somebody must want you bad." I didn't know what they meant. I returned to the recruiting office and asked the recruiter what was happening. He told me that my record would be sent to BUMED, Bureau of Medicine and Surgery; this is the governing agency of the Navy for all medical situations regarding Navy service members or candidates in question and whether or not they can serve.

I asked him if there was a phone number I could call to plead my case. He said, "No one calls BUMED; he is like the almighty OZ, nobody gets to talk to him, and you will have to wait on their decision." A few days later, I received a voice message on my cell phone. It said, "Mike Carroll, this is Captain Jim Bowen. Please call me on my cell, at work, or at home, and left me his numbers. I had no idea who this man was, but he wanted to talk to me since he gave me every phone number he had."

I called him back. "Mike, what the hell are you trying to do? I have your medical record in front of me." At this point, I now knew that Captain Bowen was with BUMED's office. He said, "You're not trying to run away to the beach away from Robin, are you?" My eyes widened. How does he know Robin? After assuring him that Robin and I were fine, he told me that he and Frank Radford used to run down the Silver Strand beach together and that he was in Franks's business. He heard me speak at an FED and would never question my patriotism. "Mike, I am looking at your record, and it appears you want to return to the Navy. What do you want to do, an admin job or what?" I said Captain, I want to kick down doors and find the bad guys. I was still a little angry after 9/11. He stamped my file R1, meaning I was fit for full operational SEAL team duty.

I remembered my prayer: God, if you don't want me to serve in the Navy, please close the door and close it hard. Please open the door if it is your will for me to serve. What are the chances that the decision was in the hands of somebody who understood and knew who I was?

Please don't judge me, but since I thought it was such a long shot, I hadn't told anyone, including Robin. I did not want her to worry about something that would probably not come to pass. Now that I had confirmed this would happen, I still had time before enlisting to get counsel and permission from Robin. I knew once in, I would work up and deploy with a SEAL team. When I let it be known that I was trying to get back in, my old buddy Rico reached out, wanting to get together for lunch. He was now the Captain of SEAL Team Five, deploying his team to Iraq in about three weeks.

He drove up to Alpine. "Mike, are you seriously considering returning? If you can do this during this deployment cycle, I could bring you over to be with SEAL Team Five." Then he interjected, "If you get killed on my watch, Robin will kill me." We both laughed, but we both knew it could happen. Iraq was still a dangerous place.

After explaining to Robin what I wanted to do, she was physically upset but tried to see it from my point of view. She reached out to our Pastor, Joe Foglio's brother Tony. They were on the phone for a while, and I was curious about their conversation. After getting off the phone, I asked Robin what he had said. Pastor Tony said, "Four years is very short to last Mike a lifetime."

That seemed to give Robin some peace; she still didn't like the idea of me going to war at 50. I reached out to Joe, and he was concerned but supportive. I hadn't sworn in, so I was still a civilian. We had our FED in October 2006, and Robin and I had an opportunity to host Paul and Billie Tsika. I explained to them what was in the works. Both being Marines during the Viet Nam conflict, Paul and Billie could relate to what I wanted to do. Paul is a warrior; he said, "Mike, anybody that has never served in the military will not understand what you are doing and don't expect their support." He had contemplated returning to service himself after 9/11 but knew there was no chance at 60 years old. After talking to Paul, my thoughts were validated, and I had more peace about the decision I was about to make.

The paperwork was taking a little longer than I had anticipated. We continued living as usual, building our business, caring for our kids, and living. In November 2006, we were off to this business achievers in Orlando, Florida. This business trip is the free trip that the direct sales coorporation sends us to every year. Orlando, Florida, has always been one of our favorite locations because we would bring our kids to enjoy all that Disney and Universal have to offer. While in Orlando our support group would also host a three day event where all the leaders would stay several days later for more fun and evening leadership meetings.

We were having a ball. The kids, Robin, and I were enjoying Universal Studios. We had just boarded the Tower of Terror ride; in our seats, the elevator was starting to go up when my phone rang. The San Diego recruiter called me to say my approval paperwork had arrived. I needed to drive to the Orlando Navy Recruiting station ASAP to swear in and sign my enlistment papers. After getting off the ride, I told Robin and the kids what I had to do. I dropped them at the hotel and drove downtown to the Navy recruiting station.

Upon arrival, the local recruiter greeted me and led me into the office, where they were already with the enlistment papers. I have to be honest; I was not nervous or excited about what I would do. Subconsciously, I wanted to do this since 9/11; something happened that day in me that I couldn't shake. Maybe it was the same kind of feeling my Dad felt when Pearl Harbor was attacked. 9/11 was the second time in history that we were attacked on our homeland in such a large scale.

The officer in charge asked me to raise my right hand. "I, Mike Carroll, do solemnly swear that I will support and defend the Constitution of the United States against all enemies, foreign and domestic; that I will bear true faith and allegiance to the same; and that I will obey the orders of the President of the United States and the orders of the officers appointed over me, according to regulations and the Uniform Code of Military Justice. So help me God."

I took that oath multiple times during my first 16 years of service; every time a member re-enlists, they must swear in again. This time, I felt like it meant something; I was swearing in as a patriot!

That evening at our emerald club meeting, I shared with Dick Davis what I was doing and asked him if I could share my journey on how I had come to this decision about what I had just committed to. He asked Ron Puryear, who thought it would be a good idea. Halfway through the meeting, they brought me up to share what and why I was re-enlisting. I want to say that all well received it, but it wasn't. Like Paul Tsika said, "They wouldn't understand nor support it."

At the time, it was painful to see the reactions of some of the people who were my friends and for whom I had the most profound respect. I can look back on it now and understand why they didn't understand what I was doing then. They probably thought I was running away from the business and going to play soldier boy, never to return, and I am sure they were all concerned for my safety. They didn't know and couldn't tell that I had a vision to build this business until the day I died, God willing. I wasn't going anywhere.

Ron Puryear was the one opinion that truly meant so much to me besides that of my mentor and coach, Joe Foglio. Ron had me send him a voicemail that he tagged and released to the entire organization. I still have that voice message in my favorite saved file. Ron is gone now, and when I'm missing him, I play that message; it is my favorite all-time message. That was one of the most pivotal times and decisions I made in my life, and to have the support and reverence that Ron gave me meant so much, and I will never forget.

Chapter Thirty-Five
Training For War

Not long after returning from Orlando, I received orders to TRADET, Training detachment. The powers that be thought that would be a great place to put me since I hadn't had eyes on SEAL operations since 1992, plus we had been at war since 2001. There is a vast difference in training between peacetime and war. The training is more intense to replicate war-like conditions. A lot of changes had been made since I was last in. One of them was that Naval Special Warfare had a pretty good budget and spared no expense for the equipment and training. SEALs had proved themselves in Vietnam, but being at war since 9/11, they had now proved they were a force to be reckoned with. The footprint size on the battlefield was small compared to the force multiplier that SEALs provided.

When I reported to the command, I was told I would work in the Department of Mobility, where the task units went through one of the last training phases before deploying down range into battle. Some of the training was as realistic as it could get. The simulations of the urban towns they would fight in were very realistic. The mock-up looked just like an Iraqi town. Cars were burning in the streets, farm animals were roaming around, and Iraqi role players looked like the families you would see down range. You could tell there wasn't any cost spared to give our guys the most realistic experience that they would have when they arrived in the Country.

I was introduced to Chris Kyle during that time. Later on, the movie American Sniper would be based on his life. But at this time, we both lived in Alpine and hit it off with that commonality. He seemed like a good old boy from Texas. His task unit was going through the mobility training where I was. A part of mobility was to teach the guys how to react if their patrol was ambushed, initiated by an IED (improvised explosive device), which was a huge problem and weapon of choice by our enemy.

The scenario was that their platoon would roll into town with their Humvees; at a predetermined place, one of their Humvees would be disabled electronically to simulate an IED; they would then have to react and get the guys out of the Humvee that was blown up and get off the X. X being the ground zero of the attack. As they rolled in, I prepared for the attack in a second-story building right above the center of the ambush. I was part of the Opposing Force (OPFOR). The enemy would be engaging the platoon to simulate the attack. All forces would be using our standard weapons, except we would be firing sim rounds (simulated rounds, steel balls, replaced with paintballs).

Even though it is all simulated and training, the adrenaline is real. The environment, the smell, and the optics all contribute to bringing your senses to almost accurate levels, which is the best preparation for the real deal. The anticipation was building on both elements, friend and foe. The platoon knew what would happen but didn't know where and how many would attack. As they were rolling in, coming closer and closer, then all at once, the Humvee was disabled, and a machine gun fired upon their vehicles; the sound was equal to actual rounds being fired, and the platoon knew they were under attack and needed to react quickly before they had the full force of the ambush element on them.

I noticed one of the vehicles was stopped right below where I was perched in the second-story window; seated in the navigator seat, out stepped Chris, ready to suppress the fire and neutralize any threat on his platoon. Immediately, I started to fire on Chris, hearing the hits on his body armor and knowing exactly where it was coming from. He did a 180-degree turn and, without hesitation, fired a round and hit me right in the face shield. I was neutralized; therefore, I was out of the fight. I thought that was a badass shot. Chris: God Bless Chris Kyle, a true American hero. RIP!

After serving at TRADET for several months, it was time to report to SEAL Team One to prepare for the Iraq deployment. I was attached to task Unit 2, which would be deployed to Ramadi, one of the Country's hottest areas. When I got to Team One, I was interviewed by the Captain. After the interview, he said he had an important job for me. I believe he saw in me what he was looking for. I was a good age to relate to the Sheiks; age meant wisdom in their culture. I could communicate confidently, a skill set I learned from our business support organization.

There was a shift in the battle plan at the time to start winning the hearts and minds of the Iraqi people. They called it Tribal Engagement. He said a great awakening was going on, and it was beginning in the Anbar province. There was a Sheik Sattar who had started this movement. He had a large following, but he was upsetting the apple cart of the insurgency that Al Qaeda was driving.

There was some coverage on the news with him and President Bush. If there was leadership in Iraq that believed the U.S. was in their Country to help the people, it could turn the tide against the insurgency that wanted to fill the vacuum that was created when Saddam Hussein was removed from power. There were a lot of casualties of war on both sides that could be lowered when the people of Iraq knew which side to stand on.

Tribal Engagement, in a nutshell, was to build relationships with the Sheiks of the villages and persuade them that we were there to improve the lives of their people. This could be done by finding out their needs and then filling them. By showing that we cared, we would win them over to our side, and in turn, they would provide valuable intel on who and where the bad guys were. I was honored to be tasked to be the Tribal Engagement guy for Task Unit Two, Charlie Platoon. This was in my wheelhouse because of the skills I learned from my business support group in the 20 years of building our business. The mission was to build relationships with the Sheiks through communicating and connecting, which is what we do to build our business.

I had several months to prepare, studying the different provinces, who the Sheiks were, and their history. The villages were broken out into three categories. One was red, which meant they were non-compliant and could be dangerous, but they had to be convinced, and we had to try to get them at least in the following category: yellow. This was neutral and probably not too risky. The last one was green, very compliant, willing to help, and would be very helpful. The Sheiks in the green hated Al Qaeda because of the personal experience they had through intimidation and murder.

I was excited about getting a chance to work directly with Sheik Sattar, President Bush's go-to guy in Iraq, whom he could rely on to help the Iraqi people realize the American soldiers were there for them. One of the tools the insurgency used was to convince the Iraqi people that we were evil and that we were there to take from and hurt their people. The insurgents would pay young teenage kids to place IEDs to kill American soldiers. If the kids wouldn't do it, they would threaten to destroy their family members. So, the Iraqi people were between a rock and a hard place.

Our job was to train the village's people to secure their area by showing them how to protect their homes against Al Qaeda. About three weeks before we were going to deploy, we got news that a car bomb killed Sheik Sattar. President Bush's most prominent advocate was dead, which would make it harder for us to do our job. Knowing that Sheik Sattar's followers would now be scared to work with us when we got down range was concerning. I was also disappointed that I would not get a chance to work with a true hero who was willing to go all in for his Country and who was willing to die for his cause.

When SEAL Team Five returned from deployment, I had a chance to meet with my close friend Rico, who, if you remember, was the Captain of Seal Team 5. Before heading down range, I went to his office to discuss their deployment and learn as much as possible. It was encouraging when he told me how excited he was when I told him I would be the tribal engagement guy for SEAL Team One. He believed in the shift in the battle plan, which was to win hearts and minds instead of having gun fights with the Iraqi people who were convinced that we were terrible. Rico knew that the T.E. piece was the tool that could change everything. After leaving his office, I believed I was in the right time of history and could make a difference. Maybe I was naive, but thinking one can make a difference was good.

The task unit continued to train and prepare for deployment. I had a lot of catching up to do. People asked me about the most significant change I noticed when I left in 1992. Everything had batteries; I had to learn to turn my weapon system on. There were switches all over that M4—different optics for every situation, day, night, and everything else.

I also noticed that peacetime training was a massive contrast from wartime training. There was more live fire training than using the blank firing device. We used this back in the day to give you the realism of sound with no rounds being shot. It was an apparatus that screwed on the end of the barrel that would cause the gas from the blank round to cycle the weapon for semi-automatic and auto.

There was a progression in training that started with the crawl, then a walk, and then to a run pace. This allowed the transition from sim rounds (paintball) to live rounds, making the training as accurate as possible. Wartime training brought another level of risk.

The brotherhood in the teams still seems to be there, except it was very competitive and more political than I remembered from the first go around. The primary reason was that the Naval Special Warfare SEAL team had created their rate as Special Operators. The Navy comprises different job descriptions and is organized by rates. In those rates, you compete with your peers by subject matter expertise, which was decided by a rate-specific test and your evaluation or fitness report, like a year-end review.

Before SEAL teams had their rate, we had what they called source ratings; for example, I was trained as a Hull Technician, as I explained earlier. So, I competed with my Hull Technician peers in the entire Navy. Since SEAL teams had the brotherhood of watching over each other and knowing we were at a disadvantage because we didn't work in those jobs, our expertise could have been more extensive. Our leaders would boost our fitness report to give us an advantage. It was still up to the individual to study the material to do well on the test.

The political environment changed after implementing the Special Operator rate, so we fought against it. Since the SEAL community is so tiny compared to the rest of the Navy, there were only so many leadership positions at the higher enlisted ranks. Other than that, it still had the camaraderie and brotherhood it always had. It became apparent that you would fight for your brother on the left and right when you went down range.

It was a great feeling to be back in the teams. The training was something that I had missed during those fourteen years of being a civilian, but there was no comparison with the training and time I got to bring to my kids. I would not trade that for anything. Being away for that long and then having the opportunity to come back during the

War on Terror was something that I will never forget. I feel very fortunate that I could have my cake and eat it, too.

All training and prep work were complete. Soon, we would load the C17 aircraft and head to Iraq, but there were some goodbyes I had to say before I did. First, I had to prepare our business team and cast a vision for them to run on why I was away. I got with Joe Foglio, and we devised a plan to unite our entire organization. Joe was going to show the plan, and after, we would let the team know how important their mission was while I was down range completing my mission. We called the meeting Operation Iraq Freedom. We wanted them to feel a part of the cause, and their part was to work hard at their operation freedom.

It was well received; they knew I was not running off without knowing when I returned; it was business as usual. While I was gone, Joe, Norma, and Robin would continue the fight in our organization. I can't thank Joe and Norma enough for their leadership and how they stood in the gap for the Carroll organization while I was away. However, the one person who had the most challenging job of all was Robin.

The military is highly trained to go to war. Still, the spouses of military personnel are not trained to be left behind and hold down the household, kids, and all the other responsibilities. Maybe in my next book, I will give tell you all of the crap Robin had to put up with while I was gone; she can assist with that story; it might be a book in itself and be a best seller.

The hardest part of this operation was the goodbyes to my dear, dear family. Robin and the kids drove me to North Island Air Base in Coronado. We had some time while the aircrew was fueling and loading all the pallets onto the plane. As the time got closer to me having to board with all of the task unit's personnel, it became evident that this would be very difficult.

I got a wave signaling me it was time; there was no easy way to do this. I started with my youngest Christian; he was reticent but strong; he gave the hug that he usually gave me, the same hug he gives me now, like hugging a cat. Michael, on the other hand, I knew he would take it the hardest; he has always been a sensitive-spirited kid who loved spending time with his Dad. He hugged me and didn't want to let go. Kaitlin, our oldest, was a little between the two; she was strong but not over-the-top emotional. It's incredible how different they all are. Robin has a tough exterior, but the longer I've been married to her, the more I realize she has a very compassionate and soft soul. Robin hugged me and said goodbye like I was going to the grocery store down the street. I never really got the true story about how they acted after the C17 rolled down the runway, taking their Daddy and husband off to war in Iraq.

Chapter Thirty-Six
Tribal Engagement

On our way to Iraq, our C-17 needed to make a fuel stop. Our leading officers told us that we would have approximately four hours on the ground to hang out in the terminal or walk into the town and see the countryside of Germany on this beautiful, warm fall day. Not knowing what would be available in town, several of us thought it better to take a walk, take our chances on a nothing burger, or sit around for four hours in the terminal, an easy choice. Not knowing how long it would be before we could enjoy a vacation or two, we were committed to taking that chance. So off to town, we went; after about thirty minutes, we stumbled across this quaint little bar and cafe. It was just the ticket we were hoping for. We ordered some food and beer, and we were not disappointed.

A couple of the guys already had a couple of deployments to Iraq, and we talked about what we could expect when we arrived. After about an hour or so of great German food and beer, we were ready to head back to the airport for the final leg into Iraq.

After another eight hours in the air, we arrived at TQ, short for Al Taqaddum, about an hour's drive from Ramadi, where our Task Unit would be based for our deployment. We only knew it was dark, and the SEALS would be transiting from TQ to Ramadi using Humvees with Team Seven leading us. All the support personnel would travel by air the next day during daylight.

We all jocked up and got ready to move out. I climbed into my designated Humvee, and we started to roll. The thought came to me:

244

we weren't in Kansas anymore, Toto. We had just arrived in a combat zone, not knowing what lurked in the darkness waiting for us. For almost a year, I prepared for the worst but hoped for the best, pouring over intel reports and AAR (After Action Reports) on what was happening in this God-forsaken place. I signed up for this, so let's get on with it.

You could tell everybody was in a heightened state called living in the red. Heads are on a swivel, looking for anything that wants to harm you. During that time of the war, the weapon of choice for the enemy was IEDs, Improvised Explosive Devices. There were more casualties caused by these devices than anything else. Our forces proved that the enemy didn't stand a chance in a firefight, so they chose the cowardly method, planting IEDs under the concealment of darkness on the roads that we needed to travel on.

It is one thing to battle in a gunfight; we are well trained for that, but to fight something you can't see and knowing you can't protect yourself when it comes is a different story. I can't train for it; it's hard to prepare mentally. I must admit that my prayer life increased while I was in the country.

Our military forces worked hard to mitigate this threat with high-tech equipment used to sweep the roads looking for IEDs. But to me, it was like a snow plow clearing the roads. What happens when you get another heavy snowfall after the plow comes through? The enemy knows that if they see the road being swept, a convoy will follow soon. So after the sweep moves through, they lay the IEDs. Needless to say, traveling in Iraq is very unnerving.

The other known threat was sniper fire; whenever you stepped out of a building or vehicle, your eyes were scanning the rooftops; it was just something that became second nature. Sniper fire was a concern, but not as much as the IED threat. Even the enemy snipers learned that it wasn't a good idea to take that shot, knowing they might get a JDAM

(Joint Direct Attack Munition) dropped on their head. By the time I got there, the enemy had learned survival tactics, and their primary weapon of choice was the IED.

Just arriving in the area, no one from our team knew what the threats were; it could change daily. So we were traveling from TQ to Ramadi, hopefully, ready for whatever would come our way. And that should be the mindset; complacency has proved to be a killer in all wars.

About an hour later, our convoy of platoons rolled into the famous Shark base. This was the base in Ramadi, where the SEAL task units were based. Camp Mark Lee was named after the first SEAL to lose his life in Operation Iraqi Freedom when he was killed in a firefight in Ramadi.

I stepped out of my Humvee at Camp Mark Lee; I felt like I was walking on hollowed ground. Just a year before my arrival, there was a huge fight called the Battle of Ramadi. There were 94 Americans killed, along with 34 from other countries.

Right before I was formally enlisted back into the Navy, I had attended a memorial service for Michael Monsoor, who was also killed in Ramadi, saving his teammates by jumping on a grenade and shielding them from the blast. He was awarded the Medal of Honor posthumously. I was walking on the same ground, using the same equipment these heroes were walking and using just the previous year.

I had read about this great battle and learned it led to the Anbar Awakening I wrote about earlier. Sheik Sattar formed the Anbar Salvation Council, the alliance of the Sunni Tribes. Taking a stand against the insurgency, he was killed for his brave actions by his enemies. My primary job was to assist in the work he had started by building relationships with the Tribal Sunni leaders who were part of the alliance. I knew this would be a considerable task and felt very overwhelmed. But I learned from being a Navy SEAL that you have to start and not quit. That evening, rolling onto that sacred ground was my start.

After settling into my designated tent, I got a tour of the camp to become familiar with the essentials, chow hall, briefing room, and which of the Humvees I would be using for my tribal engagement operations. I was pretty much left to myself to plan and make things happen. I had a map of the different villages and the tribal leaders of the Anbar province. I was introduced to the SEAL, which was to turn over the tribal engagement mission. He would brief me on who was who in the zoo—bringing me up to date on his progress since his time in the area.

As I explained earlier, the tribal leaders were designated red, yellow, and green. Red was not compliant, yellow was somewhat compliant, and green was totally with us on moving the great awakening forward.

In the first part of the war in Iraq, when Saddam Hussein was taken out of power, there was a power vacuum. Any time this happens, there is going to be a force that will try to fill that void. In this case, it was the Al Qaeda terrorist group that was seeking to fill that void. Through intimidation and murder of the Iraqi people, they were gaining a pretty good foothold. Early in the war, the Iraqi people didn't know who was good or bad.

I am telling you what I was taught before heading down range and what I experienced there. Some of you might read this and wonder if that is correct. I will tell it like I experienced it from my point of view and not as a history lesson.

The way I understood my mission was to build relationships with the tribal Sheiks and the ones that were in the yellow and red, trying to get them to know that we were there to help them improve the quality of life for themselves and their village. Basically, win the hearts and minds.

The other piece was to train the people of their village how to protect themselves against Al Qaeda, who were intimidating through torture, murder, or paying kids to plant IEDs and take up arms against the Allie forces. If we could train and equip their people to protect and fight for themselves, that would be a win-win for all.

After getting my turnover brief from my SEAL brother, my first engagement would be with Sheik Ahmed, Sheik Sattar's brother, who took over as leader of the Anbar Salvation Council. When we rolled into his compound one evening, the SEAL team platoon was escorted into his office. The entire platoon poured into his office, loaded for war, wondering how he would respond to this unscheduled visit. His attitude and arrogance took me back; it was nothing like what I had read about his brother, Sheik Sattar. It was a total power play. Here, the elite SEAL platoon entered his office to assist and be an extension of our Commander In Chief, who did not even look up or stand up to greet us. This was my first introduction to what I would have to deal with during my time in Iraq.

We accomplished nothing that night; maybe our appearance of being there did something, but it's hard to tell. After letting us sit there for about ten minutes, he stared into his computer, acting like he had something important to do before acknowledging our presence. There was some small talk, and my platoon OIC (Officer in Charge) introduced me as his liaison and said that I would be dropping in on him soon. We shook hands; I noticed there was a coolness about him. My job would be to warm up his cool somehow.

That would be my only introduction to the Sheiks, and I would be building relationships and working to get them more on our side. Once on our side, they would be helping us with actionable intel on the bad actors in their area. This was another advantage of the Tribal Engagement mission.

The following week, I planned for my first mission, assembling a crew of some of the personnel from our SEAL platoon. They were always ready to get some if they had the chance. There would be enough to man three humvees. This was our requirement. A crew no less than that in case we run into trouble. We had one 50 Cal. gunner in the Humvee turret, and the rest loaded for whatever.

My first mission would be with Sheik Ahmed. I would never give a warning or notice that we would visit. One didn't know who was friendly; if you gave notice, there was always a possibility that they could tell somebody who told somebody and...

We rolled in during broad daylight, parked our Humvees, set security around our vehicles, and proceeded toward his office by escort. Upon entering his office, he was a little warmer; he stood up and met me halfway across his office, with his hand welcoming and shaking mine. He had us take our seats. Five SEALs and the interpreter were in the office. Sheik Ahmed asked us if we would like some tea, and of course, we all said yes. I hated the tea; it was like pure sugar, sweeter than you would find in the southern states, but hearts and minds were there to build relationships. He also offered a cigarette; I hadn't smoked a cigarette since I graduated from BUD/s. I said yes, hearts and minds!

After a few minutes of small talk, a man entered his office with a folder with X-rays. He was sharing them with the Sheik, and as they looked at them and spoke in Arabic, I asked my terp (interpreter) what was happening. The terp told me that the man's son, the Sheik's nephew, was hit in the leg with a bag of cement that fell off a roof and broke his leg. I immediately had the terp ask the Sheik if he could use some help with his nephew. The term repeated what the Sheik said. He said what could I do? I told him I would go out to the Humvee, radio our command, and ask if we could bring the boy to our hospital on base and fix his leg. He got the biggest smile. I knew if I could get the green light to bring this boy on base, it would be just what I needed to gain favor with Sheik Ahmed, the leader of the entire alliance.

Mission accomplished, we got the approval, and from that day forward, every Sheik, including Sheik Ahmed, welcomed us with open arms; they could not do enough to help our mission help them.

The most significant part of my mission was I had a great latitude on the Tribal Engagement Mission. It was relatively new and the hope for progress in the Iraqi war. Fighting the insurgency was never-ending. People were dying on all sides, and there didn't seem to be any light at the end of the tunnel.

If we could get the Iraqi people to fight with us and not against us, we could drive back the insurgency that was trying to fill the power vacuum that was left when Saddam Hussein was taken out of power.

Since Tribal Engagement was so new, there was no playbook. The concept was to build relationships with the tribal Sheiks and win their hearts and minds, hopefully leading to the one team, one dream attitude.

There were still a lot of bad actors who were trying to destabilize and slow down or stop any progress we were trying to make. One of the questions I was asked by one of my superiors when I first came back into the SEAL team was, "Why did I come back in, and what did I hope to accomplish during my time?" My answer was very clear and naive. I said I wanted to make a difference.

When I was tasked to be the Tribal Engagement guy, studying and learning what that meant, I got excited and thought this would be perfect. I am going to work with Iraqi leaders who are the difference makers. When my feet hit the ground, I was determined to make things happen. I had to use the battleground network that had been put together since 2003, when the Iraq war started. I had to first build relationships with my military counterparts, such as Marine and Army resources, who had some relationships with these Iraq leaders.

My time was limited, so I couldn't take my time trying to figure it out. I had to use the limited resources given to me during the turnover from the previous SEAL team. I was on my schedule and needed to figure it out and fast.

After a month, I had a good start on some villages and their leaders. We started to see progress with the intel we were getting from the relationships that were being built. Just about that time, when I felt like I was making a difference, I was tasked to head north to a place called Therthar with a team. There was intel that there were some bad players up there who had an IED factory. We were tasked to clear some homes and see if we could find any weapon caches, talk to the local people, and find out who and where these bad actors were.

Since we were driving our Humvees, it would be about a three-hour transit. We had received a report that an IED on the same route we would be taking had just killed two army soldiers when their convoy was attacked. Knowing we were on the same route made you realize this wouldn't be your relaxing road trip while on your family vacation. I was the driver in my Humvee with a crew of five. I learned early to keep a distance of about twenty-five feet behind the vehicle in front and make sure you stay on the same tracks. This might mitigate the risk of hitting a pressure plate-activated device but not a command in control, where the enemy can be hiding a safe distance and fire the device through a cell phone or a wired ignitor when the chosen vehicle is directly over the place in the road where the device is buried. Usually, it is in the middle of the convoy. Driving with the IED threat is very exhausting because of the heightened awareness and attention to detail. This was the very reason I had gotten Lasik on

251

my eyes before I deployed. I wanted to make sure that I didn't mistake an IED for a rock.

We arrived safely and got to work, trying to find anything we could that would lead us to more intel on where we could find out where this IED factory was located. The first thing we had to do was settle where we would be staying. It was a FOB (Forward Operating Base) with no running water or bathroom facilities. Our squad was shown our tent, and it definitely would keep a cover over our head, but that was about it. It was open on both sides, and the ground was this really fine dirt that was everywhere. The Bradleys, Strykers, tanks, humvees, and all the other military vehicles were rolling in all day and night. We were all living in a dust cloud. There was bottled water to drink, and they would deliver what was called MRATS (Military Rations). It was very thoughtful to deliver these warm meals and set up a banquet line in the open air with no cover. It was very convenient for us, as the banquet line was directly across the road from our tent, where all the traffic with military vehicles came and went.

Our first meal was our last; when we returned to the tent, our lovely, warm meal had a brown layer of moon dust. I thought this was like Hell Week eating, except it was dry brown dirt instead of sand. Every meal after that was an MRE (Meal Ready Eat), which was quite tasty. They had gotten a whole lot better since my prior service. The meals came with a chemical packet that, when mixed with water, heated the water, which would heat your meal that was sealed in another packet. They worked well and without the dirt. I won't get into the details of the restroom facilities, because there were none. Camping was 5-star living comparatively. But this was war; you dealt with it with a great attitude. Watching Band of Brothers (a series about Easy Company, Army Airborne) puts things in perspective; we were living well.

We drove into a village where we believed the enemy was living and proceeded to go door to door and clear each house, looking for weapons or any indicator of where these people might be holding up. Spending most of the night going house to house, we finally concluded that they were good at hiding or holding up somewhere else. Early that morning, we got word that the IED factory was located. Due to a joint effort with other US forces, everything fell into place, and the target was taken down, hit in a predawn raid. Sorry for not wanting to get into all the details; as I said before, this was not the intention of this book.

I have a lot of fond memories of the time I spent in Iraq. I got to experience many great things while there; even though it was a war zone, I had the chance to meet many interesting people who are hopefully still alive. One of my memorable times was getting to know Sheik Sattar's son, Sattam. He was about ten years old, and I was introduced to him during one of my first meetings with Sheik Ahmed, his uncle. He was a pleasure to be around. Knowing that his father had just recently been killed, I went out of my way to spend time with him whenever we rolled into the Sheiks compound. When he would hear our humvees roar in, he would come running to greet us. I always made sure I had something to bring as a gift for him: a soccer ball, a new pair of tennis shoes, or whatever I had in my tribal engagement milvan container. I would let him climb into my Humvee and play with the radio or turn some knobs.

I mentioned I had a large container where I could store anything that I needed for my mission. I found resources that shipped me all kinds of things to help win the hearts and minds. Like most parents, you treat their kids well, and they will learn to trust you. They were there for help so we could help them. So I ordered kids' tennis shoes of all sizes and lots and lots of candy. Soccer balls were a big hit in Iraq. I learned early that was the sport of choice. Early upon arrival, when we were visiting Sheik Ahmed's compound, the Asian Cup had just been won. That's when I knew Sheik Ahmed had to be a big deal, for the actual Asian Cup trophy was being paraded in his compound when we were there.

Kids were always playing soccer. Whenever we would roll out for a mission, I would lock and load but always be loaded with soccer balls. When we would roll through town, the kids would follow alongside our Humvee, and I would hand out soccer balls and candy. I was like the pied piper; they would follow us down the street. We would read intel reports every day, and the enemy started turning soccer balls into IEDs, so I had to stop handing out soccer balls. The last thing we needed was one of our balls being turned into a bomb and killing a group of kids. It's incredible "the evil that men do!"

Part of the mission of winning hearts and minds was to assist the Sheik in helping his village. There were many ways to do that; some of their communities had water and sewage issues. We would pay contractors to build and increase their infrastructure with water purifiers and anything we could do to give the people a better quality of life.

One of my favorite Sheiks that I worked with was Sheik Heiss. He was a top priority for me to get to know because all the reports showed he was a massive supporter of Sheik Sattar and the Great Awakening. He was also shot while running from Al Qaeda in his vehicle after his brother was killed and his house was burned to the ground.

Despite all he had lost and gone through, he had the most incredible attitude. After meeting him, I wanted to do all I could for him. He was a very colorful character; he wore a holster like you would have seen in the Wild Wild West with a Colt pearl handle 45 revolver. One of the other things I liked about him was that he had this massive painting of George Washington at Valley Forge above his fireplace, kneeling in the snow, praying by his horse. You have to love a guy like Sheik Heiss.

Whenever we would roll into his compound, he would have our team escorted to his office, and of course, he would have tea brought in, and we would talk about the war. He shared unlimited stories about the last three or four years. After talking for about an hour, one of his workers would tell us that lunch was served. Sheik Heiss would always put on this big feast for us. We never knew where it came from; it would just appear. But it was always so good.

I could tell he had a genuine interest in us; he never asked for anything, so I would ask him, what can I do for you and your people, Sheik Heiss? He would share that his school for the kids needed some work. So, after leaving his home, we would drive down to the local school, do a survey, and talk to the principal; he would tell us what the school needed. One of my most significant accomplishments was getting approval to build a soccer/sports court for Sheik Heiss's village school before I left Iraq. While meeting the contractors at the school, the teacher would invite us into the classroom to meet the kids, and he would share that these brave American soldiers would build them a soccer field. They would all stand up and cheer for us. Very rewarding.

There was one other accomplishment that I was proud of; Sheik Heiss had told me that quite a few people in his province were significantly injured from the war, and they were in great need of medical care. One of the tools I had in my tribal engagement bag was that I could set up what we called a MEDAV. This is where we dedicate a day to medically evaluate and treat on location or schedule future care for those that need more advanced care. They would come to the Sheiks compound, which also had his full-size soccer field on his property that would accommodate the entire village if need be.

Somehow, the word got out that we were conducting this MEDAV, and we got a message from our command that War Stories, hosted by Colonel Ollie North, wanted to do a War Story on the humanitarian side.

Mike riding Sheik Sattar's horse

Our entire SEAL team task unit assisted with all the corpsmen and medics we could find. Although it was a huge success, and Sheik Heiss was very grateful for caring for his people in dire need of medical attention, the big takeaway was the devastation and aftermath of war. It was hard to witness the people who showed up with their family members who were forever deformed because of the wounds they had suffered from roadside bombs or small weapons fire. Most of these people were innocent children in the wrong place at the wrong time. It was great to witness firsthand the heart of my teammates and the way they served that day with compassion. I believed everyone who was there to witness what was achieved that day will be forever changed; I know I was.

I had many meet and greets with Sheik Heiss during my time in Iraq; he proved to be a precious source in assisting in our mission to help the Iraqi people. During our time together, a bond and friendship were forged. One day, he was complaining about how his back was bothering him; he had told the story that when he was shot in the back, it caused a great deal of pain. I asked our corpsman to have a look and evaluate. He had some X-rays taken, and it showed that the bullet had created some nerve damage, and he would need surgery to rectify his situation. My last act before leaving was that we get approval from the higher-ups to fly him to the States, where he would receive his surgery. I never heard the surgery's result because of the security issues involved with communicating with Sheiks when I returned home. I felt good about him getting the opportunity; he deserved the best care. I hope he received it!

When I volunteered to reenlist back in the Navy, I knew I would deploy, but one doesn't know what you are stepping into. After getting back in and getting my clearance back, I could read the After Action Reports (AAR) on what was happening in the region I was heading to. There were a lot of people dying and more returning home injured with life-altering wounds. My heart goes out to all the military personnel willing to put their lives on the line for what they believed was a just cause. I was honored during that time downrange to work with some of those heroes. They were Marines, Army Interpreters, and some Iraqi people who were not only fighting for a just cause but fighting for their lives. The most memorable time for me was being able to work with some of the Iraqi leaders and their families. They were people just like us. They loved their country and their families. Sometimes, when we see a tragedy in another country, we dismiss it. It can be an earthquake or an attack from a terrorist group. Having the chance to eat, laugh, and play with their children while their country is at war was truly a life changer for me.

From Left to Right. Mike, Sheik Heiss, Ollie North and Interpreter

When I read about a foreign country experiencing death for whatever reason, I will not ever dismiss it like before. Because of my time in Iraq, I feel closer to my fellow men and women!

Chapter Thirty-Seven
On-Time On Target

After returning from my tour in Iraq, I received orders to a command where I would be part of the training pipeline for the reserve SEAL teams that would be operationalized; for the first time in our community history, we would have two operational reserve SEAL teams. For the next three years, I would assist with writing the training program for these civilian SEALs. One weekend a month and two weeks a year, they would prepare to deploy at least every five years and more if they wanted to. The other piece of their training was their unit-level training (ULT). This was the final training all SEALs undergo before deployment to ready them for battle.

This was very rewarding to me; I knew it was essential to ensure these reserve SEALs were well-trained before they headed overseas to do whatever they had to do in the future, just like the P3 parachute program that Frank Radford and I wrote in 1987, which was implemented and is still being used today.

My job for the next three years before I hit my 20 years of active service, where I would officially retire, was pretty good. After work, I would focus on our business just like before I left my naval career in 1992. Unsurprisingly, our business grew during my first year of working and deploying. Most of the time, even during that year I was in San Diego, I could work the business like I always had.

The three years had flown by, and now it was time to officially retire and return to being a full-time Dad and husband. July 22nd, 2011, was my chosen day for my retirement ceremony. I stopped going to work in March of the same year because of the leave I had accrued during the four years. I chose my retirement day to be the same day as my Dad's birthday. My Dad had passed in 2003.

My ceremony was at a field on the Naval Amphibious Base in Coronado, where we would train. Our command, Group Eleven, would have to be in attendance; I don't think they had a choice. I also invited anybody in World Wide that was in the local area. The plan was that the Navy Parachute team, Leap Frogs, would be jumping in for the opening of my ceremony. I would augment the team, jumping in with the big American Holiday flag with smoke as the National Anthem played.

The guests were all showing up and finding their seats; our twin Otter aircraft circled above, hoping the skies would clear. It looked hopeless because the cloud cover looked like a layer of cotton candy that covered the Coronado area. The TOT (Time On Target) had passed. We discussed the alternate plan: should we abort, land back at the airfield, and drive me to the ceremony? This was not a great option because it would delay the ceremony about an hour and a half. We decide to give it a few more minutes to clear.

We started to have some hope; parts in the sky were beginning to open, but not over the drop zone. With faith, the Leap Frogs and I began preparing our gear for the jump. The aircraft made its jump run; the jump master, with his head out the door, would be looking for a hole in the clouds so that he could see the ground to put us out safely and land on the drop zone, considering it was surrounded by water.

As we approached the exit point, the jump master looked at us and, with this big grin on his face, gave us the thumbs up, then the thirty-second warning. I couldn't believe it; it was a miracle. God had parted the skies just in time before we aborted. The last command was given: go. We all exited and immediately deployed our parachutes. I hadn't jumped a flag since I was on the Leap Frogs in 1982, and never one this big. If I don't do this right, I could come up short and land right in the bay for all to see. How embarrassing would that be, landing in the water at your own retirement? The SEAL community would remember and talk about that for years.

The deployment of the flag went off without a hitch; all I had to do was stay upwind of the field; at the lower altitude, I would set up for my downwind, then base, and then final, right on the target.

I hadn't realized that the wind had picked up, and the drag of the flag was not giving me the full capability of my parachute. The sweet spot is between turning base to final, too far downwind, I could end up in the water. If I make the turn too soon, I'll overshoot the target.

I turned where I thought would be the optimum between the two. As soon as I turned from base to final, I thought oh crap, the parachute with the wind and the drag of this enormous flag was not letting me penetrate as much as I needed to. I am over the bay and not making up any ground. I have a hanging smoke on a tether that is hanging about 20 feet below me.

I had asked Summer Baker, who has a beautiful voice (daughter of our close friends Glen and Joya Baker), to sing the National Anthem; I could now hear her singing. I was getting close. My eyes are glued on the target, willing my parachute to move forward. As I get a little lower in altitude, the wind seems to be subsiding; I am thinking I am going to make the field, maybe a little short of the marker we call a T, the top of the T being into the wind, giving direction on which way to land. It's always the goal to land on the T, not today. My next concern was that somebody had parked their nice Audi on the helicopter pad. I think it was Greg Duncan; my hanging smoke just missed the top of his car; whew, that was close.

I landed a little short of the T. The crowd, unaware of all the concerns I had just gone through, clapped and cheered; the drop zone crew assisted with the American flag and kept it from hitting the ground. I pulled my harness off and stepped up on the stage for the start of the ceremony. As I looked out into the crowd, I saw my family: Robin and my daughter Kaitlin who flew in from Tucson where she was serving in the Airforce, next to her were my two sons Michael and Christian. This was the first time they had seen their Dad perform in an airshow with the Navy Leap Frogs. I could tell they were very proud to be there.

My eyes started to well up with tears as I began to recognize some of the people I greatly respect. Greg and Laurie Duncan, Joe and Norma Foglio, and so many more, too many to mention. The retirement was very ceremonious in the usual Navy tradition. I had chosen speakers that were part of my naval career; they had some excellent anecdotal stories that they remembered, which was a nice touch to the ceremony.

Still, to this day, some attendees talk about how great it was for them to be there; some brought their children and how special it was to have attended a Navy retirement. I have never heard of anybody in the history of the SEAL team who had parachuted into their own retirement; I could be wrong. It was a great end to a very memorable career.

Chapter Thirty-Eight
Borrowed Gear Borrowed Death

The second time being out of the Navy and being free to get up in the morning and not have to go to work was a much easier transition this time; I had gotten used to doing it for14 years. After living in Alpine for 17 years, we decided a change of scenery would be nice. We decided to put our house on the market and plan our next chapter.

Knowing that we were moving to a much smaller place, we decided to get rid of all the stuff we had accumulated while living in a 4000-square-foot house. Robin is the antithesis of a hoarder. We don't need it if we haven't used it in the last six months. We call it high speed, low drag. Every time we moved, we used it as an opportunity to eliminate the unnecessary.

We had a great realtor, and while in escrow, we decided to have a yard sale; the realtor said they would handle it. We pulled everything out of the woodwork, and their office did the rest. It was great. Robin and I enjoyed the day while the realtors handled the yard sale. They earned their money on this sale.

After the house sold, we decided to move into Coronado. After living inland, we thought we'd try the beach life. We found a cute little home we would rent for two years. Kaitlin was in the Air Force, so all we had left at home was our two boys. Michael was 19, and Christian was 15. It wouldn't be long before we would be empty nesters.

I got a call from Joe Foglio. He asked me if Robin and I wanted to look at a yacht with him and Norma. They thought about buying a boat for a second home on the water. Having been in the Navy for 20 years, I had never considered having a yacht. Robin nor I had ever set foot on one.

They would look at a 70' Hatteras yacht slipped in Coronado. I always jumped at any chance to spend time with Joe; even if he wanted me to watch submarine races, I would be there. He set it up with the broker, and we walked through this beautiful yacht. The entire time, I thought I would rather live on this than the place we were living in. The seed was planted; I talked to Robin and convinced her that living on a yacht would be great.

Not long after that first experience, we met with a broker and were now in the market for a yacht. He showed us some, but we knew nothing about what to look for and what we wanted. We had decided that the bigger the better. We wanted something spacious that would be like living in a condo.

While we were living in Coronado, Robin would take our dog Cooper to the park down the street, and there was this woman named Penny; she and her husband Gary would become close friends of ours. Robin finds out they lived on a boat and have done so for many years. Robin had shared that we were in the market for a 60-plus footer. Penny couldn't believe our first boat was going to be that big. She thought it was pretty humorous and would go home and share the story with her husband, Gary.

We finally got linked up with a yacht broker named Dick Simon. It turned out that Dick used to run 5 Indy car teams at one time, and one of them was the direct sales race team. Dick was an interesting character. At one point, the FBI busted through his house door, thinking he was the famous bank robber named D.B. Cooper, who had skydived out of an airliner with $250,000. Dick had all the skill sets to do the job and also had just bought a new engine for one of his race cars that cost $250,000. Who knows, maybe he was.

Dick was in his 70s when we met him; he had the energy of a 30-year-old. He went to work and found us a beautiful boat: a 78-foot Hatteras. It had everything we wanted in a yacht. If you know anything about yachts, a 78-footer is like a ship. If we had known better, we would have been looking for one a lot smaller.

We didn't know that it is hard to find a slip for a boat that big. We didn't ask the right questions. I thought it would be like airplanes; the bigger they are, the easier they are to drive. Robin and I were excited about this next adventure living on this big yacht. The financing fell through the morning it was supposed to close, so we didn't get that one. God was definitely looking out for us.

We found this 56-foot Ocean yacht that most people thought was still too big for inexperienced boaters. But being in the Navy and growing up with small ski boats, a large yacht didn't intimidate me. With Robin as my first mate, I knew the two of us could handle it.

The timing was perfect; after doing some modifications to open up the galley to the saloon, it was ready to move on. Our lease on our home in Coronado was ending, and we found a slip to accommodate our almost 60-foot boat down in South Bay, San Diego. Our boat was in Dana Point, and it would take about seven hours to bring her to San Diego. So I invited a couple of my brothers and sisters to join us. Dick Simon acted as my Co-Captain, making sure I made it the voyage safely since this would be the first time at the helm of a yacht. The trip was uneventful; everybody had a great time. It was now slipped at our new home for the next couple of years.

Because of Robins's high-speed, low-drag mentality, we had plenty of room on our boat to accommodate our personal effects. We gave the furniture we bought for our Coronado rental to our kids and anything else we needed to get rid of to live on our boat.

I have met many people who think their stuff is still worth what they paid, and you spend thousands of dollars on storage. Then, they seem to forget about their personal belongings and pay rent for things that lose any value they might have had. We tried to sell our expensive Ethan Allen furniture but gave it to the church for less fortunate people.

Robin, I, and our two boys were getting used to living on a boat; they had friends in the town, so they weren't with us full-time. When we told people we lived on a boat, they always thought it was the coolest thing. Many people love the idea, the glamor, and the mystique. They would ask us questions about what they were concerned about. Do you get seasick? Do you feel different when you step back on shore? Most of the time was spent on the bay, so there was little rough water. I think I had spent enough time on boats in the SEAL team, and growing up, it felt pretty normal. Robin didn't seem to have a difficult time either.

The cost always comes up as well. The slip fee alone can be more than most people pay for rent. Then there is maintenance fees. You have to have the hull cleaned every month, everything below the water line. It's salt water, so many things growing on your boat must be cleaned off, such as barnacles and other sea creatures. When something breaks, which it always does. Anything that has to do with airplanes and boats is expensive.

Almost every weekend, we took her out and cruised down Glorietta Bay in Coronado to get used to anchoring and learn what that entailed: living on the hook (anchor). It was like camping; your electricity came from your generator. We would run that during the day to get the refrigerator back to the desired temp and charge the batteries for the DC lights after dark.

We found out our good friends and business associates Glen and Joya Baker had a yacht, so we would raft up with them and another couple. This procedure tied your boats together as one big floating condo. We could transition from one boat to the next. We would share meals and hang out. It was some of the best times we had with the boat life. It was similar to RV traveling and meeting new friends in your RV campsite, sharing meals, and sitting around the campfire, except this was on the water in beautiful Coronado.

Every time we would go out to anchor or raft up, we would learn something new. It was a great way to get to know your boat's systems. After a few of these, we felt comfortable crossing to Catalina Island. It would take about seven hours to transit from San Diego to the Island, where we would moor up next to each other.

After planning the trip, we departed at O dark thirty, around 4 am. The three of us would rendezvous near the mouth at Point Loma, where you depart San Diego Bay and head out into the ocean. I was so excited that evening prior that I could hardly sleep. At about 3 am, I decided to take our dog Cooper for his last potty break, as he would have to hold it for most of the day until we got moored up, where I could dingy him to the beach.

After successfully getting him to do his business, we returned to the boat and fired up the engines for warm-up. This, of course, was the wake-up call for Robin. She jumped out of bed, excited to pull away from the dock and head to sea for a day cruise to the Island. Robin was an excellent first mate, always ready with a fender to ward off any dock or boat I got close to pulling out of the slip.

After cruising through the bays for about an hour, we successfully rendezvoused with the Bakers and the Tumis. It was a beautiful morning, with no wind and clear skies, no better for pleasure boating. This can definitely be the luck of the draw; it is hard to pick the perfect day for cruising on the ocean. One day can be gorgeous, whereas the next can be big swells and rough seas, where you better have everything secure and tied down. That would not be considered pleasure boating.

This day was definitely a great day for pleasure cruising. I set the autopilot for the course to Catalina and just sat out on the bow with the ocean breeze in my face while Robin cooked us a beautiful breakfast of eggs, bacon, and toast. Life couldn't be any better. Cruising with two other boats with your close friends on a beautiful day on the water with dolphins following our flotilla as if to say, let's play.

After about seven hours, we arrived at Avalon Harbor, where we would be moored for several days. It was like being in another country; the water was crystal clear and turquoise, and we knew this would be a great trip. There was great food on the Island, and scuba diving was some of the best you could ever experience off the coast of southern California. The kelp was in full bloom; from under the water, it looked like a forest you could dive through, swimming with all the local marine life. I was looking forward to putting my frogman on!

After settling in on the moorings, we started to plan our evening with the other two couples. Who would make what for dinner, and whose boat would we dine on? As we ate, we planned our activity for the next day. Robin and I wanted to dive. Robin had never had the opportunity to dive in a kelp bed forest. I couldn't wait to show her what she had missed all these years. Besides Robins's scuba training in San Diego, all her dives were done in warm water diving destinations. Our first dive trip together was in the Cayman Islands after I returned from my deployment in 1985.

So it was settled: Robin and I would be scuba diving while Glen and Craig snorkeled. Robin and I had all the equipment except for the BC (Buoyancy Compensator), which I needed to rent. As a frogman in the earlier days, we didn't use BCs; we had an inflatable life jacket

268

that you could deploy if you got into trouble and needed to get to the surface and stay afloat.

Craig said he had an extra one. When he brought the BC out of his lazzerette, I inspected it and tried it on for size. It was tight, but I was able to get it on. It has multiple purposes for those who don't know what a BC is used for. One is used to attach your scuba bottle without having a separate harness. Two, it has an integrated weight system instead of a weight belt. The extra weight can help you stay neutral in the water. Some variables need to be compensated with extra weight, such as how much. Some people are naturally more buoyant than others. Also, wearing a wet suit can change your buoyancy. The extra weight will give you the optimum neutral buoyancy, but this will change as you go from shallow to deeper water. An inflation actuator hose is connected to your scuba bottle, and you can add more air or let out to keep you neutral. Also, it can get you to the surface and keep you afloat during emergencies or just to rest while you're hanging out.

So Robin and I were all set to dive through the kelp forest in the morning. The weather and visibility couldn't have been better. So we loaded up our dingy and headed to the Avalon game reserve. Once there, we would tie up to the reserve perimeter lines. Once secured, we started to don our equipment and wait for Glen and Craig. By the time they got there, Robin and I were ready. I was anxiously waiting to enter the water. It had been years since I last dove, other than in the base pool that we used to do our qualification dive for pay. There weren't many maritime operations since the war on terror and fighting in the desert.

I could tell Robin was a little apprehensive; like me, she hadn't dove in years, and was not used to wearing a very thick wet suit that could make one claustrophobic. We both entered the water, and immediately, our breath was taken away from the cold water until we started to move the water between our skin, and the wetsuit suit started to warm.

Robin started to complain about her ankle. She had a replacement some years prior and was aggravated by the movement of the big fins she wore. So, multiple issues made Robin uncomfortable in the water. She said she wanted to get back in the dingy and maybe she would try again the next day. I told her that was fine and I wouldn't be long.

I started to descend and noticed my BC hose was leaking from a bad O ring that had probably dry-rotted. So, I decided to disconnect, not to deplete my air supply rapidly. I know what you're thinking; there were two good reasons to abort the dive: one, no dive buddy. The number one rule in diving is never dives without a buddy. Number two, don't dive with malfunctioning equipment.

As you read this, if you are a diver, you will be making mental notes of mistakes that were being made; I get it, and the only thing I can say for myself is that it was overconfidence from all the diving I had done in my 20 years in SEAL team that help lead me to make the mistakes. Experience can lead you down two different paths. The first can be caution and prudence; the second is complacency and overconfidence. The latter is sometimes one's worst enemy.

So, after disconnecting my BC hose, I descended to the ocean floor, about 40 feet. The visibility was incredible, and I started to weave in and out of the kelp forest. It looked like I was taking a stroll through the Amazon rainforest, with sunlight shining through the trees, but in this case, it was kelp vines. The memories started to rush in from doing this so many times off Point Loma during our recreational dives for groceries. We would do grocery diving when we needed a requalification dive every quarter for pay. Sometimes, we would be so busy training in other things that we wouldn't get in the water to dive.

After about 30 minutes, I decided to surface, knowing Robin was waiting patiently and probably worried. I started to swim through the kelp forest, heading to the surface, and felt the kelp snagging on my equipment, which created some resistance. The closer to the surface, the thicker it got. Kelp has this velcro cling to it, the hook side of velcro that grabs onto you as you swim through it. It started to come back to me from all the kelp dives I had done that you have to move through it slowly and brush the vines off as they snag you and not panic as it grabs you, just stay calm and release as it holds onto you, one vine at a time. When I surfaced, I was surprised to see how close I was to our dingy. Robin was excited to see me, and she could tell I had a great time with a big smile on my face. I had forgotten how much I love to dive.

After returning to our boats, we cleaned ourselves and gear up. At dinner, we compared notes about what we had seen; the marine life was plentiful. Sea Bass and Garibaldi, the California state fish, were everywhere. You had to find the good stuff under the rock ledges where the lobsters hid. I was taking notes on where I could grab a couple for dinner. I'm just kidding, game wardens.

I had a couple more scuba bottles that were ready to go for a dive the following day. Glen and Craig said they would like to snorkel again, but Robin said she wanted to relax and sunbathe with Joya and Bonnie.

The following day, I loaded up my dingy and headed to the same spot as the previous day to tie up. I started to get geared up while waiting for Glen and Craig to show. Upon their arrival, I knew they only had to put a mask and snorkel on, and they would be right behind me. They told me they would keep an eye on me since I didn't have a dive buddy. I hadn't mentioned that my BC hose was disconnected and didn't think much of it; everything went great on the previous dive.

I was feeling a little more froggy than the day before. I took off through the kelp; I'm sure I was hard to keep an eye on. I was having the time of my life, searching for all the lobsters underneath all the ledges; there was a ton. The marine life knows they are untouchable in the reserve, so they know it's a great hiding place. It's like deer; they know when hunting season starts, so they roam the woods without care until opening day and then go into hiding.

After about an hour, I looked at my air reserve and decided it was time to surface as I was down to about 500 PSI (pounds per square inch) and see where I was relative to my entry point. I came up through the kelp slowly and not to get hung up on it. I realized I was about 200 yards away from my dinghy when I reached the surface. Like so many times in my career, I had to spit my regulator out of my mouth and snorkel over to the boat on the surface to conserve air in case I needed it.

I started to swim but to no avail; the kelp was so thick, and the surge of the water was keeping me from moving forward. At this point, I thought it would be nice if my BC were working so I could put some air in it to stay afloat while I struggled to move through the kelp. Trying to swim on the surface with the kelp grabbing and pulling on you and the weight in the integrated BC got tiring quickly. At this point, I put my regulator back in my mouth, descended, and swam through the kelp underwater. One problem: I couldn't find the hose to my regulator; it was entangled with the kelp, which has the same feel and diameter as the air hose.

Now, I am vertical in the water and kicking hard to keep my head above water. The kelp is pulling me down from the surge in the water. I went from having a great dive to fighting for my life in seconds. There was nothing I could do to solve the problem. I thought of ditching the integrated BC, which would have been great; even if I could find the zipper and unzip it, I couldn't have gotten it off because it was too small; it was a struggle getting it on, and that was in a boat. I couldn't even look; I was so busy trying to keep my head from going below the water's surface. I knew I wouldn't come up again if my head dipped below.

All I could think about was staying afloat to keep breathing. There was one other thing on my mind: I'm a retired SEAL, and I am going out this way on a recreation dive. I couldn't believe it. There was nothing I could do except kick. How long can I keep this up? My legs were burning, and I was getting lightheaded. As I was contemplating life, I noticed some people on the shore. I thought about yelling for help but thinking they were too far away to get to me on time. Besides, there was a pride thing: I am a Frogman "for crying out loud!"

My pride started to dissipate quickly as my options were limited here. I started yelling for help; I knew I had no time left; all I could think about was, this is it! I had been in these situations before, but I had longer to think about my end this time. Other times, it was high speed, and I had no time to think; I worked on the problem and came up with a solution. This time, there is no solution; keep kicking to stay alive and think about the end.

I got a glimmer of hope out of the corner of my eye. Is that someone swimming towards me from shore? I immediately started to think there wasn't any way that whoever this was would not reach me in time. My legs are burning, and I don't know how long I can keep my head above water. I have to keep fighting; this could answer my prayer. He finally reaches me, and he is behind me without a word. I first told him to put my regulator in my mouth. With the weight, the surge, and the kelp pulling me down, I realize he cannot hold me up very long. He is tired from the swim from shore. If I can get my regulator in my mouth, I can descend through the kelp and be free from its death hold.

He places my BC mouthpiece in my mouth, which does me no good; God bless whoever this is behind me, but he was not a diver. He didn't know the difference between the regulator and the BC oral inflation mouthpiece. At this point, I am on my last ounce of energy to keep me above water.

I don't hear or feel the swimmer; where did he go? Whatever is keeping me up, I am about out of. Then I heard something: Is that a boat engine? Is there a rescue boat coming this way? Negative thoughts enter again; there is no way the boat I hear will make it in time; I am out of the strength that's been keeping me alive.

The boat is getting closer; will it get here in time? I can hear the boat engine next to me; I'm looking up and fighting with everything I have left; then, out of nowhere, I see a hand in front of my face; I grab it and hang on for dear life. At that Moment and not before, I believed I would make it. When I saw that hand, I knew this was not the way I was going out. "O ye of little faith!"

The rescue crew pulled me into the boat, and I immediately went to the deck, almost passing out from exhaustion. They started to treat me for a diving accident, air embolism, or bends. I could hardly get the words out. I am okay; there is no diving physics to deal with. They finally realized I was exhausted from trying to stay on the surface.

Glen and Craig realized that it was me yelling for help. When they saw the rescue team pull me into the boat, they ran their dingy over to Glen and Joya's boat to let Robin know that something had gone wrong and I had to be pulled from the water. I could only imagine what was going through her mind. Robin jumped into their dingy, and they rushed her to where I was in the rescue boat. By then, I was starting to regain my strength and coherence. After a quick examination, the rescue team was ready to release me.

I often wondered who the swimmer was, which gave me enough hope to keep fighting until the rescue boat arrived. Not one word was spoken from him, and I never saw him again; I would have thought he would have been there when they pulled me out of the water and joined me in the rescue boat to see how I was doing. There was no mention of any swimmer from anyone. It makes you wonder. Thank you, Lord, for sending my guardian angel and saving me again.

The lessons learned from that near-death experience were not to borrow dive gear; if you do, make sure it fits and test it before diving, and if it malfunctions, get it fixed or replace it. Number one rule: do not dive without a dive partner. We had a SEAL team brother who was a combat diver guru. He would start his day every morning with a dive with a closed circuit system, like the one I discussed earlier in the book. He would do an ocean dive without a dive buddy. One morning, he didn't show up for work. Knowing his morning routine, the command sent some guys over to where he dove and found his body at the bottom of the ocean. I believe he had a heart attack. He could have been saved if he had a dive buddy with him. I should have remembered that and learned that lesson from someone from the past.

That evening at dinner, we all talked about how blessed I was and were all grateful for how the day turned out. It made us all reflect on how fragile life can be, and without notice, it can be taken from us. Like Joe Foglio would always say, count your blessings one by one! Be thankful for each day God gives you; even if it seems like a bad day, it is still a blessing. Please don't take it for granted because tomorrow may not come.

Chapter Thirty-Nine
Michael Kelly Carroll Jr.

My oldest son, Michael, met this beautiful girl inside and out, named Toni. They fell in love and found themselves pregnant with our first grandchild. This was one of those times that I was so happy that I was alive to hear the news. Michael and Toni are very adventurous in their spirit, like Robin and me. Michael started skydiving a couple of years before he had met Toni. Of course, you always want to have your soul mate doing what you do, so Michael talked Toni into skydiving. I don't know how that conversation went, but knowing Toni, it didn't take a lot of arm twisting. Once they found out that Toni was pregnant, we were happy to hear she had given up the sport.

Michael mentioned they want to do something cool and unique for the reveal of the baby's gender. He said he wanted to get skydiving involved in the reveal. So they decided that Michael would jump out of an air balloon. The baby's gender would be revealed by the smoke mounted to Michael's foot right before he jumped from the balloon.

We found out that our youngest son, Christian, was the only one who would know the gender. So, for several months before the jump, Christian proved his integrity when certain family members, not to mention any names, tried to coax the information from him. Christian was tight-lipped and kept the secret to the end.

All the planning was done, and the smokes were rigged. Either it would be pink or blue smoke. We all drove up at O' dark thirty near Perris Valley, CA. The early morning is because the balloon will rise easier and faster. After all, it doesn't need as much hot air to rise. The envelope also can not get too hot, as it decreases the life of the envelope (balloon). It is time to load the balloon's gondola and rise to about 7,000 feet for Michael to leap from the balloon, with pink or blue smoke trailing behind him.

If you have ever experienced a gender reveal as a family member, you know the suspense is at an all-time high. The whole family dynamic is about to change either by a little girl or a boy. Either way, it will never be the same, and the family's legacy will be impacted like the butterfly effect. Another human being coming into the world will have a positive impact, especially if that child realizes their power.

Everybody was so excited; we were all in this balloon gondola, rising through the air, taking in the landscape on this beautiful morning, anticipating what this new addition to the Carroll legacy would be. Then there is Christian, sitting there with this grin like I know something you don't know. I do have to give Christian a huge credit. For about three months, he held on to that information that everybody wanted to know, and he would not reveal the truth.

It was time; the balloon was at 7,000 ft. Michael climbs out of the balloon onto a little step; the video is rolling, and you can cut the anticipation with a knife. Michael asks if everybody is ready. Yes, we all reply. He reaches down to his smoke and grabs the ring of the smoke canister, looking at Toni with that look; we are about to find out whether we are having a boy or girl; our lives are about to change from this day forward. Michael pops the smoke; everybody is staring at the canister on his foot; at first, you see white smoke from the ignition. Then, the white smoke turns blue; it's a boy! Michael and Toni start to cry, and then everybody else does. Blue smoke is now spewing from Michael's foot. He had this big grin when he kissed Toni and said, see you later. He goes backward on his back, and you can see him looking upward at us as blue smoke trails between his legs.

There is an excellent video on YouTube of the reveal; needless to say, it got a lot of views; there were some complaints, and people couldn't believe that they brought Rusty, their dog, in the balloon; hey, he is part of the family, too.

A couple of days later, we were all together, and the subject of names came up. To my surprise, Michael and Toni decided to name him after me, Michael Kelly Carroll! How awesome is that? I had never met a Michael Kelly Carroll, and now I will have a grandson with my name. At this time, he is about two and a half years old and the coolest, most handsome boy I have ever seen. Can you tell I am biased?

There are good days, and there are good days. Then there are great days and perfect days. The day I found out I would have a grandchild of my namesake was perfect. Thank you, Lord, for saving me so I could experience the miracle of Michael Kelly Carroll Jr., born on October 4th, 2020.

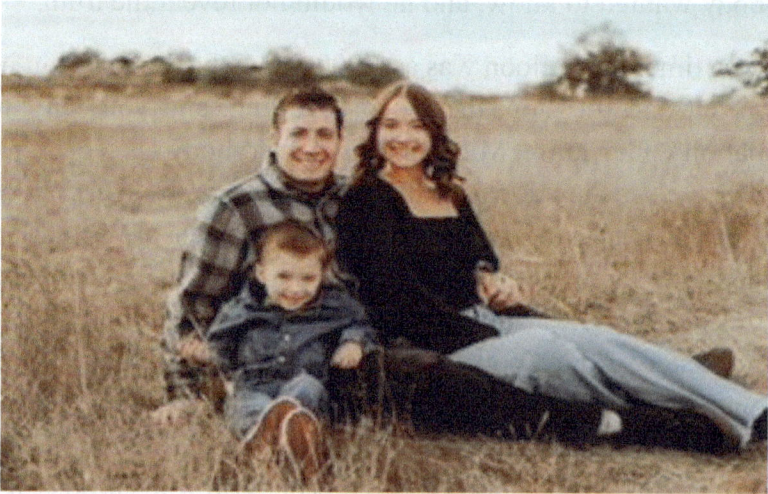

Mike And Robin's son Michael David with wife Toni their son Michael Kelly Carroll Jr.

Chapter Forty
Something Lurking

When I retired from the Navy in 2011, I had a medical exam for some added life insurance policy. When I got the results back, it seemed my PSA blood test for my prostrate was elevated. For as long as I can remember, it has always been elevated, and the Navy doctors said I should keep an eye on it, but there is no concern at this time. Now, being at another level, I decided to be proactive and get a biopsy. Sure enough, the results came back and confirmed that I had low-risk prostate cancer.

My Urologist said we could do surveillance using a PSA test every quarter and a biopsy every two years to see if it advances. I have to tell you, the biopsy is not fun. I entered into an experimental program that tries to eliminate the cancer through injections. I volunteered for the program. I didn't like the fact that I had cancer in my body and wasn't looking forward to the possibility of having a prostatectomy after hearing some of the horror stories from patients who had it done.

The first thing they wanted to do was another biopsy, but this time, they couldn't use any anesthesia. Without getting into great details, a prostrate biopsy is done by taking little bites out of the prostrate, approximately 15-20. It feels like a dull, uncomfortable pain when they numb the area. There is about a minute between each bite. The doctor will count 1, 2, 3, and pull the trigger of this gun-like device that sounds like something made from Mattel, the toy maker.

This biopsy would be different; every bite without any numbing agent would feel like I was William Wallace, lying on the table being tortured and finally yelling for freedom at the worst part. After each bite of the eighteen, I felt like screaming "freedom." Need I say more?

Of course, this experiment gave no positive results, so I continued my surveillance for 11 years. In 2022, I had my quarterly PSA, which jumped to its highest level. So another biopsy was done, and after the procedure, I decided to go back to my hanger, cook breakfast, and relax before heading home to Alpine, where we had bought our home in 2020.

After eating breakfast, I went into the bathroom, came out, and walked down the hallway; without warning, I passed out. I woke up a few seconds later from the pain in my foot. When you pass out, and the signal from your brain doesn't get to your trailing foot, it folds and can pull ligaments and break bones in the top of your foot. It is called a Les Frank fracture. Every time I tried to get up, I felt as though I would pass out from the pain which kept me from being able to get up. I called my two sons, Michael and Christian, and they got me to the emergency room.

Life is sometimes full of surprises. Just when everything seems like smooth sailing, something happens, and there is a setback. It turned out that I fractured my foot, and I was in a cast and wheeling around on a scooter for several months.

My prostrate was still on my mind; my Urologist said that we could continue surveillance but would go from low to moderate risk.

At our Free Enterprise Day function that year, I talked to Greg Duncan, and he was raving about the Urologist he was working with, Dr. Yoshida. He gave me his contact information and, through some convincing from Greg, Dr. Yoshida, who wasn't taking any new patients then, agreed to meet with me.

After meeting with Dr. Yoshida, I decided to have a prostatectomy in March of 2023. The surgery was a massive success with no adverse effects and full functionality of all systems that could be affected by the procedure.

Chapter Forty-One
It's a Miracle

I am in a slow left turn, running out of airspace; the ground is starting to come up fast, and I am doing my best glide at 75 knots. I feel the wing hit the overpass . . . I am conscious, fully aware of what's happening . . . when am I going from conscious to death? I can't believe this is it; I have never felt this close to death; this is not sudden, like all of the other times. Here, I was able to work on a solution. But now, I am a passenger; I am no longer the pilot; this airplane is taking me right to death; I am at peace; any Moment, I will open my eyes in heaven.

The crash sequence starts; the bump of my wing is just the beginning; instinctively, I close my eyes to protect them from the debris. I am now in a hurricane of crunching metal and breaking glass; the sounds are deafening, waiting for it. Will I feel anything, or will I just be gone? Within seconds, it is quiet; I hear nothing…

I have a vision. It's from above looking down; it's a crash site; it seems like my airplane, shiny polished aluminum with royal blue stripes and high lights. There is a tail number, N1097D, it is my airplane. It's a mangled mess, lying in the street; wings are bent up on both sides; the entire front of the aircraft is gone and lying to the side.

Vision changes; the airplane is flying; it looks beautiful, bright, shiny, all polished; it looks brand new. The interior smells like it was just installed from the factory. Seeing me with a big smile, it was such a beautiful day to be flying in this 1951 Cessna 195 with the big, powerful radial engine. The airplane is turning to the right for a base to final. "N1097D. You are cleared to land for runway 27, Right." Four miles out, dropping below the glide slope. Need more power, push the throttle forward. The engine quits; I couldn't hear the engine die at such a low rpm. Four miles out, there is no way it can glide that far. I am going to crash.

Did I make it? Where am I? There is no possible way that somebody would be able to survive in that mangled mess. But wait, a pair of legs are sticking out of the front where the control panel and engine would typically be. There is movement, or is it my imagination? I could have sworn I saw the left foot move.

Three men climb down the hill from the Interstate above. It looks like they are seeing if anybody is alive. I can't believe it; it looked like they were talking to an occupant in the airplane.

It's me, I open my eyes, Holy s——, I am alive.

How did I survive? All that came to mind was my guardian Angels were not asleep at the switch. Once again, they answered the call to save Michael Kelly Carroll, as they had done many times before. I couldn't believe what I saw; nothing was before me. The entire front of the airplane was gone. There was no instrument panel, yoke controls, or even the engine or cowling. It was like my seat was floating on the outside of the aircraft. How did I live through a crash that tore up my beautiful Cessna 195 like a tin can? The force it took to do what it did was incredible, and here I am in the middle of it, still alive and not cut in half like the airplane.

I could feel some blood running down my face; I had no idea what my condition was or how I looked. My attention quickly shifted toward my leg; the pain emanated from my upper right leg, which was already twice the standard size.

The next thought that came to mind was, I wonder how long it will take somebody to help me get out of the mangled airplane. My feet rested on the chainlink fence, which was being used as a barrier for construction on the road I had crashed on.

As I was thinking that, three men appeared from the Interstate above and walked down the embankment towards me. I felt a sigh of relief as my mind swirled with thoughts of fire. I didn't see or smell any signs of it, but that is a concern with any airplane crash.

One of the men took charge; he said he had medical training, which was music to my ears. As they were maneuvering around the fence that separated them from me and the plane, I asked how my face was. One of them said, "Not too bad," I could tell by their reaction that they were surprised that I was still intact and not a representation of the mangled aircraft.

As they reached me and were trying to figure out the best course of action, I explained to them how to release me from my harness system, which probably assisted in saving my life. I could feel the pressure from the harness bearing my weight, and once they unhooked me, I was carried a safe distance away from the plane.

The emergency vehicles started arriving, and the EMTs began to assess and stabilize. It was apparent that my right femur was broken; they just didn't know how bad. They had to stabilize me by straightening my leg before taking me to the hospital. One EMT warned that moving the leg would hurt badly but that they were going to administer fentanyl to get me through. I asked if this wasn't the drug killing people. The EMT said, "Not this; we have the good stuff."

The other EMT had my phone and asked me who they should call; I said, please call my wife, Robin. After getting my code to unlock my phone, she found Robins's contact and called; the EMT said she was not answering. Try my son Christian; the call was answered, and the EMT explained the situation to my son. After a short conversation, I knew Christian would inform the rest of our family what was happening and where I would be.

It was time to straighten my leg. I prepared for the worst; immediately, I knew the pain level just hit an all-time high; never before in my life had I experienced that kind of pain. I have always prided myself on my pain tolerance and not revealing the level by controlling my emotions, but there was no holding back on what I was feeling. They tried to comfort me by telling me that the hospital had better stuff and I would feel no pain soon.

Arriving at the trauma center, the pain meds they administered weren't working. I explained what the EMTs had told me about receiving stronger pain relief. The nurse said, "They lied!" You have to love their sense of humor, but it was not very comforting.

After some time, the pain subsided to the level I could bear. They took some X-rays and sutured up the laceration on my forehead caused by the shrapnel from the plexiglass of the aircraft, which was another miracle in itself. I could only imagine what was happening during those seconds and how much debris was flying around.

I hadn't been there long when Robin and our kids started filing into the room. The looks on their faces were ones of shock and amazement; husband and Dad were in a plane crash, alive and not too bad off, other than a broken leg and a laceration on the forehead. You know you are loved, but to experience the look of relief and love from your family is priceless.

Once I settled into my hospital room, the orthopedic surgeon, Dr. Sandzone, visited me to tell me the plan. He said, "I understand you are a very lucky man," I corrected him by saying, "I was blessed today; I had a front-row seat to a miracle!

I believed to the depth of my soul that a miracle saved me this time. All the other times, one could say it was a coincidence, or I was lucky, but not this time. Let me explain. It has been fifteen months since the crash; I have had a lot of time to analyze what happened that morning, all the things that had to line up for me to survive it.

Miracle #1: If I hadn't decided in the last few seconds to make that slow left turn to land on the I-8 freeway and, then made the decision not to put the airplane on the freeway, which would have been catastrophic due to the heavy traffic that morning but elected to place the aircraft, in what appeared to be a gap at that particular juncture (the overpass) which just happened to be in the exact distance away that my airplane was able to get to.

In miracle #2, the airplane's right wing tip hit part of the overpass, which caused the aircraft to lose flight, squashing all forward Momentum laterally to vertical. Not knowing at the time, but flying into the overpass only allowed approximately eighty feet of runway before the airplane would have flown directly into the structure holding the freeway over the street below, going approximately seventy-five knots, eighty-six miles per hour.

Miracle #3, squashing all the forward Momentum from the wing tip hitting the overpass, which transitioned forward Momentum to a downward force absorbing most of the energy, which on impact ripped the entire front of the airplane, everything in front of my seat away, leaving my legs dangling freely with no floor of the aircraft left and my feet resting so gently on the chain link fence.

In my mind's eye, Michael and Gabriel, the ark angels, were on each of my wings, saying, "Michael Kelly Carroll is worth saving; let him down gently but allow the passenger seat to shatter his femur, as to slow down his recovery and give him time to ponder, What is God Saving Him For? And to slow him down, we can take a break from watching over him.

There was an eraser whiteboard on the wall of my room, and Dr. Sandzone started to draw the condition of my right femur and what his plan was to fix it by surgery the following day. I immediately liked him. I could tell he loved his work by his enthusiasm for his action plan. I also had peace, knowing God wouldn't have saved me and put me in the hands of someone who wasn't good at what he did.

He said, "Michael, you shattered your femur in seven places, and we need to put it back together with a rod and some screws." I love the way orthopedics talk; they are like mechanics. Their toolbox looks like something you would see in a garage. Hammers, drills, screwdrivers, chisels. I guess that is why they talk the way they do. Deep down, they are great mechanics with degrees in medicine.

The following day, I was prepped and rolled into the operating room. It seemed like a few minutes later, and I woke up in recovery. It was about six hours—four hours of surgery and two more before I was awake and somewhat aware of where I was.

The surgery was a success; my orthopedic surgeon was very pleased. I knew it would be a rough road, and I would need a couple of months to walk without a walker, crutches, and cane, in that order. The day after surgery, the physical therapist visited me and explained the plan that I would have to accomplish before leaving the hospital. I was gung-ho to get started so I could get home as soon as possible. The first step was to be able to sit up and get my legs swung over the side of the bed. Then, using the walker, I tried to stand up on my good leg, but my good leg wasn't so good; I injured it in the crash as well. The left leg was what they called the column to support my weight, along with the walker, for at least the next four to six weeks.

I knew it would be a rough road, but I didn't know how rough it was until I tried to stand up for the first time. In the next several days, the physical therapist worked with me, and with lots of encouragement, I could stand up with a walker and walk. I could not walk very far, but I could walk. After five days of being medicated and being very well taken care of by the hospital staff, I knew it was time to go home. The biggest concern was I wouldn't have access to the same medications the hospital had me on so I could remain comfortable to sleep and recover.

I was excited to leave but very apprehensive about the recovery at home. If it weren't for Robin being with me every step of the way, I would have been a lost ball in tall weeds. She ordered a hospital bed, knowing I would be more comfortable if she could model the hospital environment. Robin was my nurse for the next five weeks, waiting on me hand and foot.

The love that I had for Robin grew immensely. I saw her in a way that I had never experienced. The old saying is that when a lemon gets squeezed, what comes out is lemon juice or lemonade. Robin got squeezed, but there was no wavering in her with the love and care she had given me for those five weeks. I am forever grateful to God for giving me such an incredible wife for the last thirty-seven years.

With the help of Robin and a physical therapist who would come into our home two days a week to get me strong enough to get out of the hospital bed and learn how to function and get back to normal.

Over the last year, I have had much time to think about what-ifs. When I opened my eyes and realized I was still alive, like I said earlier, I was surprised! If not by the grace of God, I would not have this opportunity to tell this story. It would have been just another newspaper headline. Local veteran dies in plane crash. But that isn't what happened. I am here a year later this month, writing my story about how God saved me.

In the previous chapters, I explained how I found my purpose and was inspired to write this book to help the reader realize that maybe they weren't living their life on purpose. Or perhaps they hadn't believed that God had created them for a reason. I hope that reading this book will give you pause to consider what if. What if a God knew you before you were born on this earth? And what if he had a specific reason and purpose for your life?

Even knowing and believing that God had created me for his purpose, I have realized there is so much more he has for me to do.

Sometimes, I feel like coasting; in our American culture, when you reach the age of 66 and a half years, you have reached full retirement age, at least in the eyes of the Social Security department.

Financially, my wife and I could coast, and I believed we would be ok. But I was not created to coast or retire. I believe God has so much to do, and I don't even know what he has planned for me to do. I will continue to be involved in people's lives in the same capacity I have for the last thirty-six years.

Only God knows what he will use my gifts and talents for. But I know it will be my choice, my free will, whether I allow him to continue with the plan he created me for. I believe God has everything mapped out, but somehow, HIS plan gets tucked away in the closet of life, so the journey never starts for us. Or we travel on the journey for a while, then get weary, lazy, or held up by life, and God shakes his head and says to himself, "I had such high hopes for you!"

As I write this, it scares me that it is in me to be one of those individuals. We can all have that tendency, and the enemy of God's Kingdom would love nothing more than to fool us into thinking it's ok, we have done enough and to live out the rest of our lives and not be a threat to the enemy's evil plan, to have us waste our God-given talents, that we become ineffective in the influence of other peoples lives. Our journey of purpose again turns back to the journey of pleasure.

In the last year, I have spent time with my grandson, Michael Kelly Jr., and have seen the gifts and talents that God has given him. Selfishly, I can enjoy watching him develop and learn every day and see how he is discovering those talents. I see myself in him sixty-plus years later. God is nudging him, directing him through those desires, just like he did me. Like he does for all of us, if I hadn't survived, I wouldn't be here to help his parents see what I see.

Because of the values I have learned and lived by for the last 36 years, I can continue seizing them and incorporating them into him and my three children. If I can give them my perspective, perhaps they won't just see their children's gifts and talents as something that will provide their child pleasure, but teach them that their talents are a gift from God and help direct them to their purpose.

If God hadn't saved me, I wouldn't have this opportunity to invest in my children and grandchildren. I don't know God's plan for them, but I know I am part of it. I don't know when he will not need me on earth for his plan, but I will try my hardest to take advantage of the time he has given me to assist in that plan.

We are all connected in one way or another; the words we speak to somebody or the everyday actions that somebody observes may change them and move them in a different direction. Somebody may read this book and be inspired to do something more to impact somebody in their circle.

"A good person leaves an inheritance for their children's children, but a sinner's wealth is stored up for the righteous. Proverbs 13:22:

This scripture refers to legacy: what will you leave behind from the life you lived? Some think that is a monetary sum, or maybe it's the character you lived by and sewn into your heirs. Whatever it is, have you ever asked the question, what is the purpose of the inheritance? I believe the inheritance, part of your legacy, is your purpose. Your purpose is to pass this message on to your heirs and the people you connect with to help bring them into God's Kingdom; this should be the legacy of every believer.

None of us know how much time we have on planet Earth, but with whatever time we have, we should work at living it to its fullest to impact somebody else's life. Instead of thinking life is just about going to work, earning a paycheck, and being excited about the weekend, then starting it again on Monday. There is more to do with your life, so if you don't know what God's plan and purpose are for your life, simply ask, seek Him, and never stop asking and seeking until one day you have that peace beyond all understanding what his purpose he created you for and what he is saving you for.

It has been just over a year since I started to write this book; I have started this last chapter several times and sent multiple iterations to my coconspirator, Charrie Foglio. She would respond by saying, "Mike, this is the last chapter; it needs to be all-powerful, mind-blowing, everlasting; it is too vanilla," she even used the analogy that I was waiting for a latte from the local coffee shop while writing for twenty minutes, it must have been a vanilla latte.

It is the day before Thanksgiving, and I aim to get this last chapter written before this day is over. I was reading John Maxwell's book No Limits this morning. He talked about walking into his office and how excited he was to write the chapter I was reading. The thought came to me: I don't think excitement was the word I would think of when writing this last chapter. Procrastination, apprehension, and other words come to mind, but not excitement. That's why John can make a living just off his books.

One of the things Charrie said was that I should tie all of this together. I have told you about my journey and parade today in this book. I didn't want this to be just a memoir of my life. Hopefully, your takeaway is that God created you, but for a purpose. We all have our journey in this thing called life. We were all created with different personalities from different environments, parents, cultures, and countries.

I believe God has a specific plan for all his creation. Yes, my journey is different from yours, but they are similar. That is why I wanted to share my life with you, so you could relate to some of it, knowing God created you with certain qualities, gifts, and talents explicitly designed for your life and your journey. These traits are twofold. One to guide us through God's nudging us into the direction and path laid out before our birth.

Second, we can gain influence by using our God-given gifts and talents. When we gain influence, we can say, look what God has done and given to me. For example, one person that comes to my mind is Tim Tebow. God blessed him with many gifts and talents that brought him to a place and time highlighted on national TV. Tim used that influence to give God the glory. Praying in full view of the media got much controversial attention, but through it all, it gave public praying credibility. Because of his credibility from his God-given talent, Tim Tebow made praying cool. There is so much to Tim's story, and I would encourage you to read about his journey. Don't get me wrong, I am not comparing myself to a guy like Tim Tebow, but God uses us all in small or massive ways. The point is this:

To whom much is given, much is required.Luke 12:48

There is credibility and influence in many different areas: sports, business, entertainment; the list can go on and on. The question for you is, what are you using your God-given gifts and talents for? Are you using them to gain influence for yourself or to give God the glory for giving you the ability to achieve that influence?

Some people will pick this book up because they recognize the SEAL Trident or read it because a retired SEAL wrote it. The SEAL community has acquired some credibility since the War on Terror started. Therefore, I hope being a retired SEAL brings some street cred and draws a larger audience to read this book so the reader can get some value for their life journey from reading about mine.

There are so many examples of how influence can impact people negatively or positively. I shared with you what affected me when I joined the business. When Bill Britt walked onto the stage that Sunday morning, he was given credibility through the power of edification. If you think about how one gains credibility, it has to come from somebody or something. If a tree falls in the middle of the forest and nobody hears the crash, does the tree make a sound? It is like an unknown singer; they could be great, but if nobody with influence and credibility hears them, they're just another singer singing in the shower.

I believe God opens doors for you, allowing you to be heard, but he will use somebody to whom he has given credibility and influence to open that door for you. So remember, God gave us all we have, so let us give him all the glory!

So, I have shared stories of my great adventure, and hopefully, we have all learned something from them; I know I have. I picked out some highlights from my life that I hoped would be entertaining and add value. It wasn't even clear why I was sharing these stories, but as I got closer to wrapping this book up and trying to dive deeper to answer the question, what was the meaning and value?

I believe that I have tried to share with you what I have learned so far from my life experiences, from so many different ways and directions, and I didn't want to lose you along the way from being too direct, but since this is the last chapter, here it is. God has created every one of us for his glory.

"Everyone who is called by My name, Whom I have created for My glory; I have formed him, yes, I have made Him." Isaiah 43:7 NKJV

Here answers the most critical question of all: why are we here? You are here because you have been created for God's glory. So what now? However long you have been on this earth, take a long or short look back and try to identify the specific gifts and talents you've been blessed with, however small or insignificant you may seem to think they are. Focused in the right direction, these gifts can be mighty when used correctly with the proper purpose.

You will connect or relate to somebody that only you can. Remember, God does not want anybody to perish. We have been created for a purpose, His purpose.

"Even so, it is not the will of your Father who is in heaven that one of these little ones should perish."Matthew 18:14

So, from the words of Billy Zeoli's father, Anthony, "Witness, Witness, Witness." What does that mean? Let your life be a testimony to how great God is, and let your life be a witness to that fact.

#

By Mike Carroll

Made in the USA
Monee, IL
22 September 2025

25141557R00167